Mowday, Richard T.
Employee-organization linkages

DATE DUE

APR 27 '84			

Employee–Organization Linkages

THE PSYCHOLOGY OF COMMITMENT,
ABSENTEEISM, AND TURNOVER

ORGANIZATIONAL AND OCCUPATIONAL PSYCHOLOGY

Series Editor: PETER WARR
MRC Social and Applied Psychology Unit, Department of Psychology, The University, Sheffield, England

Theodore D. Weinshall
Managerial Communication: Concepts, Approaches and Techniques, 1979

Chris Argyris
Inner Contradictions of Rigorous Research, 1980

Charles J. de Wolff, Sylvia Shimmin, and Maurice de Montmollin
Conflicts and Contradictions: Work Psychology in Europe, 1981

Nigel Nicholson, Gil Ursell, and Paul Blyton
The Dynamics of White Collar Unionism, 1981

Dean G. Pruitt
Negotiation Behavior, 1981

Richard T. Mowday, Lyman W. Porter, and Richard M. Steers
Employee–Organization Linkages: The Psychology of Commitment, Absenteeism, and Turnover, 1982

In preparation

George C. Thornton III and William C. Byham
Assessment Centers and Managerial Performance, 1982

Employee–Organization Linkages

THE PSYCHOLOGY OF COMMITMENT, ABSENTEEISM, AND TURNOVER

Richard T. Mowday

Graduate School of Management
University of Oregon
Eugene, Oregon

Lyman W. Porter

Graduate School of Management
University of California, Irvine
Irvine, California

Richard M. Steers

Graduate School of Management
University of Oregon
Eugene, Oregon

1982 AP

ACADEMIC PRESS

A Subsidiary of Harcourt Brace Jovanovich, Publishers

New York London
Paris San Diego San Francisco
São Paulo Sydney Tokyo Toronto

ACADEMIC PRESS, INC.
111 Fifth Avenue, New York, New York 10003

United Kingdom Edition published by
ACADEMIC PRESS, INC. (LONDON) LTD.
24/28 Oval Road, London NW1 7DX

Library of Congress Cataloging in Publication Data
Main entry under title:

Employee-organization linkages.

(Organizational and occupational psychology)
Bibliography: p.
Includes index.
1. Psychology, Industrial. 2. Labor turnover.
3. Absenteeism (Labor). 4. Employee morale. I. Mowday, Richard T. II. Porter, Lyman W. III. Steers, Richard M. IV. Title: Employee commitment, turnover, and absenteeism. V. Series.
HF5448.8.E493 158.7 81-17582
ISBN 0-12-509370-5 AACR2

PRINTED IN THE UNITED STATES OF AMERICA

82 83 84 85 9 8 7 6 5 4 3 2 1

Contents

Preface

Investigators do not often have the chance to reflect upon a line of research that has been conducted over many years, summarize findings from a number of different studies, integrate their own research with the work of others, and draw tentative conclusions about future research directions and implications for management practice. This book provides the authors with just such an opportunity.

Our interest in employee–organization linkages and the major thrust for the research we have conducted in this area can be traced to the University of California, Irvine, in the late 1960s. At that time a research contract was awarded by the Office of Naval Research to Professors Lyman W. Porter and Robert Dubin to establish a research project to investigate employee–organization linkages. As with many such programs, the original research project quickly expanded both in scope and in institutional setting. Parts of the project have been conducted at the University of Oregon, Purdue University, and the University of Nebraska, Lincoln, in addition to the ongoing efforts at Irvine. This book attempts to summarize the results of this research project, which has been carried out over a number of years, in many places, and by several different investigators.

The primary goal of this book is to summarize current theory and research on employee–organization linkages, including the processes through which employees become linked to work organizations, the quality of such linkages, and how linkages are weakened or severed. We have operationalized employee–organization linkages in terms of three central factors: employee commitment to organizations, absenteeism, and turnover. Attempts have been made to identify the determinants of employee commitment, absenteeism, and turnover, as well as their consequences for the individual, work groups, and the larger organization. The hypothesized processes through which employees become committed to, decide to be absent from, and decide to leave their organizations have been summarized in the form of conceptual models. It is our hope that these models will prove useful both to researchers interested in pursuing further work in these areas and to managers interested in developing a better understanding of these processes.

As with many research projects, the work reported in this book is the result of efforts made by a number of different individuals. In addition to the authors, Professors Robert Dubin and Eugene F. Stone have made important contributions to the overall project. John Van Maanen, William Crampon, Joseph Champoux, David Krackhardt, and Harold Angle, all doctoral students at Irvine at one time, worked on some of the studies reported in this volume. At the University of Oregon, Daniel Spencer, James Morris, and Thomas McDade participated in several studies. At the University of Nebraska, Lincoln, George Merker assisted in a major research project. Finally, a research project and book of this type could not be successfully completed without the secretarial assistance provided by a number of individuals. We would particularly like to thank Dorothy Wynkoop, Eve Mount, Sandra Thompson, and Nola Centuri for their hard work and patience.

Perhaps the greatest debt of gratitude for this research project and the book that has resulted is owed the Office of Naval Research for their continuing support of our efforts. The encouragement and support of Bert King and David Stonner from ONR have been particularly important in the completion of this project. It is with sincere appreciation that we acknowledge their assistance.

1

Employee–Organization Linkages: An Introduction

Costly Problem . . .
Firms Try Newer Way to Slash Absenteeism
As Carrot and Stick Fail . . .
All Cures Seem Temporary

The foregoing headline, from an article in *The Wall Street Journal* (March 14, 1979), illustrates the prominence given to how employees relate to organizations—the linkages between them—whether such relationships are in the form of attendance (or absenteeism), retention (or turnover), or loyalty or commitment to the organization. Concern about these linkages exists in all types of organizations that employ people—business firms, schools, military organizations, hospitals, government agencies, etc.

Moreover, this concern seems to be increasing as employee links with organizations tend to weaken. As William H. Whyte questions, "whatever happened to corporate loyalty?" In the 1950s, the corporation was often called the "citadel of belongingness" and the litany of the time went, "Be loyal to the company, and the company will be loyal to you." Things have clearly changed. As noted in *Fortune* (February 9, 1981):

> Although the symptoms of eroding loyalty are widely recognized, the severity of the disease is startling. Turnover among managers out of college less than five years has quadrupled since 1960. Today, the average corporation can count on losing 50% of its college recruits within five years [p. 54].

Hence, there appears to be growing and justified concern on the part of organizations regarding the causes—and cures—for reduced employee commitment and increased turnover and absenteeism. This concern, however, is not one-sided. It is not only the organization that worries about linkages, but also the employee—whether to come to work or be absent, whether to leave or stay with the organization, whether to get actively involved in and committed to the organization or not. More important, as we shall discuss later, attention to these kinds of issues is even broader than that given to them by employers and employees. The larger society also has a stake, because it is affected—at a macro level—by what happens to the collective sum of employee–organization linkages at a micro level.

We have deliberately chosen the term *linkage* to serve as a general label for the several different phenomena (commitment, absenteeism, and turnover) that we will be considering throughout this book. The dictionary definition of *link* ("anything serving to connect one part or thing with another; a bond or tie") emphasizes the focus of this book. That is, our central concern will be the types of connections (links) that individuals have to organizations, as well as the strengths of such connections. The term *linkage* ("a system of links") also has the distinct advantage of being neutral with respect to whether it is "good" or "bad" for either the individual or the organization to develop such connections. The focus is on the *nature* of such connections and an analysis of their causes and consequences, and that will be the basic thrust of the book.

Throughout the remainder of the book we will be considering two basic categories of linkages. The first category we can term *membership status*. This type of connection includes the acts of joining, and staying or leaving (which may be temporary, as in the case of absenteeism, or permanent, as in the case of turnover). If an individual is fully connected in terms of membership status it would mean that he or she had joined the organization, is not absent (on some specified criterion of amount), and has not left the organization. Obviously, if the individual has joined, has not left, but is frequently absent, then we would consider the employee to be only partially connected. The other category of linkage refers to *quality of membership*. Under this category would come such terms as *loyalty, attachment, involvement*, and *commitment*. If an employee has retained membership in an organization and has a high rate of attendance, it does not necessarily follow that his or her contributions to the organization in terms of performance or other organizationally facilitative actions are necessarily good (or bad). Individuals who have a strong and continuing membership status may or may not be regarded as high on quality of membership. Likewise, termination of membership does not necessarily indicate whether the employee or the organization will be better or worse off.

In the remainder of this chapter, we will discuss the importance of employee–organization linkages, consider the impact of societal changes on the development and nature of such linkages, and conclude with a brief description of the plan for the balance of the book.

Importance of Employee–Organization Linkages

Joint Importance to the Employee and the Organization

As indicated previously, the extent and quality of employee–organization linkages provide important consequences for the individual, for the organization, and for society.[1] They also are of central interest to organizational scholars. Let us first look at how such linkages are jointly important to the individual employee and the employing organization. When a man or woman goes to work for an organization, an exchange relationship is set up in which each party trades or exchanges something in return for receiving something of value from the other party. This exchange, which includes both economic and non economic factors, constitutes what a number of writers (e.g., Levinson, Price, Munden, Mandl, & Solley, 1962) have referred to as a "psychological contract." A chief feature of this "contract" is the nature of the employee's connection to the organization, in terms of both membership status and quality of membership.

From the perspective of the individual, joining and staying with an organization provides for a continuing source of current economic rewards (i.e., wages/salary) as well as (in most cases) some degree of future economic security in terms of retirement benefits. In addition, membership in the organization can also provide the basis for psychological rewards in terms of such factors as intrinsic job satisfaction and the support of a friendly, congenial group (i.e., a potential surrogate family). Thus, the more the employee invests of himself or herself in the organization, the more potential there is for greater rewards—both economic and psychological—from the organization. Such investment, however, like any investment, is not without costs. The employee may stay with the organization many years (thus firmly establishing the membership status connection) and may also exhibit bahavior of a loyal or committed nature (thus demonstrating a high quality of membership), and yet may not receive any extra rewards from the organization or members of the organization. An individual with many years in an organization may not necessarily receive many promotions, and an individual with a high level of organizational attachment may not necessarily receive warmer expressions of friendship from peer group members or supervisors.

Not only might extra rewards not be forthcoming in return for strong organizational connections or linkages on the part of the individual, but

[1] Much of the discussion in this and the next section of this chapter is based on two papers: Porter and Angle (1980) and Porter and Perry (1979).

there may in fact be definite negative consequences. For example, the employee may have worked for the organization for so many years that he or she has not acquired a broad range of skills that permits easy transfer to a better job in a new organization. Or the employee may have spent so much effort in maintaining a very low absence rate that irreplaceable time has been taken away from interactions with the family. In still another case, the individual may have highly praised and defended the organization in contacts with friends, only to find later that the organization has acted in a very irresponsible way and has not justified this high degree of loyalty or commitment. Thus, it is clear that, from the vantage point of the employee, efforts to increase the degree of linkage to the organization may or may not be beneficial. The consequences for the employee of having strong organizational linkages may be positive, neutral, or even negative.

From the perspective of the organization, building strong linkages would appear to be crucial. Almost all organizations need to avoid excessive absenteeism and turnover. When these two indices of non-linkage are high, costs almost always go up. Therefore, most organizations are concerned with trying to maintain strong membership status links with their employees (i.e., inducing them not only to join in the first place but also to remain as members who come to work on a regular basis).

The advantages to the organization of having long-term members who have low rates of turnover and absenteeism appear to be obvious. Less obvious, perhaps, is the necessity for organizations to develop in their members some level of spontaneous and innovative behavior that goes beyond routine prescribed behavior (Katz, 1964). One way, but certainly not the only way, to generate such behavior is to develop among employees strong feelings of psychological attachment to the organization. If this is brought about, the individual will tend to internalize the organization's goals and thus voluntarily engage in discretionary behavior of this type. If positive (i.e., organizationally beneficial) extra-role behavior can be generated by voluntary actions of the employee, rather than brought about through role prescriptions or reward system incentives, the "cost" to the organization is lowered. It is obvious that such spontaneous and innovative behavior is not necessary or even desirable in all parts of an organization. However, where it is necessary, as is often the case in management or in certain critical, highly technical jobs, then the organization has a strong stake in attempting to increase the employee's links to it.

As is the case for individuals, however, there also can be costs to the organization of having individuals too strongly linked to it. For one thing, marginally effective performers may persist in staying with the organization and thus reduce its overall effectiveness. Membership links would be strong for this group (who are not performing so poorly that they can be dismissed), but such linkages may impede the organization in bringing in new employees of higher performance capabilities. When this situation is coupled with weak membership links for the most effective performers, the organization derives the worst of both worlds: those it wants to stay proceed to leave, and those it would like to leave end up staying.

Another potential negative consequence for organizations can occur when the quality of membership linkage could be considered too strong. This is the familiar example of the "true believer," an individual who gets carried away by excessive devotion to a cause, in this case the organization. Such behavior, when it is carried to an extreme and labeled "overzealous," can cause great problems for the organization—the employee's actions may irritate other employees within the organization or antagonize persons outside the organization. Work within the organization may be interfered with, and attitudes toward the organization from outside may become less positive (or more negative) than before contact with the overcommitted zealot. In this type of case, from the organization's viewpoint, quality of membership is a good thing carried to such an extreme that it becomes dysfunctional.

Importance to Society

The membership status and quality of membership linkages that individuals have to organizations affect not only those two parties, but also society at large. For example, the larger society may need to be concerned with whether its members have sufficient commitment to its institutions, including, but not limited to, work organizations. If the general quality of membership attachment to work organizations is low, that would appear to have a number of implications for the basic fabric of society. Among these implications is the fact that without some employee commitment organizations simply would not work. Individuals would also lose one very basic source of identity and belonging, namely their employers. On the other hand, if the commitment of individuals to the organizations for which they work is so strong that these organizations are defended and protected when they are clearly and grossly acting against the broad public interest, then another type of problem is created. It would appear that society at large would have difficulty with either extreme in the quality of membership linkages when such an extreme is pervasive across a large number of individuals and organizational situations.

When both quality of membership and membership status linkages are low throughout a large number of work organizations, the level of productivity and the quality of products and services in a society would be affected. This issue is likely to become increasingly important in the next few years. The level of productivity and the quality of goods and services have become issues of national concern as the competitive position of the United States has declined. Although slow growth in productivity rates may be due to a number of complex factors, the quality of employee linkages to organizations is often mentioned as at the core of the problem. Comparisons are often made, for example, between the growth of productivity for Japan and for the United States. Comparisons between the two countries have also suggested to some that Japanese employees are more committed to their organizations and work than are their American counterparts (Marsh & Mannari, 1977). Although differences between commitment levels in the two countries are difficult to substantiate based on research, they have brought into question U.S. management practices and their resulting impact on employee–organization linkages. We can expect much more to be said about the productivity issue and how the commitment of employees influences it.

It would appear that society is best served by at least some minimum overall strength of membership status, where turnover and absenteeism are not excessively high, and where there is at least a moderate level of membership quality. In fact, it is possible to imagine that there is an optimum mean level of strength of membership status and membership quality that would best serve society. What this mean level is, and what degree of dispersion about that level would be most desirable, are matters well beyond the scope of this book. It is, however, an interesting question—for society and for researchers.

Importance to Organizational Scholars and Researchers

The topic of employee–organization linkages can also be assessed for its importance to those who study and carry out research on organizations. Certain aspects of the topic, particularly turnover and (to a lesser extent) absenteeism, have for many years engaged the interest of those concerned with employee behavior. Quality of membership, particularly organizational commitment, seems to have received increasing attention.

Probably a major reason this general topic of linkages has captured a fair degree of past and current interest of scholars in the organizational field is that it poses a number of both conceptual and empirical questions. On the conceptual level, various facets of the broad topic area, such as commitment, turnover, and absenteeism, provide rich ground for developing models of behavioral processes. For example, some 20 years ago Etzioni (1961) developed a model of the compliance structure of organizations that among other things focused on three types of organizations in relation to three types of power and (most important for this book) three types of member involvement. This theory, which we shall discuss in the next chapter, had a major impact on scholars' thinking about the nature of organizations and about members' attachment to them; it also spawned a number of studies relating to involvement and attachment. As another example, turnover is a phenomenon critical to organizations and also highly amenable to the conceptualization of the psychological processes involved. A number of partial or fully developed models of the turnover process have been proposed (e.g., March & Simon, 1958; Mobley, Griffeth, Hand, & Meglino, 1979; Porter & Steers, 1973; Price, 1977; Steers & Mowday, 1981). Mobley (1980) reminds us, however, that most of the research studies on the phenomenon of turnover have not kept pace with these conceptual advances because they have shed relatively little light on what *processes*—for example change, feedback, and interactions over time—are taking place. Thus, there is a gap between what has been *hypothesized* about turnover and the empirical data necessary to support the theory. Nevertheless, turnover, like commitment, is an intriguing subject precisely because the processes are not simple and do require considerable research efforts and sophistication to understand them.

That there has been a large number of such research efforts, even if not often sophisticated, has been well documented for various topics in the employee–organization linkage domain. Just in the area of turnover, for example (as noted in Chapter 5), well over 1000 studies have been carried out. Absenteeism, although not approaching this number, has also been the subject of a relatively large number of studies in the literature of industrial psychology and related fields. Employee commitment to organizations has not received the same empirical attention, but in the past half dozen years it also has become a frequent topic in journals reporting research results dealing with behavior in organizations. What accounts for scholars' many attempts to gather data on these topics? The answer is that the topics represent concrete manifestations of *behavioral actions,* in the case of turnover and absenteeism, or *attitudes,* in the case of commitment, that are simultaneously interesting in their own right and potentially very important to organizations. Thus, they are topics that pose issues and questions that capture the attention of those who think and study about organizations as well as those who work in and manage them.

Impact of Societal Changes on Employee–Organization Linkages

At this juncture, and as a backdrop for the presentation of the various issue and specific topics that will be taken up in the remainder of this book, it is important to consider the impact that various societal or external environment changes are likely to have on the kinds and depths of bonds between employees and organizations. This kind of consideration constitutes a critical context for any attempts to understand in more depth both the antecedents and consequences of such linkages. In effect, changes going on in the external (to organizations) environment provide a sort of "ground" for the "figure" of employee–organization linkages that is the focus of this book.

It is our view that changes going on in modern Western society generally do not affect employee connections to organizations directly. Rather, they serve to alter the work environment, and such changes in the work environment, in turn, affect individuals' attachment to organizations. That is, we see the following type of sequence in operation:

Societal changes → changing work environment → impact on E–O linkages

It should be noted that we are using the term *work environment* (or perhaps, to be more technically correct, *environment for working*) in a very broad sense to include the attitudes and behavioral predispositions that both managers and operating employees bring with them into the work situation, as well as the immediate environment in which organizations function.

Types of Societal Changes and Impacts on Work Environments

Changes taking place in society are numerous and defy any rigid classification. However, it is possible to group them under a small number of headings. Such a grouping is admittedly arbitrary, but it may be useful in attempting to identify some of the more critical changes likely to affect the work environment in major ways. Our discussion will be based on the following four categories: socionormative, demographic, economic, and technological changes.

SOCIONORMATIVE CHANGES

The socionormative part of the broad external environment refers to the cues that society provides concerning "correct" or acceptable behaviors. Socionormative influence on the work environment is brought to bear through several avenues: first, the socialization process that each person encounters in childhood and adult life before joining a particular work organization; second, the normative-type beliefs that other workers bring to the organization, which can have an impact on the focal individual (usually, but not exclusively, through the peer group); and third, the individual's general knowledge of what is happening in society, based on the media, communications, travel, and the like. Examples of socionormative changes that can have a fundamental impact on the work environment include the nature of the work ethic, aspiration levels, attitudes toward authority, sex-role stereotypes, and trust in organizations and institutions.

With respect to socionormative changes in society, Clark Kerr (1979) has referred to the current "great American cultural evolution in the work force." He refers to the fact that (a) more people want jobs; and (b) more people want "good" jobs (and are increasingly rejecting "bad" jobs). More specifically, Kerr believes that there is an increasing emphasis on personal self-fulfillment and individual rights. He states, "We have a crisis of aesthetics, not ethics—tastes have changed, and the indulgence of psychic satisfactions has increased [p. xi]." Daniel Yankelovich (1979b) similarly has identified a "New Breed of Americans" who "feel that success is not enough to satisfy their yearnings for self-fulfillment. They are reaching out for something more and for something different . . . in effect, they demand full enjoyment as well as full employment [pp. 10–11]." Likewise, still another observer of the contemporary American social scene, Amitai Etzioni, (1979) talks about the development of a "preponderant value system leaning toward the pursuit of self-satisfaction, the challenging of deferred gratification—labor now for the promise of future rewards—[as] an unsurprising consequence [p. 30]."

In the same vein, Katzell (1979) has provided an excellent summary list of current cultural trends that could be expected to have strong influence on the working environment:

— Revised definitions of success, with less emphasis on material achievement and more on personal fulfillment.
— More flexible and equal division of work roles between the sexes.
— Growing psychology on entitlement to the good life.
— Shifting emphasis from bigness and growth to smallness and conservation.
— Growing beliefs that work organizations are obliged . . . to contribute to the quality of life and society.
— Rising concern with the welfare of consumers.
— Greater awareness of issues pertaining to health, both physical and mental.
— Greater social acceptance of ethnic minorities.
— Growing conviction that there is more to life than working [p. 48].

Speaking even more directly to the impact of societal changes on the working environment, Katzell goes on to identify several trends in employee work attitudes that he believes flow from these changes:

— [More concern with] the long-range implications of . . . jobs, in contrast to here-and-now considerations.

— [Greater relative importance of] autonomy, responsibility, achievement, and related psychic rewards in relation to material or comfort considerations.
— [Desire for] more of a voice in what goes on [in one's own organization].
— [More concern with] conditions furthering ... "quality of working life" even at the expense of productivity and profits.
— [Less motivation] to work long and hard just out of habit or conscience; increasingly [greater expectations of] explanations and payoffs in both material and psychological terms [p. 49].

It seems clear that in contemporary American society changes are taking place that are and will be altering individuals' basic beliefs about what is acceptable, indeed even encouraged, in how they relate to the work situation. Socionormative changes thus may be more profound than any other category of the external environment in having the potential for affecting employee–organization linkages.

DEMOGRAPHIC CHANGES

The primary demographic change of interest with respect to ultimate impacts on employee–organization linkages relates to the changing composition and characteristics of the labor force. In particular, such characteristics include the educational level of the work force, the average age, the percentage of women and minorities (especially at managerial levels), and the percentage of dual-career or multiple wage-earner households.

Changes in the profile of the labor force, of the type just enumerated, can be expected to have diverse impacts. For example, the continuing increase in the educational level of the work force, particularly in white-collar types of jobs, will (and is) affecting what people want, and especially what they *expect*, from their jobs. These changing expectations, or aspirations, will in turn affect the types of incentives and the types of supervision that will be effective. They will also affect the *amount* of outcomes and opportunities that will be desired—and, in many cases, demanded. Similarly, an increase in the average age level of the work force—with a large increase in the 25–44 age-group by the end of the 1980s—will almost certainly affect what employees want, not only from the job but also from the organization.

The increasing percentage of women and minorities in the work force, particularly in managerial-level jobs for the former, and managerial and white-collar jobs for the latter, points to the development of a much more heterogeneous labor force than has been the case in the past. Also contributing to a more diverse work force is the decline in the percentage of male wage-earner families with a set of non-wage-earners dependent on the male. Such a set of households is rapidly diminishing (currently estimated at about 25% of all households by Clark Kerr [1979]). These several factors contributing to heterogeneity and diversity indicate that if organizations attempt to respond to employees as if they were one single type of group they will run into great difficulty. As Yankelovich (1979b) has noted, for example, "The work of managing diverse incentive packages poses an administrative and bureaucratic nightmare. Understandably, therefore, most managers choose to ignore the problem. Under the old value system they could do so with impunity; under the new value system they cannot. In the 1980's they will be obliged to face this new reality [pp. 21–22]."

ECONOMIC CHANGES

The general economic environment in which organizations operate can have powerful short-term effects on the working environment. It also, however, can have more subtle and more long-lasting effects. With respect to the former, one hardly needs to point out that the relative prosperity of the economy at any particular time can strongly influence the motivation of employees to maintain membership in their present organization (as is typical in times of recession) or look for more attractive opportunities in other organizations (as is frequent in times of prosperity). A more subtle type of impact of short-term fluctuations in the economy can occur in relation to employee mental health (Catalano & Dooley, 1977). Such changes in the status of employee mental health can in turn affect work behaviors such as absenteeism and tardiness.

Economic changes with longer-term impacts include the generally rising level of affluence (subject, of course, to short-term fluctuations) and the relative economic independence of multiple wage-earner households. If affluence is generally improving—even if slowly and with interruptions—this permits a greater increase in employee leisure time. This, in turn, suggests that the immediate job would occupy a relatively smaller portion of the total life space, indicating that efforts to motivate attention to the organization and the job would be more difficult than in the past. The rise of multiple wage-earner households has one clear-cut effect: Fewer families are dependent on a single employing organization; hence the psychological linkage of any particular household member to his or her organization is decreased. This relative economic "independence" can in turn be presumed to have an effect on an employee's willingness to join and stay with a particular organization and also to perform at an exceptionally high level. Likewise, although not strictly an economic effect, any organizational action (such as a job transfer) may be resisted because of a possible effect on the linked wage-earner.

TECHNOLOGICAL CHANGES

Changes in technology in the broad society can have numerous effects on the work environment beyond simply substituting machines for labor or more efficient equipment for less efficient equipment. One type of impact of technology is the creation of rapid obsolescence in particular jobs or sectors of the economy. This, in turn, affects employees' relations to their organizations and their desires and efforts to prevent such obsolescence from occurring. More important (for our purposes) than obsolescence, perhaps, is the technologically based information explosion. Not only is there more information available than before, but there is also an increased ability—due to technological advances in communication and transportation—to exchange information. The ease with which information can be obtained enables employees to find out about alternative job and organizational possibilities. This increased capacity to learn more about what is taking place in other organizations can be expected to have a direct impact on the ability of organizations to hold on to their most valuable employees. As Porter and Perry (1979) stated,

> The general "grass is greener" tendency will be sharpened and increased because the typical employee will know about more plots of grass, so to speak, and will be directly exposed to the best examples of what is considered "green." In effect, technological advances, cumulatively, will provide each employee with more visible options and with the means to explore those options [p. 54].

Another effect of the technologically based increase in knowledge availability is the concomitant increase in specialization of expertise within organizations. This results in a greater need for professionals in various areas. A shift from employee focus on the organization to a focus on the profession—in sociological terms, a shift from a local to a cosmopolitan orientation—often takes place. The implications for the work environment seem obvious.

Impact of Work Environment Changes on Linkages

The collective impact on employee–organization linkages of all the changes noted—socionormative, demographic, economic, and technological—seems to point in one general direction: *significantly reduced or weakened linkages*. This is not to say that every single change will have this effect, or that all changes are equally important; rather, there appears to be a distinct and probably irreversible trend toward diminished linkages.

Membership status will be attenuated by such factors as changes in the work ethic that place less value on the belief that work is "good" in its own right; societal norms that may call into question an organization's values and lead to a change in an individual's definition of what constitutes a good job or a good organization; demographic changes, such as an increase in the educational level of the work force that in turn results in changes in what is expected from an organization and how careers should be evaluated; economic changes that make it easier to leave a particular organization without undue financial hardship; and technological changes that facilitate obtaining knowledge about other organizations and other jobs.

Quality of membership, in terms of loyalty and commitment, is likely to be reduced by many of the same factors discussed in the preceding section. From the employee's point of view, the incentives for, and the value of, becoming committed to one particular organization are called into question by many of the societal changes we have listed. Furthermore, even if an individual does not actually change from one organization to another, many of the trends (e.g., the increasing opportunity for leisure time activities, the trend toward professionalism) have the effect of lessening the tendency to believe that one "owes" something to an organization beyond basic fulfillment of adequate job performance.

Implications of Reduced Employee–Organization Linkages

Implications for Employees

If linkages of employees to organizations are generally becoming weaker for the types of reasons just outlined, it might seem that this would be of great benefit to the individual employee but of great harm to the organization. This may not be the case, either for the employee or for the organization. Certainly, from the employee's perspective, weakened ties to the organization will provide a kind of freedom that will make it less difficult, both psychologically and physically, to leave a given organization. A number of trends, as noted earlier, combine to increase the ease with which a person can change actual membership from one organization to another, as well as decrease any feelings of guilt regarding transferring loyalties between organizations or simply investing less of oneself in the organization at hand.

Even though the environmental trends seem to favor the individual employee at the expense of a particular organization, that may not always be true. For example, it is problematical whether high performance accomplishments can be transferred easily and readily from one organization to another. As Porter and Angle (1980, p. 282) have noted,

> Just because an individual was highly successful in a particular organizational setting—thereby being sought after by other organizations—does not guarantee similar success in the next organization. (See the examples of American professional baseball or football players.) Even if the [employee] acts and thinks like a professional and thus is more bound to a specialized area of competence than to an employing organization, it is likely that particular organizational environments may have considerable effects on the tangible enactment of the professional performance. Therefore, while the transfer possibilities are greatly aided and abetted by environmental trends, the transplant may not take hold in the new surroundings.

There is another reason why reduced linkages might not always work to the advantage of the employee. This is the issue of how much it matters to the individual whether or not he or she experiences a reduced sense of identification with an organization and a related lessened sense of continuity and stability. Obviously, we would expect rather large individual differences in this respect. For some who change organizations, the potential problem may not be too great *if* they can concentrate on the practice of their professional skills rather than on their organization "homes," or if the new home turns out to be far superior to the old one. Those who do not have high levels of expertise may find such a transfer of organizations to be more difficult psychologically, though again this will depend on how the new organization compares to the previous one. Also, even for those who decide to stay with a particular organization but invest less of themselves in it, the "freedom" may have its costs. As a number of psychologists have stressed (e.g., Levinson, 1965), many individuals need to have an attachment to *something*. Depending on the other circumstances in their outside-of-work lives, it may not always be easy for some people to substitute other "somethings" for the work organization. Thus, a reduced feeling of attachment to an organization could have, though certainly need not have, some degree of adverse impact on one's psychological well-being.

Implications for Organizations

The implications of weakened linkages for organizations are many, and only a few examples will be mentioned here. A more extensive discussion about organizational actions that could be used to deal with the situation will be presented in the final chapter in this book.

On the negative side, from the perspective of organizations, are the obvious cost implications of reduced linkages. If those weakened bonds come in the form of greater turnover and absenteeism, there will be direct costs of replacing departing and absent employees. New employees or (in the case of absenteeism) temporary replacements must be obtained, and normal operating routines are likely to be disrupted. Furthermore, training and development costs increase directly with increases in the rates of turnover and absenteeism. Of course, the severity of such costs will depend on the types of skills and expertise lost through temporary or permanent separation of membership, and on the ease or difficulty with which new job incumbents can be obtained and brought up to the operating levels of those who left or who do not appear at work. Other, less obvious, costs include a possible decrease in the general social integration of the organization as a cohesive work force and an increase in bureaucratic control systems for dealing with turnover and absenteeism problems (Price, 1977).

If the reduced linkages appear in the form of lowered organizational commitment, organizations face the problem of how extra-role behavior (e.g., innovations that help the organization, proactive behavior that protects or advances the organization) will be engendered. There are many instances where organizations need individual members, especially those in critical positions, to perform "above and beyond the call of duty" for the benefit of the *organization*. Although the trend for many employees, especially at managerial levels, to develop more professionalism in their work may be part of the answer, such cosmopolitanism by its very nature does not guarantee extra-role behaviors on behalf of the specific organization. In fact, it could be argued that with increased professionalism attention is more often diverted to satisfying the needs of the profession, and especially one's professional peers, than to satisfying the needs of the organization. The latter's requirements may not be opposite those of the profession, but they often will be quite independent of them.

Another possible negative consequence for organizations of reduced commitment linkages could occur if low commitment were to appear among those at the topmost levels of the organization. Any evidence that the upper-level executives of an organization do not have sufficiently high commitment to it can have devastating effects on the morale and performance of those at lower levels. Behavior by example is known to have a powerful impact on observers, and operative employees could be expected to adopt quickly the attitude of "If the boss doesn't care about the organization, why should I?" in cases of demonstrable weak commitment on the part of those most influential in the organization.

The consequences of reduced linkages for organizations are not all negative, however. As we will discuss in detail in Chapter 6, reduced membership status linkages via turnover and absenteeism may produce some unexpected dividends. For one thing, it is possible that some of the worst-performing employees may leave or be absent, thus permitting more productive replacements. Also, if disruptive or disliked employees sever their relations with the organization, permanently or temporarily, this may result in increased morale and better attitudes of those who remain. Furthermore, new employees may bring new energy and fresh ideas into the organization, thus helping to promote innovations. In addition, new employees may not be subject to existing patterns of work-group conflicts and thus may be less likely to encounter distracting influences on their performance. Finally, with greater turnover and absenteeism there is more opportunity for some of the remaining employees to develop new skills or move up into more challenging jobs, thus creating the conditions for improved motivation.

Weakened quality of membership linkages may not seem to have any obvious advantages for organizations. However, as will be discussed in Chapter 6, it is possible to envision that for some types of individuals in particularly stressful work situations, a reduced commitment to the organization (and, concomitantly, a likely greater commitment to off-the-job endeavors) could have positive mental health benefits. Also, as mentioned earlier in this chapter, the general performance of the organization may be facilitated by a reduction in the number of overly committed employees who may be so oriented to the narrow and short-term interests of the organization that they are blinded to its broader and longer-range interests.

Implications for Society

We have previously conjectured that society at large is probably best served by a level of employee linkages to work organizations that is neither excessively high nor excessively low. If the various environmental trends are generally pushing in the direction of weakened linkages, as we have argued, is this good or bad for society at large? Part of the answer depends on an assessment of how strong those linkages have been up to the present time. If one could make the case that there has been too much employee linkage to organizations in the past—that there has been too little turnover, too little absenteeism, and too high a level of organizational commitment—then the general movement toward reduced linkages would be seen as being positive for society. This would be summed up in the following line of reasoning: Individuals who work for organizations are becoming more independent of those organizations and this "freedom" is healthy for individuals and not damaging for organizations; hence, it is good for society. On the other hand, if one starts with the assumption that linkages have not been too high in the past, that they have been adequate, or less, then reduced linkages in the future may be seen as presenting a problem for society. Will such reductions result in reduced productivity and reduced quality of products and services? The answer is not obvious, but the question is important.

Plan of the Book

In the remaining chapters of this book we will attempt to summarize and interpret the available literature—both conceptual and empirical—that deals with employees' linkages to work organizations. In particular, we will try to organize this literature, focusing largely but certainly not exclusively on our own work in the area, and provide as much perspective as possible on the numerous findings and conceptualizations.

The following two chapters will deal with membership quality—that is, organizational commitment. Chapter 2 focuses on the nature of organizational commitment, including its definitions, antecedents, and consequences. Chapter 3, on the other hand, provides an in-depth examination of the commitment process, especially how commitment develops in the pre-entry and early employment period and how it is maintained and continued in mid- and late-organizational career periods.

Chapters 4 and 5 provide coverage of membership status issues. The first of these two chapters concentrates on employee absenteeism and presents a detailed model of employee attendance and research findings related to the model. Also, future research issues relating to absenteeism are identified. In the next chapter, the focus is on employee turnover. Again, a comprehensive model of the turnover process is provided as well as an integration of the available research results and a specification of needed research studies.

In Chapter 6, the consequences of employee linkages are examined, with reference to effects on individuals, work groups, and organizations. Both the positive and negative impacts of commitment, turnover, and absenteeism are explored in detail in this chapter. Chapter 7 provides a follow-up to the previous chapter by focusing on the cognitive accommodations that individuals, both those who stay and those who leave, make to the decision to withdraw from an organization. Although withdrawal can be temporary (as in the case of absenteeism) as well as permanent, the latter type receives primary attention in this chapter.

In the final chapter, Chapter 8, we attempt to draw a set of conclusions from all that has gone before in the book. Although the broad topic of employee linkages has implications for individuals and for society at large as well as for organizations, in this last chapter we will concentrate on the question of how organizations can cope with linkage issues and how researchers can contribute to a deeper understanding of them.

2

Nature of Organizational Commitment

One aspect of employee–organization linkages that has received considerable attention from both managers and behavioral scientists is the topic of employee commitment. This interest has been demonstrated not only in theoretical efforts to explicate the construct but also in empirical efforts to determine the primary antecedents and outcomes of organizational commitment (Buchanan, 1974; Hall & Schneider, 1972; Hrebiniak & Alutto, 1972; Kanter, 1977; Mowday, Porter, & Dubin, 1974; Porter, Steers, Mowday, & Boulian, 1974; Salancik, 1977; Sheldon, 1971; Staw, 1977; Steers, 1977a; J. M. Stevens, J. Beyer, & H. M. Trice, 1978). Throughout these studies, commitment has been repeatedly shown to be an important factor in understanding the work behavior of employees.

Why has the topic of organizational commitment received so much attention? Several possible reasons can be identified. To begin with, the theory underlying commitment suggests that employee commitment to an organization should be a fairly reliable predictor of certain behaviors, especially turnover. Committed people are thought to be more likely to remain with the organization and to work toward organizational goal attainment. Second, the concept of organizational commitment is intuitively appealing to both managers and behavioral scientists. Interest in enhancing employee commitment, almost for its own sake, dates from the early studies of employee "loyalty" in which loyalty was seen by many as a desirable behavior to be exhibited by an employee. Third, an increased understanding of commitment may help us comprehend the nature of more general psychological processes by which people choose to identify with objects in their environment and to make sense out of this environment. It helps us to some degree to explain how people find purpose in life.

In this chapter, we wish to discuss three related aspects of organizational commitment. First, approaches to the definition of commitment are examined. Second, the literature pertaining to antecedents of commitment is reviewed. Finally, the literature focusing on the consequences of commitment is discussed. This information, when taken as a whole, will set the stage for our discussion in Chapter 3 of the manner in which employee commitment develops in work organizations.

Definition of Organizational Commitment

Competing Definitions of Commitment

When one considers the literature on the topic of organizational commitment, it becomes apparent that little consensus exists with respect to the meaning of the term. As the area grew and developed, researchers from various disciplines ascribed their own meanings to the topic, thereby increasing the difficulty involved in understanding the construct. For instance, a review of 10 different studies on organizational commitment reveals the following widely divergent definitions:

— An attitude or an orientation toward the organization which links or attaches the identity of the person to the organization [Sheldon, 1971, p. 143].

— The willingness of social actors to give their energy and loyalty to social systems, the attachment of personality systems to social relations which are seen as self-expressive [Kanter, 1968, p. 499].

— A structural phenomenon which occurs as a result of individual–organizational transactions and alterations in side bets or investments over time [Hrebiniak & Alutto, 1972, p. 556].

— A state of being in which an individual becomes bound by his actions and through these actions to beliefs that sustain the activities and his own involvement [Salancik, 1977, p. 62].

— The process by which the goals of the organization and those of the individual become increasingly integrated or congruent [Hall, Schneider, & Nygren, 1970, p. 176].

— The nature of the relationship of the member to the system as a whole [Grusky, 1966, p. 489].

— (1) It includes something of the notion of membership; (2) it reflects the current position of the individual; (3) it has a special predictive potential, providing predictions concerning certain aspects of performance, motivation to work, spontaneous contribution, and other related outcomes; and (4)it suggests the differential relevance of motivational factors [Brown, 1969, p. 347].

— Commitments come into being when a person, by making a side-bet, links extraneous interests with a consistent line of activity [Becker, 1960, p. 32].

— Commitment behaviors are socially accepted behaviors that exceed formal and/or normative expectations relevant to the object of commitment [Weiner & Gechman, 1977, p. 48].

— A partisan, affective attachment to the goals and values of an organization, to one's role in relation to goals and values, and to the organization for its own sake, apart from its purely instrumental worth [Buchanan, 1974, p. 533].

Typologies of Organizational Commitment

From these definitions, it is clear that no real consensus exists with respect to construct definition. In an effort to shed some light on this problem, several researchers have suggested typologies into which the various approaches to commitment can be organized. Although many such typologies can be identified, a review of three approaches should highlight the nature of the problem. These three approaches, shown in Table 2.1, have been presented by Etzioni (1961a), Kanter (1968), and Staw (1977) and Salancik (1977).

ETZIONI

One of the earliest attempts to develop a typology of commitment was made by Etzioni (1961a). Etzioni suggested a typology based on a larger model of member compliance with organizational directives. It is argued that the power or authority that organizations have over individuals is rooted in the nature of employee involvement in the organization. This involvement or commitment can take one of three forms: (*a*) moral involvement; (*b*) calculative involvement; and (*c*) alienative involvement.

Moral involvement represents a positive and intense orientation toward the organization that is based on the internalization of the organization's goals, values, and norms and on an identification with authority. Hence, an employee may become involved in organizational activities because he or she feels the organization is pursuing useful societal goals (e.g., the Red Cross). *Calculative* involvement, on the other hand, represents a less intense relationship with the organization and is largely based on the exchange relationship that develop between members and the organization. That is, members become committed to the organization because they see a beneficial or equitable exchange relationship between their contributions to the organization and the rewards they receive for service. This notion is similar to March and Simon's (1958) inducements–contributions theory in which employees consider the balance between their contributions and the inducements, or rewards, offered by the organization. Finally,

Table 2.1
Typologies of Organizational Commitment

Author(s)	Typology	Definition
Etzioni (1961)	Moral involvement	A positive and high-intensity orientation based on internalization of organizational goals and values and identification with authority
	Calculative involvement	A lower-intensity relationship based on a rational exchange of benefits and rewards
	Alienative involvement	A negative orientation that is found in exploitative relationships (e.g., in prisons)
Kanter (1968)	Continuance commitment	Dedication to organization's survival brought on by previous personal investments and sacrifices such that leaving would be costly or impossible
	Cohesion commitment	Attachment to social relationships in an organization brought on by such techniques as public renunciation of previous social ties or engaging in ceremonies that enhance group cohesion
	Control commitment	Attachment to organizational norms that shape behavior in desired directions resulting from requiring members to disavow previous norms publicly and reformulate their self-conceptions in terms of organizational values
Staw (1977); Salancik (1977)	Organizational behavior approach	Commitment viewed in terms of a strong identification with and involvement in the organization brought on by a variety of factors (attitudinal commitment)
	Social psychological approach	Commitment viewed in terms of sunk costs invested in the organization that bind the individual irrevocably to the organization (behavioral commitment)

alienative involvement represents a negative orientation toward the organization, which is typically found in situations where individual behavior is severely constrained. In a prison, for example, inmates are "involved" in the organization as a result of societal action, not by their own choosing.

For each form of commitment, Etzioni suggests primary control mechanisms that organizations often employ to secure compliance with organizational directives. Normative power, which rests largely on the allocation of symbolic rewards, is most often associated with moral involvement, whereas remunerative power is typically associated with calculative involvement. Coercive power is used in a situation involving alienative involvement. Hence, it is argued that organizations attempt to secure compliance behavior on the part of their members by tying influence attempts to the nature of the involvement by the member.

KANTER

In a somewhat different vein, Kanter (1968) has argued that different types of commitment result from the different behavioral requirements imposed on members by the organization. She suggests three different forms of commitment (see Table 2.1). *Continuance* commitment is defined in terms of a member's dedication to the survival of the organization. It is believed to be caused by requiring members to make personal sacrifices and investments to the extent that it becomes costly or difficult for them to leave. In other words, when members have made significant sacrifices to join or remain with an organization (e.g., an apprenticeship program for a particular trade, or simply a long tenure with the organization), they are more likely to feel a strong need for system survival. The individual may come to feel that "I have sacrificed so much for this organization that we must keep it going."

In addition to continuance commitment, Kanter identifies *cohesion* commitment as an attachment to social relationships in an organization brought on by such techniques as public renunciation of previous social ties or by engaging in ceremonies that enhance group cohesion. The process involved in pledging a fraternity or sorority, for example, signifies a public transition for a pledge from a state of being an outsider to a state of being a member. Organizations typically engage in a variety of such activities to develop a member's psychological attachment to the organization (e.g., first-day employee orientations, public notices of new members, the use of uniforms or badges). All such efforts are aimed at developing increased cohesion among group members and hence increased cohesion commitment.

Finally, Kanter (1968) identifies *control* commitment as a member's attachment to the norms of the organization that shape behavior in desired directions. Control commitment exists when an employee believes that the norms and values of an organization represent an important guide to suitable behaviors and is influenced by such norms in everyday acts. Such commitment is thought to result from having members publicly disavow previous norms where they exist and reformulate their self-conceptions in terms of the organization's norms and values. For instance, the widely cited "organization man" syndrome in which the lives of employees are largely determined by a concern for what is best for the organization (and what the organization would approve of) represents a good example of organization norms and values shaping one's behavior and attachment.

In contrast to Etzioni (1961a), Kanter views her three approaches to commitment as being highly interrelated. That is, organizations often use all three approaches simultaneously to develop member commitment. For example, an employee may be committed to an organization as a result of a dedication to system survival, a feeling of group cohesion, *and* an identification with organizational norms and values. In many ways, each of these three aspects of commitment is seen as reinforcing the others as they jointly influence the individual to increase his or her ties with the organization. Etzioni, on the other hand, attempts to develop somewhat broader definitions or categories of commitment and suggests that influences on employee commitment largely fall into one of three categories.

STAW AND SALANCIK

In one of the most significant developments in the literature on organizational commitment, both Staw (1977) and Salancik (1977) emphasized the need to differentiate between commitment as seen by organizational behavior researchers and commitment as seen by social psychologists. Basically, the point is made that the term *commitment* has been used to describe two quite different phenomena. Organizational behavior researchers, on the one hand, use the term to describe the process by which employees come to identify with the goals and values of the organization and are desirous of maintaining membership in the organization (see, for example, Buchanan, 1974; Porter *et al.*, 1974). This approach is also referred to as *attitudinal* commitment by Staw (1977).

Staw suggests several problems with the attitudinal approach to defining commitment. To begin with, commitment is conceptualized largely from the standpoint of the organization, "and because of this we may have missed some of the psychological processes central to the individual's own perception of being commited [p. 4]." In addition, Staw suggests that many of the aspects of attitudinal commitment (goal identification, desire for continued membership) may be constructs in their own right and that summarizing them into a single concept may lose information and may not be justified on theoretical grounds. (This same point is made by Hall [1977].) Finally, some aspects of attitudinal commitment (e.g., a willingness to exert effort on behalf of the organization) are simply verbal expressions of the behaviors that one seeks to predict.

In contrast to the notion of attitudinal commitment, Staw, Salancik, and others have suggested the concept of *behavioral* commitment. This approach draws heavily on the work of several social psychologists (e.g., Kiesler, 1971) and focuses on the process by which an individual's past behavior serves to bind him or her to the organization. Much of the initial work on behavioral commitment was done by Becker (1964), who describes commitment as a process in which employees make "side bets" with the organization. This side-bet notion represents a process of linking previously irrelevant or extraneous actions and rewards to a given line of action in such a way that the individual loses degrees of freedom in his or her future behaviors. As Becker (1964) notes,

> if a person refuses to change jobs, even though the new job would offer him a higher salary and better working conditions, we should suspect that his decision is a result of commitment, that other sets of rewards than income and working conditions have become attached to his present job so that it would be too painful for him to change. He may have a large pension at stake, which he will lose if he moves; he may dread the cost of making new friends and learning to get along with new working associates; he may feel that he will get a reputation for being flighty and erratic if he leaves the present job. In each instance, formerly extraneous interests have become linked to his present job [p. 50].

Similarly, Salancik (1977) writes,

> Commitment comes about when an individual is bound to his acts. Though the word bound is somewhat clumsy, what we mean by it is that the individual has identified himself with a particular behavior. Three characteristics bind an individual to his acts and hence commit him. They are the visibility, the irrevocability, and the volitionality of the behavior. By manipulating these three characteristics, an individual can be made to be more or less committed to his acts and their implications [p. 64].

Once these commitments are made, individuals must find mechanisms for adjusting to such commitments psychologically. This is often done through cognitive dissonance (Festinger, 1957). As Salancik (1977) notes, "The power of commitment in shaping attitudes stems from the fact that individuals adjust their attitudes to fit the situations to which they are committed [p. 70]." Hence if an employee has worked for a major corporation for 20 years, he or she is likely to develop attitudes that justify remaining with the organization in the face of alternative positions. Again, Salancik (1977) notes,

> You act. You believe your action was valuable, worthwhile, desirable. You act again, renewing the belief. In time, without realizing it, you have made a myth; your sense of veracity and value has been merged into the pattern of action. The myths sustain the action; and the action sustains the myth [p. 20].

In short, a self-reinforcing cycle emerges in which a behavior causes the development of congruent attitudes, which in turn lead to further behaviors, and so forth. As a result, the individual slowly increases both behavioral and psychological linkages with the organization.

Although the distinction between attitudinal and behavioral commitment is a useful one (and will be used throughout this book), the assertion that one approach is superior to the other is questionable. Rather it would appear that both concepts are useful. Attitudinal commitment focuses on the process by which people come to think about their relationship with the organization. In many ways, it can be thought of as a mind set in which individuals consider the extent to which their own values and goals are congruent with those of the organization.

Behavioral commitment, on the other hand, relates to the process by which individuals become locked into a certain organization and how they deal with this problem. Clearly, these two phenomena are closely related. Hence, if we are to make progress in understanding the commitment construct, it is necessary to consider both forms as they relate to each other and to the broader issue of organizational behavior.

Toward a Definition of Organizational Commitment

When this attitudinal–behavioral dichotomy is used, the seeming heterogeneity permeating the 10 different definitions of commitment given at the beginning of this chapter begins to simplify. That is, most of these disparate definitions can be classified as based on either attitude or behavior. For example, when we talk about someone becoming "bound by his actions" or "behaviors that exceed formal and/or normative expectations" we are in effect focusing on overt manifestations (behaviors) relating to commitment. On the other hand, when we discuss commitment in terms of when "the identity of the person [is linked] to the organization" or when "the goals of the organization and those of the individual become increasingly integrated or congruent," we are in effect focusing on employee attitudes toward the organization.

Since the object of attitudinal commitment is the organization (that is, the extent to which an individual identifies with his or her employer), we shall use *attitudinal commitment* and *organizational commitment* interchangeably in this book. Behavioral commitment, on the other hand, where the primary object is *behavior,* will be specifically designated as such. In order to do justice to both concepts, we shall focus exclusively in this chapter on commitment as an attitude and examine the pertinent literature therein. On the basis of this analysis, we then turn in Chapter 3 to a more detailed consideration of behavioral commitment and the interactive relationship between the two forms of commitment. It is hoped that in this way both approaches as well as their interrelationships will be highlighted.

Following Porter and Smith (1970), we define *organizational commitment* for our purposes as the relative strength of an individual's identification with and involvement in a particular organization. Conceptually, it can be characterized by at least three factors: (*a*) a strong belief in and acceptance of the organization's goals and values; (*b*) a willingness to exert considerable effort on behalf of the organization; and (*c*) a strong desire to maintain membership in the organization. When organizational commitment is defined in this fashion, it represents something beyond mere passive loyalty to an organization. It involves an active relationship with the organization such that individuals are willing to give something of themselves in order to contribute to the organization's well-being. Hence, to an observer, commitment can be inferred not only from the expressions of an individual's beliefs and opinions but also from his or her actions.

It is important to note that this definition does not preclude the possibility (or even probability) that individuals will also be committed to other aspects of their environment, such as family or union or political party. It simply asserts that regardless of these other possible commitments the organizationally committed individual will tend to exhibit the three characteristics identified in the foregoing definition.

A common theme that runs through much of the conceptual work on organizational commitment is the notion of *exchange* (Farrell & Rusbult, in press; March & Simon, 1958). Individuals come to organizations with certain needs, desires, skills, and so forth, and expect to find a work environment where they can use their abilities and satisfy many of their basic needs. When an organization provides such a vehicle (for example, when it makes effective use of its employees and is dependable), the likelihood of increasing commitment is apparently increased (Steers, 1977a). However, when the organization is not dependable or fails to provide employees with challenging and meaningful tasks, commitment levels should diminish.

This notion of exchange is valuable both from a conceptual standpoint in understanding the construct and from a societal standpoint in understanding that commitment is not simply a means of managerial exploitation of employees. As Buchanan (1975) argues,

> the commitment attitude is reciprocally valuable. It advances the interests of the individual as he develops the patterns of his work life just as surely as it furthers the ends of the organization. This is important, for it is easy to misconceive commitment as an Orwellian device for subverting individuality in the service of the corporate organization [pp. 70–71].

When viewed as an attitude, commitment differs from the concept of job satisfaction in several ways. To begin with, commitment as a construct is more global, reflecting a general affective response to the organization as a whole. Job satisfaction, on the other hand, reflects one's response either to one's job or to certain aspects of one's job. Hence commitment emphasizes attachment to the employing organization, including its goals and values, whereas satisfaction emphasizes the specific task environment where an employee performs his or her duties.

Moreover, organizational commitment should be somewhat more stable over time than job satisfaction. Although day-to-day events in the work place may affect an employee's level of job satisfaction, such transitory events should not cause an employee to reevaluate seriously his or her attachment to the overall organization. Available longitudinal evidence supports this view (see, for example, Porter *et al.*, 1974). Commitment attitudes appear to develop slowly but consistently over time as individuals think about the relationship between themselves and their employer. Such findings would be predicted from the definition and available theory. Satisfaction, on the other hand, has been found to be a less stable measure over time, reflecting more immediate reactions to specific tangible aspects of the work environment (e.g., pay, supervision). Evidence for this transitory nature of satisfaction can be found in Smith, Kendall, and Hulin (1969) and Porter *et al.* (1974).

Antecedents of Organizational Commitment

The empirical studies carried out on the topic of organizational commitment represent a rich collection of findings with respect to both the antecedents and the consequences of the construct. The vast majority of these studies are correlational in nature. As a result, although we know a good deal about variables that are empirically related to commitment, we know far less about the psychological processes involved in its development. In the remainder of this chapter we shall provide an overview of the correlational findings with respect to both the antecedents and the outcomes of commitment. On the basis of these results, we then suggest in the next chapter how these findings may fit together from a modeling point of view to help explain the psychological and behavioral processes through which commitment to an organization develops over time.

It should be noted here that throughout the various studies on organizational commitment many different measures of the construct were employed. These various measures are discussed briefly in the Appendix. Also discussed in the Appendix are the development and validation procedures used for the Organizational Commitment Questionnaire (OCQ), the instrument upon which our own findings are based.

Several years ago, it was suggested that the major influences on organizational commitment could be grouped into three categories: (*a*) personal characteristics; (*b*) job- or role-related characteristics; and (*c*) work experiences. Replicated results by Steers (1977a) support the importance of all three of these categories as major influences on employee commitment. In this study, commitment as measured by the OCQ was regressed on several personal characteristics, job characteristics, and work experiences. Results, shown in Table 2.2, demonstrate that each set of factors is significantly related to commitment for two diverse samples of hospital employees and research and development (R&D) scientists. More recent research sugests the need to add a fourth category of antecedents, namely, structural characteristics (Morris & Steers, 1981; J. M. Stevens *et al.*, 1978). These categories of antecedents, along with hypothesized outcomes of commitment, are shown in Figure 2.1 and are intended to provide some structure for our review of the correlational findings

Table 2.2
Multiple Correlations between Antecedents and Organizational Commitment for Samples of Hospital Employees and Scientists and Engineers

	Hospital employees ($N = 382$)		Scientists and engineers ($N = 119$)	
Antecedents	*R*	*F*-value	*R*	*F*-value
Personal characteristics	.55	24.96**	.42	3.28*
Job or role-related characteristics	.64	47.86**	.38	3.89*
Work experience	.71	89.26**	.64	20.04**

Source: Steers *Administrative Science Quarterly*, 1977, *22*, 46–56.
*Significant at .01 level.
**Significant at .001 level.

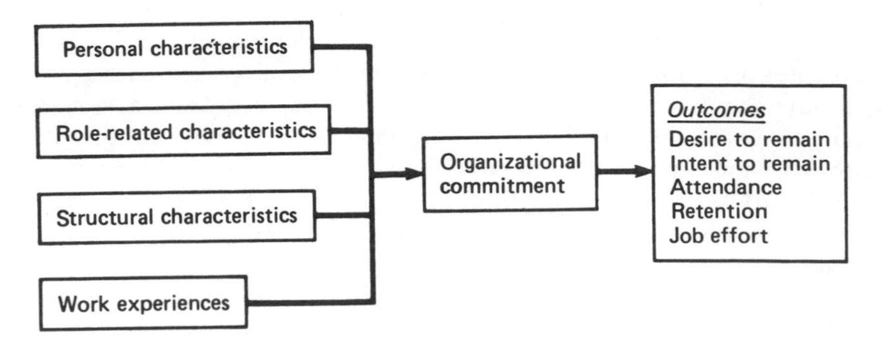

Figure 2.1. Hypothesized antecedents and outcomes of organizational commitment (adapted from Steers, 1977a).

concerning organizational commitment. We shall now briefly summarize the research pertaining to each of the antecedent categories.

Personal Correlates of Commitment

Numerous studies have examined the effects of various personal characteristics on organizational commitment. Personal characteristics studied have included age, tenure, educational level, gender, race, and various personality factors. In general, commitment has been found to be positively related to both *age* and *tenure* (Angle & Perry, 1981; Brown, 1969; Hall *et al.*, 1970; Hrebiniak, 1974; Lee, 1971; Morris & Sherman, 1981; Sheldon, 1971). Some mixed findings have also emerged, however, indicating that age and tenure are not direct correlates of commitment (Hall & Schneider, 1972; Steers, 1977a). In support of at least a moderate relationship between these variables, March and Simon (1958) noted that as age or tenure in the organization increases, the individual's opportunities for alternative employment become more limited. This decrease in an individual's degrees of freedom may increase the perceived attractiveness of the present employer, thereby leading to increased psychological attachment.

In contrast to age and tenure, *education* has often been found to be *inversely* related to commitment (Angle & Perry, 1981; Morris & Sherman, 1981; Morris & Steers, 1980; Steers, 1977a), although the results are not entirely consistent (Lee, 1971; Steers & Spencer, 1977). It has been suggested that this inverse relationship may result from the fact that more highly educated individuals have higher expectations that the organization may be unable to meet. Moreover, more educated individuals may also be more committed to a profession or trade. Hence, it would become more difficult for the organization to compete successfully for the psychological involvement of such members.

In other research, it has been fairly consistently found that *gender* is related to commitment. That is, in studies by Angle and Perry (1981), Gould (1975), Grusky (1966), and Hrebiniak and Alutto (1972), women as a group were found to be more committed than men. Grusky (1966) explained this relationship by arguing that women generally had to overcome more barriers to attain their positions in the organization, thereby making organizational membership more important to them. This is similar to the concept of initiation rites as an influence on behavioral commitment, as discussed by Salancik (1977).

Finally, a series of studies have examined various *personality* factors as they relate to commitment. In isolated findings, commitment has been found to be related to achievement motivation, sense of competence, and other higher-order needs (Koch, 1974; Morris & Sherman, 1981; Rotondi, 1976; Steers, 1977a; Steers & Spencer, 1977). It would appear that commitment to the organization can be bolstered to the extent that employees see the organization as a source of need satisfaction. Hence, again we see an exchange relationship developing between the individual and the organization in which commitment attitudes are "exchanged" for desirable outcomes for the employees. A related aspect of personality involves the values held by employees. In this regard, modest support has emerged to suggest that individuals with a strong personal work ethic tend to be highly committed to the organization (Buchanan, 1974; Card, 1978; Goodale, 1973; Hall *et al.*, 1970; Hall & Schneider, 1972; Hulin & Blood, 1968; Kidron, 1978; Rabinowitz & Hall, 1977). Finally, one study discovered that workers with a work-oriented central life interest were also highly committed to the organization (Dubin, Champoux, & Porter, 1975).

In summary, a variety of personal characteristics have been found to be related to organizational commitment in various correlational studies across diverse work samples. These findings indicate rather clearly that individual differences must be taken into account in any model of commitment processes in organizations. In the next chapter, we shall return to this point as we examine the developmental processes relating to employee commitment.

Role-Related Correlates of Commitment

The second group of correlates of organizational commitment that have been identified in the literature relate to employee roles and job characteristics. We are concerned here about the extent to which variations in the task requirements of jobs influence employee commitment. There appear to be at least three related aspects of work role that have the potential to influence commitment: job scope or challenge, role conflict, and role ambiguity.

A good deal of work has been carried out examining the relationship between *job scope* and commitment. The basic hypothesis here is that increased job scope increases the challenge employees experience and thereby increases commitment. Again, implicit in this hypothesis is the notion of exchange. Employees are thought to respond positively when provided with more challenge in their jobs. Fairly consistent data from various work samples support this position (Brown, 1969; Buchanan, 1974; Hall *et al.*, 1970; Hall & Schneider, 1972; Marsh & Mannari, 1977; Steers, 1977a; Steers & Spencer, 1977; J. M. Stevens *et al.*, 1978).

In addition, several studies have examined the related concepts of *role conflict* and *role ambiguity* as they relate to commitment. Role conflict was found to be inversely related to commitment in two separate studies; mixed results emerged for role ambiguity (Morris & Koch, 1979; Morris & Sherman, 1981). Relatedly, J. M. Stevens *et al.* (1978) found that role overload was strongly and inversely related to employee commitment. Hence, the portrait that emerges with respect to the impact of role-related factors on commitment is that such influences may be positive so long as the employee has clear and challenging job assignments. Where the assignments become ambiguous, place the employee in conflict, or provide excessive role stress, the effects on commitment tend to be adverse.

Structural Correlates of Commitment

A relatively new area of investigation of correlates of organizational commitment has dealt with the influence of organizational structure on commitment. Significant attention has been focused on the manner in which structure affects other attitudes, such as job satisfaction (Cummings & Berger, 1976; Porter & Lawler, 1965), but little has been done with respect to commitment.

The first study in this area was carried out by J. M. Stevens *et al.* (1978), where four structural variables were considered (*organization size, union presence, span of control,* and *centralization of authority*). None were found to be significantly related to commitment. Subsequently, however, Morris and Steers (1980) examined the effects of structural variables and found as did Stevens *et al.* that size and span of control were unrelated to commitment. However, it was also found that *formalization, functional dependence,* and *decentralization* were related to commitment. That is, for the sample studied, employees experiencing greater decentralization, greater dependence on the work of others, and greater formality of written rules and procedures felt more committed to the organization than employees experiencing these factors to a lesser extent. With one exception (centralization), these findings do not contradict the earlier results of Stevens *et al.* The two studies simply examined different aspects of structure as it related to commitment.

Rhodes and Steers (in press), in studying the effects of *worker ownership* on commitment, found that when employees have a vested financial interest in the organization they are significantly more committed than when they are simply employees. This study was carried out among matched plywood mills, one owned by the employees and the other owned by a major wood-products firm. This study also found that increased *participation in decision making* (a related aspect of decentralization) was related to commitment.

Finally, in unpublished findings emerging from our own series of studies on commitment using the OCQ, the issue of *occupational groupings* was examined. As shown in Table 2.3, though mean commitment levels differ significantly across the four organizations studied, no significant differences in mean commitment levels were found across occupational level for the two samples for which data were available. Hence, these preliminary data suggested that although different organizations manifest different overall levels of employee commitment, this commitment is

Table 2.3
Comparison of Commitment Scores within and between Organizations[a]

Organizational commitment	State university	Major hospital	Research and development firm	Industrial firm	*F*-ratio
Total organization	4.73	5.21	4.43	5.37	17.94
Occupational groupings					
Administrative	4.84	5.14			
Professional		4.86			
Technical		5.34			
Clerical	4.55	5.02			
Service	4.57	5.36			
F-ratio	1.19	2.83			

[a]The *F* ratio comparing the total organizational commitment scores (17.94) is significant at the .001 level, whereas the two *F*-ratios comparing within-organization commitment scores (1.19 and 2.83) are insignificant. Because of the homogeneity of samples for the other two studies, no occupational differences were available. Details concerning samples and measures are available in Steers (1977a), Steers and Spencer (1977), and Morris and Steers (1980).

equally strong up and down the organizational hierarchy. Top executives as a group are *not* more committed than service workers or blue-collar workers. Although these data are tentative, results suggest that a favorite stereotype concerning lower levels of loyalty among rank-and-file workers may in fact be a myth.

From the foregoing evidence, the structure of the organization does appear to have an influence on commitment outcomes. This trend parallels research relating structure to job satisfaction (Cummings & Berger, 1976) and illustrates how structural variation can combine with personal and role-related variables to influence the extent to which individuals see it in their best interest to attach themselves psychologically to the organization.

Work Experience Correlates of Commitment

The fourth category of major antecedents of organizational commitment represents those work experiences that occur during an employee's tenure with the organization. Work experiences are viewed as a major socializing force and as such represent an important influence on the extent to which psychological attachments are formed with the organization.

Several work experience variables have been found to be related to organizational commitment. In three studies, *organizational dependability*, or the extent to which employees felt the organization could be counted upon to look after employee interests, was significantly related to commitment (Buchanan, 1974; Hrebiniak, 1974; Steers, 1977a). These findings by Steers were replicated in two divergent samples. Moreover, Buchanan (1974) and Steers (1977a) also found feelings of *personal importance to the organization* to be related to commitment. That is, when employees felt they were needed or important to the organization's mission, commitment attitudes increased. Again, in the study by Steers, the findings were replicated. Grusky (1966) and Steers (1977a) also found commitment to be related to the extent to which employee *expectations were met* in the work place, although the finding did not replicate in the Steers study.

A further factor relating to work experiences focuses on the extent to which employees sense that their co-workers maintain *positive attitudes toward the organization*. Buchanan (1974) has argued that such perceptions "rub off" on employees, leading to heightened commitment. Data in support of this contention can be found in Buchanan (1974), Patchen (1970), and (replicated) in Steers (1977a). In addition, research by Rhodes and Steers (in press) found that *perceived pay equity* and *group norms regarding hard work* were also related to commitment for a sample of wood-products employees. This latter finding also emerged in the Buchanan (1974) study.

Only two studies were found relating commitment to *leadership style*. In both studies, commitment was found to be related to leader initiating structure (Brief, Aldag, & Wallden, 1976; Morris & Sherman, 1981); in the latter study, commitment was also found to be related to leader consideration.

Finally, an important factor in facilitating commitment appears to be the degree of an employee's *social involvement* in the organization. This idea was first introduced by Sheldon (1971) and subsequent support has been found by Buchanan (1974) and Rotondi (1975). Such findings suggest that the greater the social interaction, the more social ties the individual develops with the organization. As a result, the individual becomes further linked to his or her employer.

In all, then, at least 25 variables have been found to be related in some way with organizational commitment. These variables trace their origins to various aspects of organizational life, including personal characteristics of the individual members, role-related characteristics of the work place, structural aspects of the organization, and the various work experiences encountered by the employees. What is clearly lacking in many of these findings is an explanation for the *dynamics* of organizational commitment. That is, we know little about the processes by which the identified factors interact to influence employees' affective responses to the organization. What is needed, then, is some effort toward constructing a model of the commitment process. This is attempted in the next chapter, based in part on the data reviewed here. Before we begin this analysis, however, we should first summarize much of what is currently known about the *consequences* of organizational commitment.

Consequences of Organizational Commitment

What, then, are the consequences of organizational commitment? At least five possible outcomes have been studied, including job performance, tenure with the organization, absenteeism, tardiness, and turnover (see also Chapter 6). On the basis of our own work and the work of others, we can summarize the current level of knowledge on each of these topics (see Table 2.4).

Commitment and Job Performance

Clearly, the least encouraging finding that has emerged from studies of commitment is a rather weak relationship between commitment and job performance. In both individual and group-level studies, few important correlations emerged, although the correlations are consistently in the predicted direction and often reach statistical significance (Mowday *et al.*, 1974; Porter, Crampon, & Smith, 1976; Steers, 1977a).

Several factors may account for this. In particular, following contemporary theories of employee motivation, performance is influenced by motivation level, role clarity, and ability (Porter & Lawler, 1968). Attitudes like commitment would only be expected to influence one aspect of actual job performance. Hence, we would not expect a strong commitment–performance relationship. Even so, we would expect commitment to influence the amount of effort an employee puts forth on the job and this effort should have some influence on actual performance.

Commitment and Tenure

If highly committed employees are desirous of remaining with the organization, as our conceptual model suggests, then we would expect to see commitment and actual job tenure related. In fact, such is the case. Highly significant positive correlations have been found between increased tenure and increased commitment (see Table 2.4). What remains to be established, however, as we shall see in the next chapter, is the nature of the causal relationship between these two variables. That is, does commitment lead to increased tenure or does increased tenure cause changes in commitment levels?

Commitment and Absenteeism

Theory would predict that highly committed employees would be more motivated to attend so they could facilitate organizational goal attainment. This motivation should exist even if the employee does not enjoy the tasks required by the job (e.g., a nurse's aide may not like certain distasteful aspects of the job but may feel that he or she is contributing to worthwhile public health goals). Modest support for this relationship can be found in several studies (F. J. Smith, 1977; Steers, 1977a), but this support is not entirely consistent (Angle & Perry, 1981). On the other hand, where an employee's commitments lie elsewhere (e.g., a hobby, family and home, or sports), less internal pressure would be exerted on the employee to attend (Morgan & Herman, 1976).

It should be clearly noted here that it is not suggested that a direct commitment–attendance relationship would be expected. In Chapter 4, we have suggested what the major influences on attendance might be; these include but certainly are not limited to commitment (Steers & Rhodes,

Table 2.4

Summary of Empirical Findings with Respect to the Consequences of Organizational Commitment

Sample	Reference	Performance	Tenure	Absenteeism	Tardiness	Turnover
Public employees 1	Koch and Steers (1978)					−.38***
Public employees 2	Mowday *et al.* (1979)		.23***	−.13**		−.19***
Hospital employees[a]	Steers (1977a)	.05 .07 .11* .10*	.26**	.08		−17**
Scientists and engineers	Steers (1977a)			−.28**		
Psychiatric technicians[b]	Porter *et al.* (1974)					−.02 −.32* −.43** −.43**
Retail-management trainees[c]	Porter *et al.* (1976)	.36 .35[d] .33[d] .20				−.41* −.43*
Part-time military personnel	Hom, Katerberg, and Hulin (1979)					−.58*
Transit workers	Angle and Perry (1981)			.05	−.48*	−.48**

*Significant at the .05 level.
**Significant at the .01 level.
***Significant at the .001 level.

[a]For the hospital sample, four separate measures of performance were available for the one time period.

[b]Results presented here are from four data points of a longitudinal study. Hence, the relationship between commitment and turnover increased over time.

[c]Results for the turnover analysis presented are from two data points of a longitudinal study representing measures taken on the employees' first day and the last two months in the organization. Analyses for performance were available for measures taken at three points in time and represent cross-lag relationships between commitment and subsequent performance from 4 to 6 months, 6 to 9 months, and 4 to 9 months.

[d]Correlations approached significance at the .05 level.

1978). It is suggested only that commitment may represent one influence on attendance motivation.

Commitment and Tardiness

In a study by Angle and Perry (1981), commitment was found to be strongly and inversely related to employee tardiness ($r = -.48$). Again, the theory underlying the construct suggests that highly committed employees are likely to engage in behaviors consistent with their attitudes toward the organization. Coming to work on time would certainly represent one such behavior.

Commitment and Turnover

Following the theory, it is our belief that the strongest or most predictable behavioral outcome of employee commitment should be reduced turnover. Highly committed employees by definition are desirous of remaining with the organization and working toward organizational goals and should hence be less likely to leave. Thus, we feel it is important to recognize the importance of organizational commitment, along with other variables, in any comprehensive model of employee turnover.

In an effort to examine the commitment–turnover relationship, a series of studies has been undertaken to determine the extent to which this relationship holds. In all, eight studies of the commitment–turnover relationship have been carried out. Five of these studies represented predictive correlational designs among various samples (see Table 2.4). In all five studies, highly significant correlations were found between commitment and subsequent turnover (Angle & Perry, 1981, Hom *et al.*, 1979; Koch & Steers, 1978; Mowday *et al.*, 1979; Steers, 1977a). In a more detailed analysis of data originally reported by Mowday *et al.* (1979), Mowday, Koberg, and McArthur (1980) found that the impact of commitment on turnover may be indirect through its relationship to other variables, such as desire to stay and intention to search for another job. This finding is consistent with the intermediate-linkages model of turnover processes proposed by Mobley (1977) and discussed in Chapter 5.

In a sixth study, a longitudinal design was used to track commitment levels over time among a sample of psychiatric technicians (Porter *et al.*, 1974). Again, commitment was found to be significantly and inversely related to subsequent turnover. In addition, it was found in this longitudinal study that the magnitude of this relationship between commitment and turnover *increased* over time. That is, as we would expect, commitment attitudes strengthened over time for those who chose to remain with the

Table 2.5
Discriminant Analysis between Stayers and Leavers for Commitment and Job Satisfaction for Psychiatric Technicians

Variable[a]	Time period 1	2	3	4
Standardized discriminant weights				
Organizational commitment	−.12	1.04	1.04	1.43
JDI—supervision	−.25	.05	−.24	−.12
JDI—co-workers	.48	−.38	−.19	−.25
JDI—work	.57	.10	−.50	−.39
JDI—pay	.85	−.18	−.01	−.28
JDI—promotion	−.40	.19	.52	.01
Test statistic	5.1	4.7	13.5*	13.0*
Degrees of freedom	6	6	6	6
Total discriminatory power	12.5%	7.4%	20.7%	21.0%

Source: Porter *et al. Journal of Applied Psychology,* 1974, *59,* 603–609.
*Significant at the .05 level.
[a]JDI = Job Descriptive Index.

organization but declined for those who left. These findings are shown clearly in Table 2.5. Such findings reinforce the statement made earlier that commitment attitudes develop slowly over time and increase with employee tenure. Parenthetically, it should also be noted in this study (and two others—Hom *et al.,* 1979; Koch & Steers, 1978) that in all four time periods of the longitudinal design, commitment proved to be a moderately better predictor of subsequent turnover than did the more traditional attitude measure of satisfaction as measured by the Job Descriptive Index (JDI).

The seventh commitment–turnover study also used a longitudinal design among a sample of retail-management trainees (Porter *et al.* 1976). Several features of this study set it off from the typical turnover study: (*a*) the sample is composed of individuals starting out in managerial careers; most studies dealing with turnover focus almost exclusively on rank-and-file employees who possess varying amounts of tenure with the organization; (*b*) the attitude measured is the individual's commitment to the organization as noted earlier; most other turnover studies involving employee attitudes deal simply with job satisfaction; and (*c*) most important, the study is longitudinal—individuals' commitment patterns are tracked from the first day on the job through the end of the first 15 months of employment. From what we know from other literature on turnover, this beginning period of membership in an organization is the most critical period for turnover, since that is where most of it occurs.

What did these data show? First, and most strikingly significant (statistically and otherwise), the eventual leavers had lower attitudes along the way than did the stayers. More specifically, the eventual leavers were significantly lower in commitment attitudes than stayers ($p < .05$) on the *first day* on the job, and were even more separated from the paired stayers in the 2-month period just prior to leaving (whether they left in the first month or so, or in the twelfth or fifteenth month). Put another way, stayers maintained a fairly constant level of commitment throughout the first 15 months on the job, whereas those who would eventually leave sometime during the first 15 months started out on the job (first day) with lower commitment and their commitment declined (though not statistically significantly so for this relatively small matched sample) as they got closer to the point of leaving the organization. These results are based on a strict longitudinal analysis of the data.

A somewhat different analysis that involved cross-sectional comparisons demonstrated the same effect. This analysis, however, showed the differences between the two groups (stayers and leavers) in somewhat more dramatic form. It used a "last back" technique of analysis. That is, leavers' commitment attitudes measured within 1.5 months of the time they actually left were compared with those of the matched stayer group at the same point in time; likewise, leavers' commitment attitudes 3 months prior to leaving and 5 months prior to leaving were also compared with the attitudes of the stayer group measured at the same point in time. What this analysis shows clearly is that the closer an eventual leaver comes to the point of termination, the more his or her attitudes separate from the comparable stayer (see Figure 2.2). Thus, if a leaver is within a couple of months of leaving, his or her attitudes are clearly lower than those of comparable stayers; on the other hand, if he or she is at least 6 months away from leaving, his or her attitudes are indistinguishable from those of someone who is not going to leave in 6 months.

To put the total set of findings from this study in perspective: The respondents—that is, the management trainees—who left the organization voluntarily sometime during the first 15 months of employment typically had begun to show a marked decline in commitment to the organization prior to actually leaving it. These findings, taken together, would seem to point to the following conclusion: If an individual member of an organization begins to show or demonstrate a definite decline in commitment, it is a clear warning that a voluntary termination may occur in the near future. Termination can occur without this decline, but if it appears it probably has meaning for subsequent behavior.

The eighth and final study represented an attempt to reduce turnover in a controlled field experiment using 50 branches of a large West Coast bank

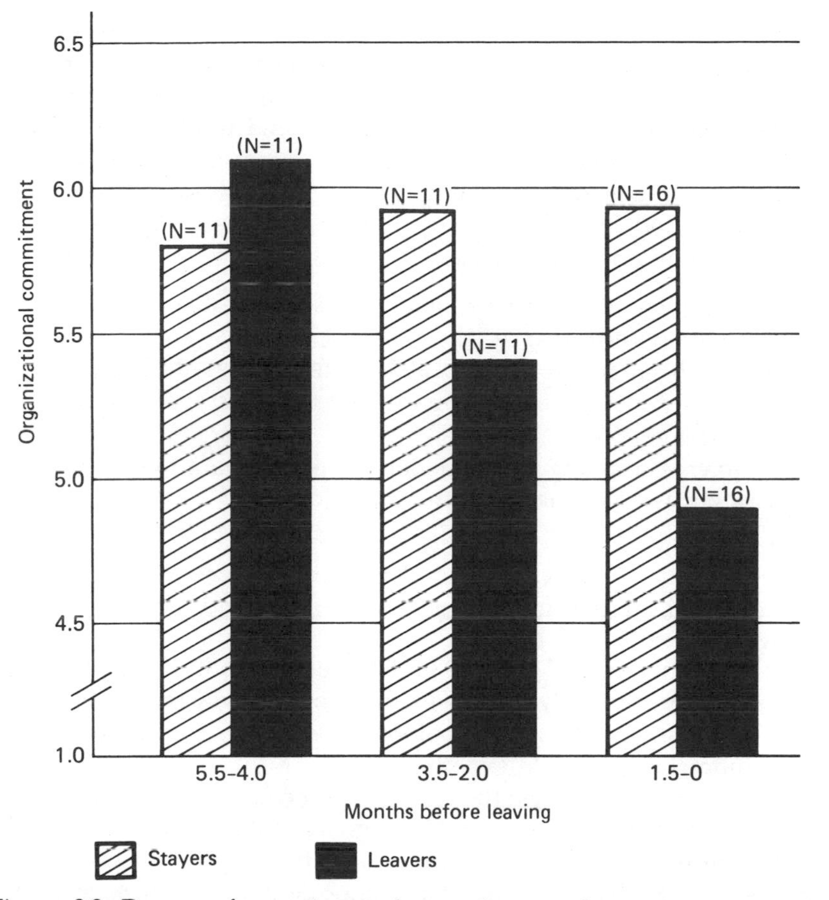

Figure 2.2. Degree of organizational commitment of stayers versus leavers; months before leavers terminate (Source: Porter *et al.*, *Organizational Behavior and Human Performance*, 1976, *15*, 87–98).

(Krackhardt, McKenna, Porter, & Steers, 1981). Twenty-five experimental branches were matched with 25 control branches based on branch size, location (residential versus commercial), and average income level of depositors. Based on pilot interviews with tellers and branch managers, it appeared that major factors influencing turnover among tellers included the following: (*a*) lack of opportunities for professional growth and development; (*b*) poor working conditions; (*c*) poor relationships with supervisors; and (*d*) communications problems.

As a result of these findings, a relatively simple experiment was initiated, aimed at building commitment and reducing turnover by changing supervisory behavior. Specifically, a supervisory workshop was developed and instituted for branch managers in the experimental branches. The workshop consisted of two sessions. At the first session, supervisors were asked to identify factors they felt were contributing to turnover among subordinates. Then they were asked to go home and think about possible solutions. At the second session, 1 week later, supervisors were asked to generate several specific goals that they felt could be accomplished within a 4-month period and would help reduce turnover. Agreement was reached on three primary goals:

1. Meet individually with each teller to discuss problems and provide feedback on performance.
2. Meet with tellers as a group at least four times during the study period to exchange information on work issues and problems and possible solutions.
3. Set up cross-training programs for those who want to broaden their skills. Focus on avenues of career development.

After the intervention, questionnaries were sent to tellers as a manipulation check and to measure attitudes. It was expected that the intervention would lead to both increased commitment and reduced turnover over the next year.

What were the results? Several findings emerged. To begin with, the initial finding was that only some of the branches actually implemented the goals. This was, of course, disappointing and shows the importance of manipulation checks in field experiments.

Of those who implemented the goals, an immediate *drop* in commitment was found rather than an increase. Although it is not known for certain, it is possible that this initial drop was caused by the heightened sensitivities raised by the problem-solving discussions and the expectations that changes must occur. Problem-solving sessions focused on the negative aspects of the job and this focus may have led employees to question their level of attachment to the job and the organization. Subsequent measures showed a belated *increase* in organizational commitment. Finally, the intervention did lead to a significant decrease in turnover compared to the matched control groups. Hence, it was felt that for this particular sample, the intervention did have some impact on raising attitudes and reducing turnover.

Summary

In this chapter, the topic of organizational commitment was introduced. It was noted that several typologies of commitment have been suggested. On the basis of this work, it was suggested that one meaningful way to organize our thoughts about this topic is to differentiate between commitment as an attitude and commitment as a behavior.

Our approach to defining attitudinal commitment suggests that commitment be viewed as the relative strength of an individual's identification with and involvement in a particular organization. According to this approach, commitment can be characterized by at least three factors, including (*a*) a strong belief in and acceptance of organizational goals and values; (*b*) a willingness to exert considerable energy on behalf of the organization; and (*c*) a strong desire to maintain membership in the organization. Commitment as an attitude was contrasted with the more commonly studied attitude of job satisfaction.

A major portion of this chapter attempted to summarize the available empirical work that has emerged concerning antecedents and outcomes of organizational commitment. It was noted that antecedents of commitment could be found in at least four separate areas: (*a*) personal characteristics; (*b*) role-related characteristics; (*c*) structural characteristics of the organization; and (*d*) work experiences. In addition, several consequences of commitment were discussed, the most prominent one being employee turnover.

Having reviewed the literature, we are now in a position in the next chapter to attempt some form of synthesis. That is, we shall make an effort in Chapter 3 to suggest how many of these variables fit together to influence employee commitment processes. We then suggest, at the end of Chapter 3, a future research agenda for additional empirical research on the topic of organizational commitment.

3

Development of Organizational Commitment

The research studies reviewed in the previous chapter suggest that a number of variables have been viewed as antecedents of employee commitment to organizations. In interpreting the results of these studies, however, it is important to recognize that previous research on the antecedents of organizational commitment has, almost without exception, been cross-sectional in design. In other words, investigators have collected questionnaire data from employees at one point in time and correlated commitment with a number of different measures. Although these studies are useful for identifying the types of personal, job-related, and organizational factors that may be related to organizational commitment, they provide less insight into the causal nature of these relationships.

The identification of causal relationships in the study of commitment represents an important area of theoretical concern. Unlike job satisfaction, which is viewed as a less stable attitude that may reflect contemporaneous job conditions, commitment is viewed as a more stable attachment to the organization that develops slowly over time. The commitment of employees to organizations is perhaps best characterized as a *process* that unfolds over time. This process may begin before the employee enters the organization and may extend over successive years of employment. To develop a better understanding of employee commitment it is necessary to focus attention on the factors that may influence the development of commitment at different stages of an employee's career, and on the process through which employees become committed to organizations (cf. Buchanan, 1974).

The purpose of this chapter is to examine the commitment process. Although the discussion will draw upon existing research, it should be apparent that the lack of rigorous longitudinal studies limits discussion to a more speculative nature. The goal of this chapter is to identify relevant variables and develop a conceptual model that can serve to guide future research on the commitment process. The discussion of the commitment process will be divided into three stages: (a) anticipation or pre-entry and job choice influences on commitment; (b) initiation or the development of commitment during the first few months of employment; and (c) entrenchment or the continuing development of commitment through mid and late career stages. The three stages in the development of organizational commitment are summarized in Figure 3.1. Following this discussion, data from two previously unpublished longitudinal studies will be presented. Both studies focus on the development of commitment during the early employment period and suggest several factors that may influence the commitment of new employees.

Development of Organizational Commitment: A Conceptual Framework

Before discussing specific factors that may influence employee commitment at different career stages, it is useful to discuss in more general terms the process through which commitment is developed. As suggested in Chapter 2, two major theoretical approaches have emerged from previous research on commitment. First, commitment has been viewed as an attitude of attachment to the organization that leads to particular job-related behaviors. The committed employee, for example, is absent less often and is less likely to leave the organization voluntarily than are less committed employees (Mowday *et al.*, 1979). The focus of this line of research has been on the implications for behavior of commitment

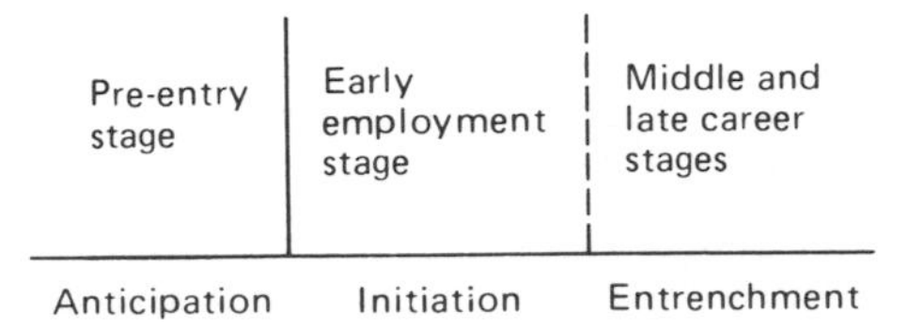

Figure 3.1. Stages in the development of organizational commitment.

attitudes. Second, a line of research in organizations has emerged that focuses on the implications of certain types of behaviors for subsequent attitudes. A typical finding in this research is that employees who freely choose to behave in a certain way and who find their decision difficult to change become committed to the chosen behavior and develop attitudes consistent with their choice (Salancik, 1977). In summary, one approach has emphasized the influence of commitment attitudes on behaviors, whereas the other has emphasized the influence of committing behaviors on attitudes.

Although the commitment attitude–behavior and committing behavior–attitude approaches emerge from different theoretical orientations and have generated separate research traditions, understanding the commitment process is facilitated by viewing these two approaches as inherently interrelated (cf. Mowday & McDade, 1979; Staw, 1977). Rather than viewing the causal arrow between commitment attitudes and behaviors as pointing in one direction or the other, as many researchers have done, it is more useful to consider the two as reciprocally related over time, as shown in the simple diagram in Figure 3.2. The view taken in this chapter is that it is equally reasonable to assume that (*a*) commitment attitudes lead to committing behaviors that subsequently reinforce and strengthen attitudes; and (*b*) committing behaviors lead to commitment attitudes and subsequent committing behaviors. The important issue is *not* whether the commitment process begins with either attitudes or behaviors. Rather, what is important is to recognize that the development of commitment may involve the subtle interplay of attitudes and behaviors over time. In other words, the process through which commitment is developed may involve self-reinforcing cycles of attitudes and behaviors that evolve on the job and over time strengthen employee commitment to the organization. The basic theoretical orientation underlying the discussion in this chapter is that the process of commitment is characterized by the reciprocal influence of attitudes and behaviors.

Although viewing the commitment process in terms of reciprocal influence makes sense from a theoretical standpoint, it raises the difficult question of where to begin a discussion of the process. Most writers have chosen to view the early employment period (first several months to 1 year on the job) as the career stage during which the commitment process begins (e.g., Bray, Campbell, & Grant, 1974; Buchanan, 1974). The early employment period has a major influence on the development of employee commitment, as will be discussed later. However, it is likely that the commitment process begins before employees formally start work in the organization. Pre-employment and job choice influences on commitment

Figure 3.2. Reciprocal influences between attitudinal and behavioral commitment.

will be discussed in the next section. Since the decision to join an organization involves a definite behavior, the discussion will emphasize the linkage between committing behaviors and subsequent attitudes. The discussion will also focus, however, on pre-employment influences other than job choice on subsequent commitment.

Anticipation: Pre-employment and Job Choice Influences on Commitment

Although the different goals, values, and expectations new employees bring to organizations have been extensively investigated (Wanous, 1980), fewer studies have questioned whether new employees enter organizations with different propensities to become committed. Several studies have found reliable differences in the level of commitment new employees report on their first day at work. Moreover, one study even found that the level of commitment expressed by employees their first day in the organization predicted turnover up to several months on the job (Porter *et al.*, 1976), although this finding was not replicated in another study (Mowday & McDade, 1980). Although commitment levels among new employees have been found to vary even before any work in the organization has begun, it is unlikely that this early commitment reflects a stable attachment. Rather, differences in commitment that new employees bring to the job may reflect different propensities to become committed to the organization. This type of propensity may provide a foundation for commitment that can be either strengthened or weakened by subsequent job experiences. In addition, initial levels of commitment may influence how the new employee experiences his or her job during the first few months at work. New employees entering the organization with high levels of commitment, for example, may be more likely than uncommitted employees selectively to perceive positive features of the job and work environment.

The question to be addressed in this section is what types of pre-employment and job choice factors influence the level of commitment of new employees as they enter the organization. The several categories of factors that appear important are summarized in Figure 3.3.

Personal Characteristics

A number of personal characteristics found to be related to commitment were discussed in the previous chapter. Since many of the findings among existing employees appear relevant to new employees as well, relationships between personal characteristics and the development of initial commitment among new employees will be discussed only briefly. In considering the development of initial commitment, however, it is useful to highlight several of the more relevant personal characteristics.

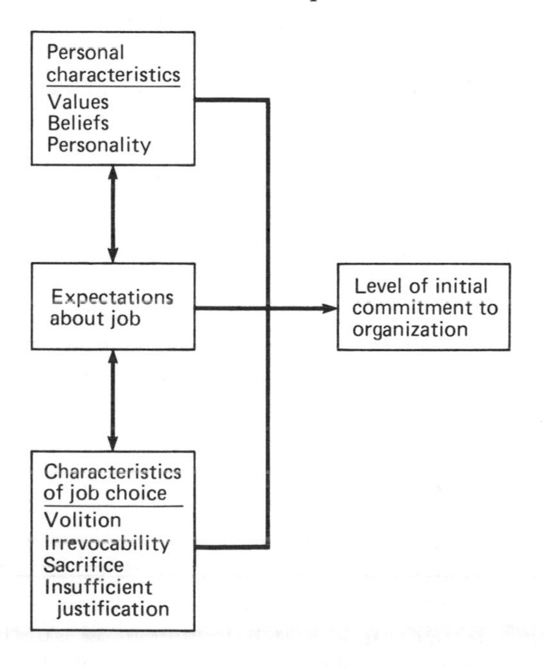

Figure 3.3. Major determinants of initial commitment to the organization.

New employees entering organizations have different goals and values that they seek to satisfy through employment. Initial levels of employee commitment are probably related to employee perceptions of congruence between the organization's values and their own and the extent to which valued goals are seen as attainable on the job. Unfortunately, little research exists among newly hired employees to support this assertion directly. Evidence of a more indirect nature is provided in a study by Mowday and McDade (1980). They found the need for achievement to be related to commitment expressed by new employees on their first day at work, although the relationship was not particularly strong ($r = .20, p < .05$). New employees with a high need for achievement in this sample probably expressed higher initial commitment because they viewed the organization as a place in which their need could be satisfied. Similar relationships might also be found for other needs such as affiliation and power, although additional research will be required to establish a direct relationship between initial commitment and the extent to which new employees view organizational membership as instrumental to need satisfaction.

In addition to direct influences on initial commitment, employee needs can also be viewed as interacting with early job experiences to influence commitment during the first several months at work. In other words, the needs employees bring to the job may interact with their experiences once at work to influence commitment. The highest levels of commitment during the early employment period, for example, may be found among employees who brought a high need for achievement to the job and who subsequently perceive their work as challenging. The question of whether employee needs directly influence commitment or interact with job experiences to influence commitment will require further research before firm conclusions can be drawn.

New employees are also likely to enter organizations with differing work-related values, such as belief in the Protestant work ethic and work as a central life interest. These values are likely to result from the early socialization of the individual. Research evidence suggests that employees who have a strong belief in the value of work or who see work as central to their self-concept are also more likely to become committed to the organization (Dubin *et al.*, 1975; Hall & Schneider, 1972; Rabinowitz & Hall, 1977). Although such a general relationship is likely to hold, it is important to recognize that new employees with a strong personal work ethic may become more attached to their jobs than to the organization in which the job is performed. Such a pattern of attachments is often characteristic of professions where individuals identify more strongly with the profession than with the organization in which they are employed.

Accountants may be less committed to an accounting firm than to the accounting profession, for example, and lawyers less committed to a corporation than to the profession of law. The development of professional attachments that transcend organizations is often given as one explanation for the negative relationship observed between commitment and education.

The socialization of individuals, both in the family and through educational experiences, and the resulting values and beliefs appear to represent important influences on the propensity of employees to become committed to organizations. Research in this area remains limited, however. In general, much greater research attention has been given to the socialization of new employees by organizations than by nonorganizational sources. Since new employees may enter organizations with strongly held beliefs and values that are difficult to change, nonorganizational sources of socialization represent an important influence on commitment.

Employee Expectations

Research on the early employment period has most often focused on the impact of employee expectations on attitudes and turnover. Several studies have found that employees who enter organizations with more realistic expectations are less likely to leave voluntarily than employees whose expectations are unrealistic (Wanous, 1980). In addition, several studies have found a positive relationship between commitment and the extent to which employees who had been on the job for some time believed their expectations had been realized (Buchanan, 1974; Steers, 1977a). The recall nature of the measures used in these studies, however, makes it more difficult to draw conclusions about the effect of met expectations on commitment.

Mowday (1980) directly investigated the influence of met expectations on commitment for a sample of newly hired employees. He compared the expectations of new hires with job incumbent perceptions of supervisory behavior, reward practices, role characteristics, and job challenge in two hospitals. This study found no relationship between the accuracy of expectations new hires brought to the job and commitment after 1 month at work. Additional analyses on data from this same sample by Mowday and McDade (1980), however, did find the expectations of new hires were related to the level of commitment reported the first day at work. Initial commitment was found to be positively related to expected job challenge, rewards that are likely to result from high performance, and several dimensions of supervisory behavior. The causal nature of these relationships was impossible to determine from the data collected, although Mowday and McDade (1980) interpreted these results as suggesting that high expectations about the job lead to high levels of initial commitment.

On the basis of evidence from one study, it is difficult to draw conclusions about the influence of expectations on commitment. No direct evidence exists that met expectations are related to commitment, however, and the evidence relating met expectations to other attitudes such as job satisfaction is mixed (cf. Wanous, 1980). The existing evidence permits us to conclude tentatively that the level of expectations new hires bring to the job has a direct relationship to commitment very early (e.g., within the first week) at work but only a limited influence, if any, on commitment after several months on the job. Employees who enter organizations with high expectations may have a greater propensity to become committed, although continued commitment during the early employment period may be more sensitive to actual job experiences than to initial expectations (or any comparison between the two).

Job Choice Factors

Research on job choice in organizations has traditionally focused on the factors causing employees to select one job rather than another. More recent research has investigated the implications of job choice and circumstances surrounding the choice process for subsequent attitudes toward the job. In an early study, Vroom and Deci (1971) found that graduate students from a business school systematically reevaluated job alternatives following their choice. The chosen job was rated as more attractive and more likely to lead to the attainment of goals the student valued highly after the choice had been made than before the decision. Moreover, unchosen job alternatives were evaluated more negatively following job choice than before. In interpreting these results, it is important to recognize that students had little or no additional information about the jobs following their choice than they had before a decision was made. Similar research findings have been reported by Lawler, Kuleck, Rhode, and Sorensen (1975) in a study of accounting students. As predicted by dissonance theory (Festinger, 1957), these two studies suggest that the act of selecting a job may influence the new hires' attitudes toward the job, at least initially.

Both research and theory have tried to refine the general predictions made by dissonance theory. Several investigators have attempted to identify those circumstances surrounding the selection of a job that are likely to lead to a high commitment to the choice. Salancik (1977) has identified several important characteristics of behaviors that make them committing. First, the decision or behaivor must be explicit. In other words, the act is unequivocal and observable to others. Second, the choice must be difficult to revoke or change. Third, the decision is public in the sense that it is widely known to others. Finally, the decision or behavior must have been freely engaged in. Freedom of choice is increased when the individual has several alternatives from which to choose and there is limited external pressure to choose one alternative over another. When job choices are characterized by these factors, Salancik (1977) predicts that individuals will become behaviorally committed to their decision. Moreover individuals will develop more positive attitudes toward their chosen job in an effort to justify their decision. As suggested earlier, decisions characterized by high behavioral commitment should also lead to greater attitudinal commitment.

Two studies are available that have examined the predicted relationship between behavioral commitment in job choice and subsequent attitudinal commitment to the organization. Mowday and McDade (1979) found commitment for new hires the first day at work positively related to the amount and accuracy of information about the job, two factors that were thought to influence perceived freedom of choice. Contrary to predictions, commitment was also positively related to several variables reflecting the perceived revocability of the choice (i.e., intended length of tenure, perceived ease of transfer to another job within the organization, and perceived ease of finding another job in a different organization). In other words, high initial commitment was more likely to be associated with revocability of the job choice than with irrevocability.

In a second study, O'Reilly and Caldwell (1980b) studied job choices made by MBA students and the students' attitudes after 6 months at work. They found that attitudinal commitment to the organization after 6 months was positively related to both perceived freedom and irrevocability at the time the job choice was made. No significant relationships were found between commitment and either explicitness or public knowledge of the job choice. In their study, behavioral commitment features associated with job choice accounted for 12% of the variance in organizational commitment after 6 months at work. It should be noted that O'Reilly and Caldwell's (1980b) study differed from the research of Mowday and McDade (1979) in that only 6 months commitment was measured. It is possible that if O'Reilly and Caldwell (1980b) had measured first-day commitment, however, even stronger relationships would have been found. Mowday and McDade (1979) reported that their behavioral commitment items accounted for 40% of the variance in first-day commitment although common methods may have inflated this percentage.

Another set of findings emerging from these two studies suggests that the amount of external justification individuals have for their job choice may influence subsequent commitment. O'Reilly and Caldwell (1980b) found high levels of commitment among students who reported taking a job that did not offer the highest salary and who also believed that they were making other sacrifices to take the job. Similar but more complex results were reported by Mowday and McDade (1979). They found that the attractiveness of alternative job offers received by the individuals but forgone was negatively related to commitment the first day at work, although this relationship became positive when commitment was measured after 1 month. This finding suggests that passing up attractive alternatives may have caused individuals to question their job choice the first day at work. After 1 month on the job, however, these same individuals appear to have engaged in postdecision justification of their job choice by bolstering attitudes, similar to the pattern of findings among the MBA students studied by O'Reilly and Caldwell (1980b). In general, it might be predicted that low extrinsic justification and sacrifices in job choice are associated with higher commitment after the choice is made. In a related finding, O'Reilly and Caldwell (1980a) reported that individuals who were intrinsically motivated in their job choice were more committed than those whose choice was extrinsically motivated.

The results of these studies suggest that the circumstances associated with the new hire's decision to join the organization may have important implications for his or her organizational commitment. The study by Mowday and McDade (1979) suggests that individuals who make job choices that are behaviorally committing enter the organization with a greater propensity to become attitudinally committed, whereas O'Reilly and Caldwell's (1980b) findings suggest these effects may persist for up to 6 months on the job. Both studies also suggest that insufficient justification and sacrifices made in the decision to join an organization may lead to greater commitment. These findings provide empirical support for the hypothesized relationship between committing behaviors and attitudinal commitment to the organization (cf. Staw, 1977).

In summary, the research in this section has examined several different factors that may cause new employees to have a high level of commitment when entering an organization. The model of antecedents of first-day commitment that emerges from the discussion is presented in Figure 3.3. Initial commitment to the organization appears to be influenced by personal characteristics of the new hire, expectations about the job, and the circumstances associated with the decision to join the organization. It is also suggested that interrelationships exist among the different sets of variables that may lead to initial commitment. Mowday and McDade (1980), for example, found that individuals who made behaviorally committing job choices also reported higher expectations about the job.

Though the commitment of new employees their first day in the organization is considered important (cf. Porter *et al.*, 1976), it should be recognized that commitment at this stage probably does not represent a very stable attachment to the organization. Rather, the commitment level a new employee brings to the job may be interpreted in terms of the propensity to develop a longer-term commitment to the organization. First-day commitment may be the initial step in the much longer process through which employees develop a stable attachment to the organization. Whether or not new employees who bring a high level of commitment to the organization continue to maintain high commitment, however, may depend to a large extent upon their initial job experiences. The influence of initial job experiences on continuing commitment to the organization will be discussed in the next section.

Initiation: Early Employment Influences on Organizational Commitment

The first several months that a new hire spends in the organization are thought to be particularly crucial in the development of lasting attitudes and expectations (cf. Hall, 1976). This time provides the new hire with his or her first direct experience with the new organization, job, supervisor, and co-workers. Although prior to entry the new hire had only expectations about what the job might be like, the first several months provide firsthand experience. Studies of the early employment period suggest that the type of experiences provided new employees on their first job can influence success in the organization up to several years later (Berlew & Hall, 1966; Bray *et al.*, 1974). Moreover, most new employees who eventually leave the organization will actually terminate during the first 6 months to 1 year on the job (Wanous, 1980). The experiences of new employees shortly after joining the organization therefore appear crucial to the development of lasting commitment.

Influences on organizational commitment during the early employment period are numerous, as suggested by the discussion of antecedents of commitment in the previous chapter. To simplify the discussion, these influences will be categorized as personal, organizational, or nonorganizational. They are summarized in Figure 3.4.

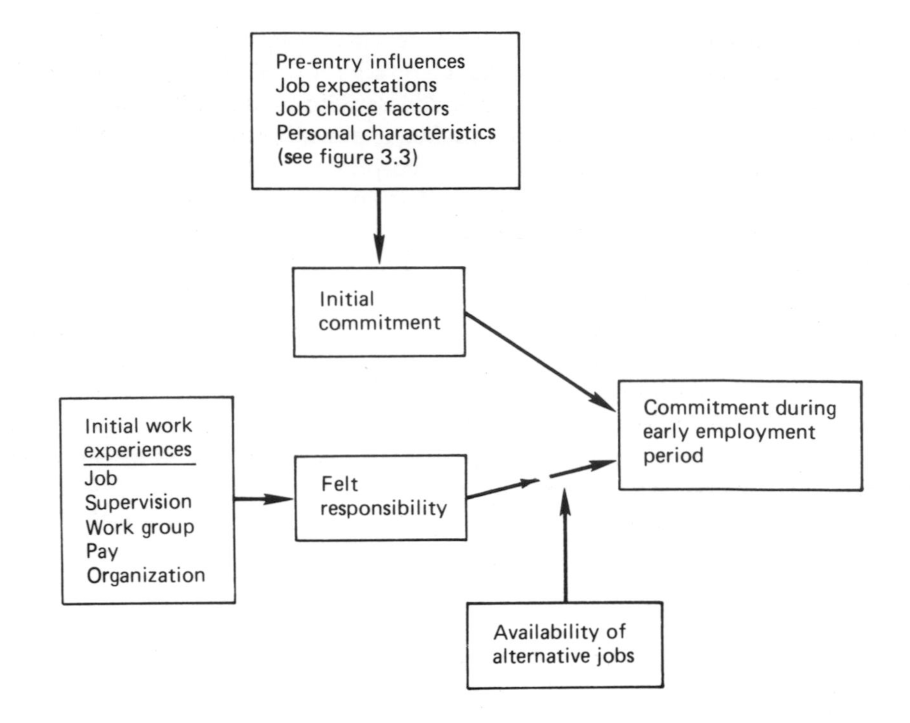

Figure 3.4. Major determinants of commitment during the early employment period.

Personal Influences

As suggested earlier, the characteristics that individual employees bring to the organization represent potentially important influences on commitment. One characteristic that has already been extensively considered is the level of commitment of new employees on their first day at work. First-day commitment was interpreted as a propensity to develop more stable attachment. Although research is limited, there is some evidence that employees who enter the organization with a high level of commitment tend to maintain commitment at a high level through the first several months of employment. Mowday and McDade (1980), for example, found first-day commitment related to commitment after 1 month on the job ($r = .19, p < .05$). The strength of the relationship between first-day commitment and commitment at 3 months was about the same ($r = .21$), although this correlation was not significant because of a decrease in sample size. Crampon, Mowday, Porter, and Smith (1978) found rather stable means for commitment across the first 9 months of employment for a sample of retail-management trainees. In this sample, new hires who eventually stayed with the organization had a higher first-day commitment than eventual leavers. Moreover, the level of commitment for stayers was relatively stable across the first 15 months of employment, whereas commitment for leavers increased during the first month and then decreased shortly before leaving (also see Porter *et al.*, 1976).

The importance of first-day commitment in the development of greater commitment during the early employment period may be understood in terms of behaviors new employees are likely to engage in. Individuals who enter the organization with high levels of commitment may be more likely to put forth extra effort, volunteer for tasks, and take on added responsibilities. To the extent the new employees freely choose to engage in behaviors beyond those expected, the behaviors themselves may be committing and thus may reinforce the commitment cycle. The new employee who puts in extra hours learning the job or who completes a task ahead of schedule, for example, may justify these behaviors by even more positive attitudes in the future. Such a reinforcing commitment cycle may be particularly likely when few extrinsic inducements are provided for behaviors that exceed the organization's expectations.

The likelihood of developing a self-reinforcing cycle of commitment, however, is largely dependent on the opportunity to engage in behaviors that are committing. In other words, the opportunities provided to new employees are crucial in determining whether initially high levels of commitment are translated into more stable attachments. The nature of the job opportunities that are most likely to induce increasing commitment is discussed in the next section.

Organizational Influences

In the previous chapter we reviewed a number of job and work environment characteristics that have been found to be related to commitment. Although most of these studies did not examine the development of commitment during the first few months of employment, it is likely that many of the characteristics related to commitment during later years on the job are relevant to commitment during the early employment period as well. Previous research on the antecedents of commitment, however, has often lacked theoretical focus. In other words, it is sometimes difficult to discern why a particular job or work environment factor *should* be related to commitment. The general theoretical ambiguity associated with most previous research on commitment is evident when it is considered that many, if not all, of the antecedents of commitment have also been investigated as determinants of job satisfaction. Before a theory of commitment can be developed that differentiates this construct from other job-related attitudes, it is necessary to identify a conceptual model that helps integrate and tie together previous research into a more coherent framework.

Salancik (1977) has proposed one conceptual framework that helps integrate previous research. In general, he proposes that "any characteristic of a person's job situation which reduces his felt responsibility will reduce his commitment [p. 17]." The key determinants of commitment are therefore found in characteristics of the job and work environment that increase the employee's felt responsibility. From a behavioral perspective, felt responsibility induces employees to become more behaviorally involved in the job. Greater behavioral involvement should, other factors held constant, lead to greater attitudinal commitment as employees develop attitudes consistent with their behavior. From an inducements–contributions perspective (March & Simon, 1958), however, it should also be noted that felt responsibility may increase employee contributions to the organization. From this perspective, whether high contributions lead to high commitment depends on the level of inducements provided for employes. March and Simon (1958) suggest that high commitment is most likely to occur when the inducements offered to employees match their contributions. In contrast, those working in the behavioral commitment tradition suggest that high commitment may be more likely to follow when contributions exceed inducements (e.g., the case of insufficient justification). As we shall see, the general prediction that felt responsibility increases employee commitment becomes a good deal more complex when the roles of inducements and external job alternatives are considered. Research evidence suggests that employee commitment to the organization may be the result of complex interactions between job-related and external factors. This complex interaction will be discussed in a separate section dealing with nonorganizational influences on commitment.

In this section several characteristics of the job and work environment that may serve to increase felt responsibility will be indentified. This discussion will be brief, since many of these variables were reviewed in the previous chapter.

JOB CHARACTERISTICS

It has commonly been found that job scope is positively related to organizational commitment (Buchanan, 1974; Marsh & Mannari, 1977;

Steers, 1977a; J. M. Stevens *et al.*, 1978). When job scope is viewed as a summary construct composed of separate task dimensions such as variety, autonomy, challenge, significance, and feedback, it is clear why higher levels of commitment are generally found among employees on higher scope jobs. Such task characteristics as autonomy, challenge, and significance may increase the behavioral involvement of employees in their job and thus increase their felt responsibility. Another task characteristic that may be expected to foster commitment is task interdependence (Salancik, 1977). Felt responsibility generally increases among employees when tasks are interdependent (i.e., employees depend upon each other in the performance of their jobs). Morris and Steers (1980), for example, found that commitment was positively related to functional dependence among work roles.

SUPERVISION

In general, high levels of employee commitment should be associated with supervisoin that is not overly tight or close (Salancik, 1977). Supervisors who allow their employees greater discretion over how the job is performed increase the employees' felt responsibility. Although this prediction may appear to conflict with the positive relationship that has been found between leader initiating structure and commitment (Brief *et al.*, 1976; Morris & Sherman, 1981), this conflict may be more apparent than real. Leader initiating structure can involve clarifying job expectations for employees and setting clear task goals, both of which may increase the employee's felt responsibility on the job. In addition, it would be expected that felt responsibility and thus commitment would increase when supervisors allow employees to participate actively in decision making on the job (Rhodes & Steers, 1978) and when organizations are characterized by a high degree of decentralization (Morris & Steers, 1980).

WORK GROUP

Group cohesiveness is generally associated with a high degree of interaction and felt responsibility among members of the group (Cartwright, 1968). High levels of interaction among members of the group are likely to lead to greater social involvement in the organization. The degree of social involvement of employees in organizations has been found to be positively related to commitment in several studies (Buchanan, 1974; Rotondi, 1975; Sheldon, 1971). Previous research has also found organizational commitment to be positively related to positive group attitudes toward the organization and group norms about hard work. Although general relationships between commitment and group attitudes and norms have been found, we would expect these relationships to be particularly strong in cohesive groups since such groups are better able to ensure member compliance with group beliefs and norms.

PAY

Because pay provides an important inducement for employees to remain as members of organizations, it might be predicted that level of pay would be positively related to commitment, particularly where employee contributions are high. Empirical support for such a prediction is weak. Data presented in Table 2.3 in Chapter 2 suggest that better-paying positions are not necessarily associated with higher commitment in organizations. In addition, there is some research to suggest that perceived equity of pay may be a more important determinant of commitment than level of pay (Rhodes & Steers, in press). There are also theoretical reasons to doubt that level of pay will always be associated with high commitment. Salancik (1977) suggested that level of rewards influences the perceived instrumentality of work. Moreover, he suggested that when instrumental rewards for work are salient it reduces the employee's felt responsibility. This follows from the view that salient extrinsic rewards provide external justification for engaging in the task and lower the need for employees to provide internal justification for task involvement. More will be said about the role of extrinsic rewards in the section on nonorganizational influences on commitment.

One interesting example of how pay systems may enhance organizational commitment is provided by Eastern Airlines ("The Spirited Turnaround," 1979). Faced with high current and long-term liabilities, Eastern asked its employees to contribute voluntarily 3.5% of their salaries to a fund that would ensure the company's netting 2% of its gross revenue. As described by Charles J. Simons, Eastern's executive vice-president and vice-chairman, the fund works as follows:

> *Take a hypothetical example of a man earning $100 a month. We carry on the books that we paid him $100 but actually pay him only $96.50. If at the end of the year we make our 2%, we pay him 12 times the $3.50 that was in escrow; if we fall short, we have that cushion to bring our net up to the target amount.*

In addition, Eastern employees were also given an incentive. They could share in one-third of the net profits above the 2%, up to 103.5% of their salaries. The fact that this deal was not entirely equitable from the employee's perspective was made clear (i.e., employees could share in 100% of any shortfall but only 33% of any profits). Despite this, Eastern's 32,000 employees and the leadership of the union accepted the plan.

What makes this example particularly interesting is that it has many of the elements of behavioral commitment discussed by Salancik (1977). For example, the plan was voluntarily accepted by Eastern's employees. Moreover, the inequitable nature of the arrangement was made clear to employees before they accepted. The potential negative consequences of the arrangement were made known in advance and employees may not have felt there was sufficient justification for entering into such an agreement. It would be predicted that the employees at Eastern would become behaviorally committed to their decision and ultimately become more attitudinally committed to the organization. This appears to be exactly what happened. The productivity of Eastern employees increased after the agreement and the company recorded record earnings.

Although many factors in this example may account for the increased effectiveness of Eastern Airlines, the unique pay system implemented in this organization suggests one way in which employee commitment to the organization can be enhanced. In general, any reward system in which employees share in the success of the firm through profit sharing or stock options should increase the felt responsibility of employees and thus their commitment to the organization. This effect may be particularly pronounced when, as in the case of Eastern, employees voluntarily agree to share in both the success of the firm (i.e., its profits) and some of the failures (i.e., its losses).

ORGANIZATION CHARACTERISTICS

Several organization characteristics that have been found to be positively related to commitment have already been mentioned (e.g., functional dependence, decentralization). In addition, Rhodes and Steers (in press) found that employee ownership of organizations was positively related to commitment. This finding is consistent with Salancik's (1977) view that felt responsibility on the part of employees (which would undoubtedly be higher when employees hold stock or ownership shares in the organization) leads to greater commitment. In addition, several studies have found that commitment is related to organization dependability or the extent to which organizations are viewed as looking after the best interests of employees (Buchanan, 1974; Steers, 1977a). This finding suggests a reciprocation norm in which employees develop greater feelings of responsibility when organizations are viewed as caring about employee well-being. The paternalistic management practices and job security found in Japanese organizations, for example, have often been cited as one factor leading to high levels of commitment among Japanese employees (cf. Marsh & Mannari, 1977).

The discussion of organizational influences on commitment during the early employment period would not be complete without mentioning socialization processes organizations establish for their new members. The socialization practices of organizations provide the stimulus for creation of employee attachment to the organization through many of the mechanisms that we have discussed. In some organizations, socialization of new members may be more or less random and unplanned. In other organizations, however, newcomers are introduced to the organization through a carefully planned series of steps and experiences designed to transmit important values and norms about behavior. Despite the importance of socialization practices in organizations, we currently have a poor understanding of how specific socialization practices influence employee commitment. In one interesting study, Kanter (1972) investigated commitment mechanisms used by communes and utopian communities. She found that such total organizations elicit high levels of commitment among their members by requiring explicit sacrifices to become a member, investments in terms of resources or time and energy, public renunciation of previous social relationships, and mortifying experiences designed to increase the dependence of the individual on the group. Van Maanen and Schein (1979) identified several dimensions along which the socialization practices of organizations may differ and how specific practices may influence employee responses. Although not addressing the issue of employee commitment specifically, they suggested that unquestioning acceptance by newcomers of their new role is more likely when certain socialization practices are followed:

> the conditions which stimulate a custodial orientation derive from processes which involve the recruit in a definite series of cumulative stages (sequential); without set timetables for matriculation from one stage to the next, thus implying that boundary passages will be denied the recruit unless certain criteria have been met (variable); involving role models who set the "correct" example for the recruit (serial); and processes which, through various means, involve the recruit's redefinition of self around certain recognized organizational values (divestiture) [p. 253].

The propositions set forth by Van Maanen and Schein (1979) suggest several interesting areas of inquiry concerning the development of commitment during the early employment period. Additional research will be required, however, before firm conclusions can be drawn about the influence of socialization practices on employee commitment.

Nonorganizational Factors

Although attitudinal commitment of employees is likely to be largely influenced by characteristics of the organization in which they are employed, commitment levels can also be influenced by characteristics of *other* organizations in which they might be employed. This follows from Thibaut and Kelley's (1959) early suggestion that satisfaction with a group is dependent on the individual's evaluation of that group (comparison level) and his or her evaluation of alternative groups he or she might join (comparison level for alternatives). In general, the availability of attractive alternative job opportunities should result in less positive attitudes toward the job and organization (Farrell & Rusbult, in press; O'Reilly & Caldwell, 1980b; Pfeffer & Lawler, 1980). Research evidence suggests, however, that the availability of alternative jobs (i.e., revocability of job choice) may interact with both the circumstances surrounding job choice and the sufficiency of extrinsic rewards provided by the organization in influencing commitment.

O'Reilly and Caldwell (1980b) found that MBA students who had not taken the job offer with the highest salary (insufficient justification for job choice) reported significantly higher commitment after 6 months when no alternative job offers had been received since joining the organization than when alternative jobs were available. In contrast, students who had accepted the job offer with the highest salary (sufficient justification for job choice) reported similar levels of commitment when alternative job offers had and had not been received. In interpreting this finding, it appears that new employees who had insufficient justification for their original job choice had a greater need to justify their decision to join the organization. This need was greatest when the decision was not easily revoked (no alternative job offers received), resulting in higher commitment to the organization. O'Reilly and Caldwell's (1980b) findings suggest that the highest levels of initial commitment may be found among new employees who had insufficient justification for their job choice and who subsequently find their decision cannot easily be changed.

Using data collected among university and college faculty by the Carnegie Council on Higher Education, Pfeffer and Lawler (1980) also found evidence of a complex interaction when the effects of alternative job offers on attitudes toward the organization were considered. In their study, sufficient justification for employment reflected the level of extrinsic rewards (pay) provided by the organization. They found that level of extrinsic rewards was positively related to attitudes only for faculty who had received alternative job offers. No relationship was found between extrinsic rewards and attitudes among faculty who had not received job offers from other institutions. This finding suggests that receiving job offers from other organizations may make the level of pay available in the present job salient to employees. Employees who do not receive offers of alternative employment, however, may be far less sensitive to the level of extrinsic rewards provided by the organization.

Though it is difficult to integrate the results of these two studies since common variables were defined differently, both suggest that the availability of alternative job opportunities may not affect all employees in the same fashion. Rather, the availability of alternative employment appears to influence the employee's need to justify original job choice and make salient extrinsic rewards provided by the organizaiton. For organizations operating in competitive job markets (e.g., engineering), high levels of commitment are most likely to be maintained by providing employees with high levels of extrinsic rewards.

In summary, the discussion in this section has focused on the development of commitment during the first few months of employment in the organization. The discussion is summarized in Figure 3.4. Three broad sets of influences on commitment during the period can be indentified. First, individuals are thought to enter organizations with different levels of propensity to become committed. The initial level of commitment reported by new employees their first day at work appears to be a function of personal characteristics, expectations about the job, and the circumstances associated with job choice. Second, the job-related experiences of new employees during the first several months of employment have a major influence on the development of commitment. The discussion of these experiences was organized around Salancik's (1977) view that factors that serve to increase the employee's felt responsibility to the organization lead to higher levels of commitment. Such factors were discussed in terms of job characteristics, supervision, work groups, pay, and characteristics of the organization. Finally, nonorganizational influences on employee commitment were considered. In general, it was suggested that the availability of alternative job opportunities would lead to less positive attitudes, although this influence may result from more complex interactions between job offers and job-related factors.

Although the commitment process extends beyond the early employment period, the development of commitment during the first few months of employment appears particularly important to the continued attachment of employees. Most new employees who eventually leave the organization will terminate within the first 6 months to 1 year on the job (Wanous, 1980). The development of organizational commitment during the first several months decreases the likelihood of early termination. Moreover, the commitment levels of new employees appear to stabilize beyond the first month or so of employment. Mowday and McDade (1980) found commitment at 1 month highly related to commitment after 3 months of employment (r = .83). In addition, Crampon *et al.* (1978) reported test–retest correlations between commitment at 4 and 6 months and between commitment at 6 and 9 months of r = .72 and .62, respectively. Although levels of commitment developed during the early employment period appear to stabilize, it is apparent that the development of organizational commitment is a process that continues through subsequent years of employment. Factors that influence the development of commitment beyond the early employment period will be considered in the next section.

Entrenchment: Continuing Commitment to Organizations

Previous research suggests that one of the strongest predictors of commitment is tenure in the organization. The longer employees work in the organization, the more likely they are to report high levels of commitment (Angle & Perry, 1981; Brown, 1969; Hall *et al.*, 1970; Hrebiniak, 1974; Lee, 1971; Morris & Sherman, 1981; Sheldon, 1971). A number of explanations can be offered for why continued employment is a strong influence on the development of commitment. The discussion is summarized in Figure 3.5.

First, length of service increases the likelihood that employees will receive more challenging job assignments, be given greater autonomy and discretion at work, and receive higher levels of extrinsic rewards. In general, higher-tenure employees hold more desirable positions than lower-tenure employees. The positive features of jobs that lead to commitment during the early employment period may also facilitate commitment for employees with longer service.

Second, investments made by the employee in the organization may also increase with length of service. Increasing investments in the form of time and energy may make it increasingly difficult for employees to leave

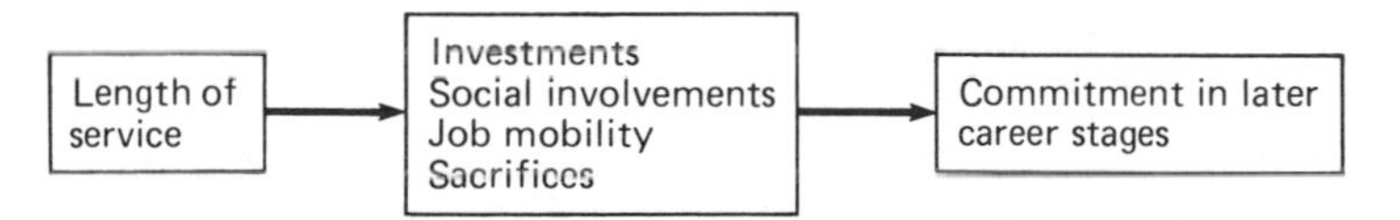

Figure 3.5. Major influences of the continuing development or organizational commitment during the later career stages.

their jobs voluntarily, although this tendency may differ across occupations (e.g., young accountants may often join auditing firms for 5–10 years with the goal of gaining experience that will allow them to move later to corporate accounting positions).

Third, increasing length of service also brings increasing social involvement in the organization and community. For many individuals, work provides the basis upon which social relationships off the job are formed. Many people socialize with co-workers, and they may hesitate to jeopardize these relationships by moving to another job. In addition, both the employee and members of his or her family develop increasing social involvement in the community. As social relationships on the job and in the community grow stronger, the probability of leaving the organization, particularly to take a job in another city, may grow more remote.

Fourth, increasing length of tenure in an organization may serve to decrease the employee's job mobility. Some individuals develop specialized roles in organizations with job skills that would be difficult to transfer (Salancik, 1977). In addition, the availability of alternative jobs may decrease with age. Even with state and federal laws concerning age discrimination, many organizations hesitate to hire older workers whose length of contribution to the organization will necessarily be brief.

Finally, increasing length of service may have a more subtle influence on the development of commitment. Tenure in an organization has associated opportunity costs, even though they may not be apparent to employees at early or mid-career stages. The individual who has sold insurance for one organization for 25 years, for example, may suddenly realize that his or her dream of becoming a teacher is no longer feasible. Alternatively, employees who have neglected their family to pursue a career actively may come to realize that the opportunity to develop close relationships with their children and watch them grow has passed. Most employees have goals or aspirations in life that will never be attained. Increasing investments in a job and organization for most people involve the sacrifice of other important goals. In order to justify this sacrifice, attitudes toward the organization may become more positive. In other words, increasing commitment with length of service may be one way individuals rationalize their decision to forgo some important goals in the pursuit of other goals.

As Salancik (1977) has suggested, interpreting relationships between organizational commitment and tenure is difficult because so many factors may covary with length of service. In the foregoing brief discussion, it was suggested that length of service may be associated with increasing investments and social involvements, decreased mobility, and sacrifices. Each of these factors, alone or in combination, may serve to strengthen commitment to the organization.

Longitudinal Studies of the Commitment Process

As suggested at the beginning of this chapter, the process of becoming committed to an organization may involve relationships among attitudes, perceptions, and behaviors that grow stronger over time. Individuals who make behaviorally committing job choices, for example, may enter organizations with higher initial commitment and subsequently engage in committing behaviors on the job. The commitment process may be characterized by increasing consistency among attitudes, perceptions, and behaviors as length of service in the organization increases. Although empirical evidence on reciprocal relationships among attitudes, perceptions and behaviors is limited, two unpublished studies provide data that highlight this process. These studies will be discussed next.

Retail-Management Trainees

Crampon *et al.* (1978) conducted additional analyses on data collected from a sample originally reported by Porter *et al.* (1976). Participants in the study were management trainees entering a large retailing organization. Most of the trainees were male and were entering their first full-time job after graduating from college. Each trainee was assigned to one of 12 training centers for the first 9 to 12 months of employment in the organization. The training centers were regular retail stores that had a training director responsible for supervising training. After completing training, trainees were assigned to management positions in the organization's stores.

Data were collected from trainees at regular intervals during their first 15 months of employment. Data collection began the first day the trainees entered the organization and questionnaires were again distributed after 2 weeks and 2, 4, 6, 9, 12, and 15 months of employment. The relationships reported by Crampon *et al.* (1978) of particular interest were between attitudinal commitment to the organization as measured by Porter's scale and rated job performance. The performance of each trainee was rated by a training director after 4, 6, and 9 months of employment. The repeated-measures nature of this study makes possible cross-lag correlations between commitment and performance at three points in time (Figure 3.6).

The pattern of correlations emerging from the cross-lag analyses suggests reciprocal relationships between commitment and performance across the 5-month period. Organizational commitment measured at 4 months was more strongly related to job performance at 6 months ($r = .36$, $p < .05$) than the alternative causal relationship ($r = .00$). The difference

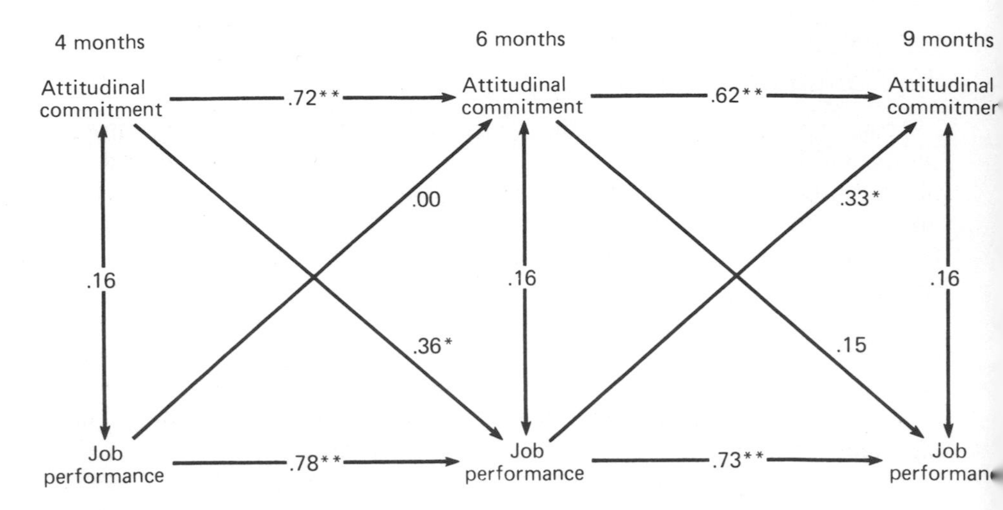

Figure 3.6. Relationships between attitudinal commitment and job performance during the early employment period; $*p < .05$, $**p < .01$ (Crampon *et al.*, 1978).

between these correlations was significant. In contrast, job performance at 6 months was a better predictor of commitment at 9 months ($r = .33$, $p < .05$) than commitment at 6 months was a predictor of performance at 9 months ($r = .15$), although the difference between correlations failed to reach significance. Moreover, the cross-lag correlations were generally larger than the concurrent relationships between commitment and performance at each of the three points in time.

Although the results of this study must be interpreted with caution because of the small sample size ($N = 46$) and the marginal difference in correlations at the later time periods, the pattern of correlations suggests the following sequential relationships between commitment and performance:

attitudinal commitment → job performance → attitudinal commitment

This pattern of results is consistent with the view that attitudinal commitment leads employees to engage in committing behaviors on the job, which in turn result in higher subsequent attitudinal commitment.

Hospital Employees

The second study that has longitudinally examined the development of organizational commitment during the early employment period was reported by Mowday and McDade (1980). They studied newly hired employees in two large state-run custodial hospitals. Participants in the study were primarily females hired for lower-level patient-care positions. Because of the relatively routine nature of these jobs, training was primarily provided on the job. Newly hired employees reported for an orientation session their first morning at work and were then assigned to a ward in the hospital.

Questionnaire data were collected from this sample during the orientation session and again after 1 and 3 months of employment. This study focused on the expectations and initial commitment brought by new hires to the job and the influence of these variables on later commitment and job perceptions. The relationships to be considered here concern attitudinal commitment to the organization and expected and perceived job challenge. Job challenge during the early employment period is of particular interest, since previous research has suggested that it is an important determinant of later success in the organization (Bray *et al.*, 1974). The longitudinal nature of this study allows cross-lag correlations to be calculated between commitment and job challenge measured at three points in time over a 3-month period. The correlations are presented in Figure 3.7.

The results suggest that expected job challenge the first day at work was a better predictor of commitment after 1 month ($r = .19$, $p < .05$) than commitment the first day was a predictor of perceived job challenge at 1 month ($r = .02$). In contrast, commitment at 1 month was a better predictor of perceived job challenge at 3 months than the alternative causal relationship ($r = .67$ versus .54). As with the previous study, these results must be interpreted with caution since the sample size was small ($n = 43$)

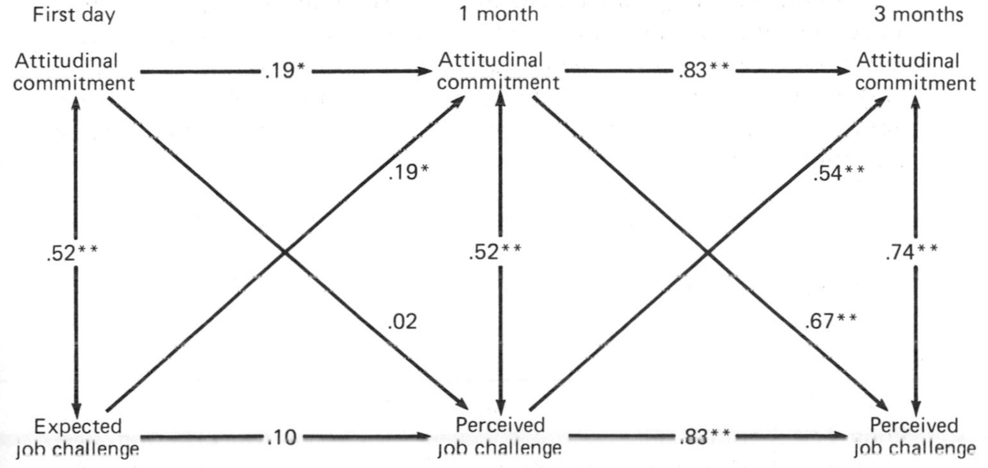

Figure 3.7. Relationships between attitudinal commitment and job challenge during the early employment period; $^{*}p < .05$, $^{**}p < .01$ (Mowday & McDade, 1980).

and differences between correlations were not significant. In addition, concurrent correlations were generally large and commitment at 1 month was predicted equally well by expected job challenge and commitment the first day.

Keeping these study limitations in mind, the pattern of correlations suggests the following sequential relationship:

expected job challenge → attitudinal commitment → perceived job challenge

Moreover, the strength of these relationships appeared to grow stronger over time. Considering relationships between commitment and other variables that were measured in addition to job challenge (but that did not always exhibit the same pattern of results), it was found that the median cross-lag correlation between the first-day and 1-month measures was $r = .01$, and the median cross-lag correlation between the 1- and 3-month measures was $r = .46$. Mowday and McDade (1980) generally reported low relationships between measures taken on the first day and again at 1 month. Between 1 and 3 months, however, relatively strong relationships were found between all of the measures. They interpreted this finding as indicating that relationships between commitment and perceptions of the job had started to stabilize after the first month of employment, whereas during the first month attitude–expectation/perception relationships were generally low and unstable. In this particular study the first month of employment appeared to be a particularly volatile period in the development of attitudes and commitment.

In summary, design limitations and the sometimes marginal findings associated with the two studies reviewed in this section indicate these results must be interpreted with caution. However, both studies do offer a suggestive view of the process through which commitment is developed during the early employment period. The first study suggested a pattern of sequential relationships in which

commitment attitudes→behavior→commitment attitudes

whereas the second study suggested a sequence in which

job expectations→commitment attitudes→job perceptions

Moreover, the second study suggested that commitment and perceptions had become much more consistent between the first and third months of employment. The sequential pattern of relationships found in these studies suggests that commitment may develop through a self-reinforcing cycle similar to the process suggested in Figure 3.2. Commitment appears to influence other variables, which in turn, influence subsequent commitment. Whether future research finds that commitment→behavior or vice versa may depend more on the particular point in time that a study enters the process than on any underlying causal relationships. When sufficient measurement periods are included in future research designs, it appears likely, based on these two studies, that the cyclical nature of the relationships proposed here will be found.

Organizational Commitment: A Future Research Agenda

A large number of studies on the topic of employee commitment to organizations have been sumarized here and in Chapter 2. Although Chapter 2 focused primarily on various personal, work, and organizational variables that have been found to correlate with commitment, this chapter has attempted to place the discussion of commitment and its correlates within the context of a process that may develop across different career stages. Judging from the number of studies available in the literature, organizational commitment is a concept that has attracted considerable attention. Interest in organizational commitment is likely to increase in the future as our concern for the quality of working life and the basic relationship between employees and organization grows. Additional work of both a theoretical and an empirical nature will be required before a full understanding can be developed of the conditions that foster employee commitment and the processes through which organizational commitment grows. The success of future research in increasing our understanding of organizational commitment, however, is less likely to depend on the amount of research interest generated in this area than on the direction this research may take. Because the questions asked in future research on commitment will be crucial to our understanding of the concept, it is useful to summarize several areas of study that appear particularly important.

Agenda item 1. Despite a number of studies on commitment in organizations, our understanding of the commitment process remains largely speculative. As noted previously, most research on commitment has been cross-sectional in design. Causal relationships hypothesized in previous research on the antecedents of commitment have largely been limited to inferences based on theory or intuition (e.g., it is intuitively unlikely that high levels of commitment lead to lower educational attainment). Although some studies have reported multiple measures of commitment (e.g., Van Maanen, 1975), the two studies reviewed in the previous section are among the few that have examined *relationships* between commitment and other variables across time. What are needed, if progress is to be made in our theoretical understanding of the commitment process, are additional longitudinal studies that view commitment *as a process* developing over time. Although static correlational analyses have contributed to our understanding of the types of variables that may be related to commitment, the payoff from additional studies of this type appears to be minimal. Researchers interested in commitment must show a greater willingness to undertake longitudinal investigations if our understanding of commitment is to increase.

Agenda item 2. In addition to the need for longitudinal investigations, there is also a need to expand the area of inquiry into antecedents of commitment. Studies that have correlated commitment with behaviors, for example, have most often viewed behavior as a consequence rather than as an antecedent of commitment. A number of studies that have examined the influence of commitment on such behaviors as turnover, absenteeism, and job performance (Mowday *et al.*, 1979). It would be useful if future research also conceptualizes specific behaviors as a cause of commitment. Several studies on the circumstances surrounding job choice have shown that the behavior of selecting among alternative jobs can influence subsequent commitment, in one study up to 6 months after employment in the organization (O'Reilly & Caldwell, 1980b). The influence of additional behaviors on commitment also needs to be investigated. For example, it might be predicted that new employees who volunteer to work on weekends or take extra job assignments would become more committed to the organization, particularly in the absence of extrinsic inducements to engage in such behavior. Research that focuses on job-related behaviors leading to commitment will help integrate the behavioral and attitudinal approaches to the study of commitment that have emerged in previous theory.

Agenda item 3. Another potentially important area for future inquiry can be found in more complex predictions between variables that are thought to influence commitment. The need for achievement, for example, has been found to have a direct influence on commitment in several studies (e.g., Steers, 1977a). It is probable, however, that employees who bring a high need for achievement to the job situation will only become committed if the job provides the opportunity to satisfy this need. In other words, employee needs such as achievement may interact with characteristics of the job to influence commitment. The highest levels of commitment, for example, may be found among high need achievers who are placed in jobs that are challenging, provide some autonomy in how the work is performed, and provide frequent and concrete feedback about task performance. Previous research has generally failed to consider more complex interactions between variables in relationship to commitment, although such interactions appear to be important.

Agenda item 4. Although most of the longitudinal studies of commitment have focused on the early employment period, there is a need to consider the development of commitment at mid- and late-career stages as well. Buchanan (1974) suggested that influences on commitment may differ across employees at different career stages. With the exception of his exploratory investigation, few researchers have pursued this possibility. Research has continued to focus on the early employment period, perhaps because the first few months in the organization have been found to be particularly important and attitudes undergo rapid changes. However, the importance of the early employment period should not cause us to neglect the continuing development of commitment as length of service in the organization increases.

Agenda item 5. Another question of some importance concerns multiple commitments employees in organizations may hold. Separate areas of research inquiry have examined commitment to different referents such as job, organization, career, and nonwork factors. However, few studies have simultaneously examined the impact of multiple commitments on employees. Dubin *et al.* (1975) found that employees who were committed to the organization were also more likely to identify work as a central life interest. Weiner and Vardi (1980) reported positive relationships between commitment to the job, organization, and career among a sample of employees in diverse occupations. However, there is some suggestion in the literature that commitment to one area of an individual's life may prevent commitment to other areas (e.g., Gouldner, 1958). The employee who is highly committed to family and community activities, for example, may be less likely to develop strong commitments to the job or organization. The influence of multiple commitments and the conflicts they may create for employees represent an important area for future research.

Summary

Employee commitment to organizations is a topic that has generated considerable research interest in the past and is likely to be given increasing attention in the future. The literature reviewed in this chapter and the one preceding it suggests that a great deal is already known about individual and job-related factors associated with employee commitment. In contrast to the largely bivariate correlational tradition of most research on commitment, this chapter attempted to examine commitment as a process that develops slowly over time. The commitment process was viewed as something that may begin before employees enter organizations and extend throughout the career of the individual in the organization. Although some research is available that has examined the development of commitment during the early employment period, relatively few studies have systematically incorporated a process approach to the investigation of commitment. The discussion in this chapter suggests that different factors may influence employee commitment at various career stages. Moreover, the development of commitment may be a cyclical process in which attitudes and behaviors relevant to commitment continuously reinforce each other. Additional research will be needed before a comprehensive understanding of the commitment process can be developed. One goal of this chapter is to urge researchers to move away from studies conducted at one point in time and toward research that examines relationships between commitment and other variables longitudinally.

4

Determinants of Employee Absenteeism

There are at least three approaches to the study of employee absenteeism in organizations. To begin with, many managers approach the subject by using various rules of thumb derived from their years of experience and personal assessments concerning the major causes of absenteeism. For example, we sometimes hear that "when it is harder to stay off the job than it is to come to work, employees will have regular attendance." Such rules of thumb, though interesting, typically fail to get at the heart of the problem. More seriously, such an approach tells us little about the more scientific aspects of the problem.

A second approach to understanding absenteeism involves considering various isolated facts that are made known about it. For example, we hear that females in general have higher absence rates than males. In a book on the subject by Yolles, Carone, and Krinsky (1975), several such isolated facts were presented: (*a*) Absenteeism is far more severe in major cities than in smaller towns and rural areas. (*b*) Absenteeism among females tends to decrease during their careers, whereas absenteeism among males tends to increase. (*c*) Cigarette smokers experience 45% more days lost due to illness and injury than nonsmokers. (*d*) In Belgium, which has very little absenteeism, the law requires there to be a bar in every factory where wine, beer, brandy, and vermouth are served. Here again, the researcher or manager is faced with a problem of integrating these various pieces of information and determining the relative importance of each.

A more useful approach than either of the first two is to view absence behavior systematically and to attempt to gain a portrait of the various major influences on such behavior and how they are interrelated. Toward this end, we shall present a model of employee absenteeism aimed at highlighting many of the more important determinants (Steers & Rhodes, 1978). Although no model can be all-inclusive, it is felt that such an effort can provide a relatively clear portrait of the general processes leading up to attendance or absenteeism.

Extent and Cost of Absenteeism

Before we examine this model, however, it is helpful to consider briefly just how serious a problem absenteeism has become for organizations. One way to answer this question is to look at nationwide absenteeism statistics (Yolles *et al.*, 1975). In many industries, daily absence rates approach 15–20% per day! If we take one commonly accepted estimate of the average daily cost per employee per absence of $66 including wages, fringe benefits, and so forth (Mirvis & Lawler, 1977), the estimated annual cost of absenteeism in the United States is about $26.4 billion. Even if we take a more conservative approach and use the minimum-wage rate, the estimated annual cost of absenteeism in the United States is $8.5 billion.

The situation in other countries is no less severe. In Canada, for example, estimates of the annual cost of absenteeism range from $2.7 billion to $7.7 billion (Gandz & Mikalachki, 1979). Moreover, in Western Europe, overall absenteeism rates range from 14% in Italy to a low of 1% in Switzerland (Yankelovich, 1979a). In Italy, absenteeism has become so institutionalized that many organizations cannot cope on those rare days—usually twice a month on paydays—when everyone shows up. This problem is serious enough to merit its own name, *presentismo*, and results because many Italian manufacturers must hire 8–14% more workers than they need just to get the work out (after controlling for absenteeism). When most everyone attends to collect his or her paycheck, there is not sufficient work to go around.

France ranks second in Western Europe (after Italy) in absenteeism. One study found that one-half of French workers never miss a single day of work. However, of the remaining half, over 80% take at least 40 "sick days" per year. Even Germany, with a reputation for a disciplined work force, exhibits a 9% absenteeism rate, well above the roughly 3% rate in the United States. Clearly, then, absenteeism represents a signficant problem of international concern.

A further way to understand the costs of employee absenteeism in the United States is to examine patterns of absenteeism rates across time and across industries. Figures 4.1 and 4.2 are illustrative in this regard. Figure 4.1, based on national U.S. data, indicates that absenteeism often increases around holiday seasons and that in recent years absence rates have remained relatively constant from year to year. Figure 4.2 shows that absenteeism is generally somewhat higher in larger organizations and in manufacturing. Few regional differences are detected.

In considering the costs associated with absenteeism, it is important to note that absenteeism does not invariably lead to reduced operating efficiency. Staw and Oldham (1978), for example, point out that some absenteeism may actually facilitate performance instead of inhibiting it. That is, absenteeism relieves dissatisfied workers of job-related stress and in some cases may allow them to be more productive when they return to work. Furthermore, Moch and Fitzgibbons (1979) have identified at least three conditions or situations that might mitigate or even eliminate the effects of absenteeism on operating efficiency. These situations are (*a*) jobs that have been "people proofed" by automating production and reducing the role of employees to machine monitors; (*b*) work environments that anticipate and adjust for expected absenteeism (for instance, many companies use "floater pools," where people are employed primarily to replace absent employees throughout a plant); (*c*) instances where employees have little direct effect on plant-level efficiency. Based on a study among blue-collar workers, Moch and Fitzgibbons found that absenteeism influences plant efficiency primarily in situations where (*a*) production processes are not highly automated; and (*b*) the absences cannot be anticipated. Hence, managers can have a significant influence on improving operating efficiency in certain types of work environments if they can succeed in reducing absenteeism.

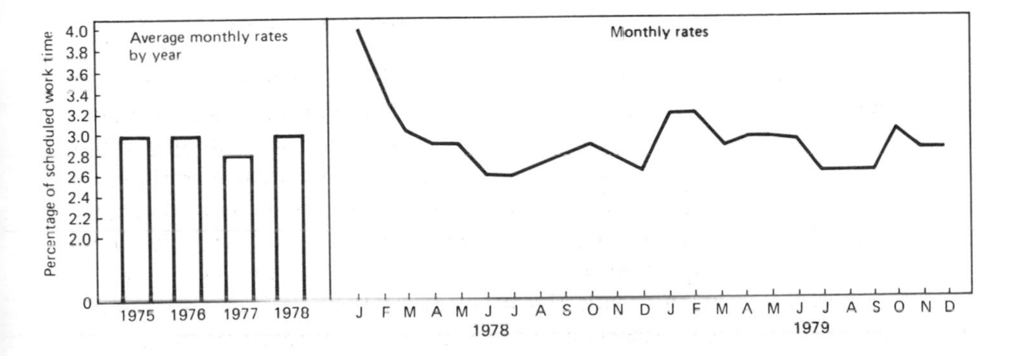

Figure 4.1. Median job absence rates: all companies (*job absence and turnover: 1979*, Bureau of National Affairs, 1980).

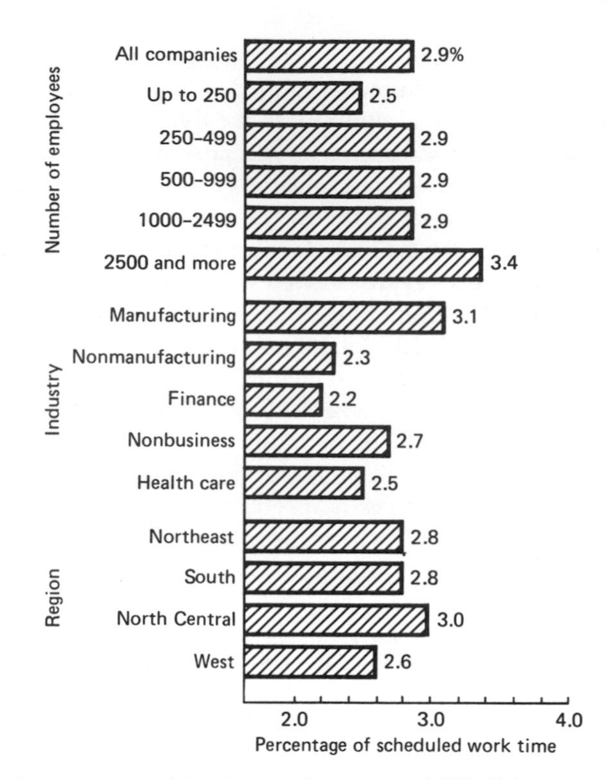

Figure 4.2. Average monthly absenteeism rates: 1979 (*job absence and turnover: 1979*, Bureau of National Affairs, 1980).

Relationship between Absenteeism and Turnover

Most research into withdrawal behavior has focused on employee turnover and has treated absenteeism with subsidiary interest. Moreover, it is often stated in the literature that turnover and absenteeism share common antecedents and hence can be treated with similar techniques. A review of the available evidence by Porter and Steers (1973) argued against this assumption noting that absenteeism as a category of behavior differs in three important respects from turnover: (*a*) The negative consequences associated with absenteeism for the employee are usually much less than those associated with turnover; (*b*) absenteeism is more likely to be a spontaneous and relatively easy decision, whereas the act of termination is typically more carefully considered over time; and (*c*) absenteeism often represents a substitute form of behavior for turnover, particularly when alternative forms of employment are unavailable. Of the 22 studies cited by Porter and Steers (1973) that examined influences on both turnover and absenteeism, only 6 found significant relations in the same direction between the factors under study and *both* turnover and absenteeism. Muchinsky (1977) found evidence of a relationship between the two forms of withdrawal at the individual level of analysis but not at the group level of analysis. However, the magnitude of the relationships were sufficiently modest to demonstrate that the two variables were not caused by the same forces.

As noted by Mobley (1980), these findings should not be surprising. In fact, there are many situations in which absenteeism and turnover would not be expected to be related. These include the following:

> (a) When turnover is a function of the positive attraction of an alternative job rather than escape, avoidance, or "withdrawal" from an unsatisfying or stressful current job.
> (b) When absenteeism is a function of the need to attend to non-job role demands (e.g., parents, sports person, etc.).
> (c) When the consequences of quitting relative to the consequences of being absent have little in common.
> (d) when absenteeism and turnover are constrained, e.g., a monetarily enforced absenteeism control policy and no job alternatives respectively.
> (e) When absenteeism or turnover is a spontaneous or impulsive act.
> (f) When the work role is structured so as to permit discretionary non-recorded, time away from the job (e.g., professional, managerial positions).
> (g) When non-used days of absence are "vested" and can be taken with pay at the time of termination.
> (h) When absenteeism serves a "safety value" to dissipate work pressures that otherwise might precipitate turnover [pp. 9–10].

Even so, Mobley notes that there are at least three situations where we would expect a relationship. These include situations in which: (*a*) the employee takes time off to engage in job search; (*b*) absenteeism represents avoidance of a dissatisfying or stressful job and alternative jobs are available; and (*c*) the consequences of absenteeism and turnover have high communality (e.g., both serve to facilitate nonwork values or activities). On the whole, then, although we would expect some modest relationship between factors that influence absenteeism and turnover, the relationship would clearly not be a strong one. As a result, it must be concluded that sufficient reason exists to justify the study of employee absenteeism in its own right, and not simply as an analogue of turnover.

Measuring Employee Absenteeism

If we are to understand the nature of employee absenteeism in various organizations, we must first understand how (or whether) it is measured in empirical studies. Rather surprisingly, it was found in one survey of 500 U.S. firms that fewer than 40% kept absenteeism records (Hedges, 1973). Moreover, a similar survey of 1600 Canadian firms found that only 17% kept such records, despite the fact that 36% of these firms ranked absenteeism among their most severe problems (Robertson & Humphreys, 1978).

From both an organizational and an empirical standpoint, this is unfortunate. It would appear that there are several reasons why organizations should insist on keeping accurate records of attendance (Gandz & Mikalachki, 1979). Among these reasons are the following (*a*) to administer an organization's payroll and benefits program more accurately and equitably; (*b*) to aid in manpower planning and production scheduling; (*c*) to identify absence problems; and (*d*) to measure and control personnel costs.

Assuming one wishes to measure absenteeism, there are several methods that have been used to collect such data. Unfortunately, there is no uniformly accepted classification scheme for assessing this form of behavior. Huse and Taylor (1962) examined four indices, including the following:

1. Absence frequency—total number of *times* absent
2. Absence severity—total number of *days* absent
3. Attitudinal absence—frequency of *1 day* absences
4. Medical absences—frequency of absences of *3 days* or longer

A different approach has been taken by Chadwick-Jones, Brown, Nicholson, and Sheppard (1971). Here seven indices of absenteeism were used:

1. Absence frequency
2. Attitudinal absence
3. Other reasons—number of days lost in a week for any reason other than holidays, rest days, and certified sickness
4. Worst day—difference score between number of individuals absent on any week's "best" and "worst" days
5. Time lost—number of days lost in a week for any reason other than leave
6. Lateness—number of instances of tardiness in any week

7. Blue Monday—number of individuals absent on a Monday minus number of individuals absent on a Friday of any week

Muchinsky (1977) reviewed the reliabilities of each of these indices using data from both Chadwick-Jones *et al.* and elsewhere.These results, shown in Table 4.1, suggest that absence-frequency measures tend to exhibit higher reliability than the other measures.

Further compounding the problem of measuring absenteeism is the fact that the various measures used in empirical studies are not typically related to one another. For example, one study by Nicholson and Goodge (1976) compared absence severity for employees for 2 consecutive years (labeled AS 1 and AS 2), absence frequency for each of 2 consecutive years (AF 1 and AF 2), unsanctioned (or noncertified) absences (UCA), absences before or after a holiday (AH), and lateness frequency (LF). Results of the various measures were then correlated, yielding the results shown in Table 4.2. As can be seen, little correspondence was found between the

Table 4.1
Studies Computing the Reliability of Various Absence Measures

Investigator	Absence measure	Type of Reliability	Reliability
Turner (1960)	Frequency	Spearman–Brown	.74 (plant 1)
			.60 (plant 2)
Huse and Taylor (1962)	Frequency	Test–retest	.61
	Attitudinal		.52
	Severity	(1 year)	.23
	Medical		.19
Ronan (1963)	Time lost	(Estimated from factor analysis)	.70
Chadwick-Jones *et al.* (1971)	Frequency		.43
	Attitudinal		.38
	Other reasons	Test–retest	.27
	Worst day	(1 year)	.20
	Time lost		.19
	Lateness		.16
	Blue Monday		.00
Farr, O'Leary and Bartlett	Days absent	Spearman–Brown	.35
	Times absent		.39
Latham and Pursell (1975)	Frequency	Test–retest (12 weeks)	.51

Source: Muchinsky *Journal of Vocational Behavior,* 1977, *14,* 43–77.

Table 4.2
Correlations between Various Measures of Absenteeism[a]

As 2	.99					
AF 1	.29	.29				
AF 2	.18	.27	.57			
AH	.10	.12	.45	.30		
UCA	.17	.17	.88	.63	.43	
LF	−.07	−.05	.09	.09	.05	.15
	AS 1	AS 2	AF 1	AF 2	AH	UCA

Source: Adapted from Nicholson and Goodge (1976, p. 238).

[a]AS = *absence severity; AF* = absence frequency; AH = absence before or after a holiday; UCA = unsanctioned absence; LF = lateness frequency; 1 and 2 represent year 1 and year 2 of a 2-year study.

variables. Hence, the problem of measuring absenteeism remains a serious one for researchers on the topic.

A Model of Employee Attendance

If we examine the current state of the art in studies of employee attendance or absenteeism, the results are not encouraging.[1] A review of existing research shows that investigators have typically examined bivariate correlations between a set of variables and subsequent absenteeism (Muchinsky, 1977; Nicholson, Brown, & Chadwick-Jones, 1976; Porter & Steers, 1973). Little in the way of comprehensive theory building can be found, with the possible exception of Gibson (1966).

Moreover, two basic (and questionable) assumptions permeate much of the work that has been done to date. First, the current literature typically assumes that job dissatisfaction represents the primary cause of absenteeism. Unfortunately, however, existing research consistently finds only weak support for this hypothesis. For example, Locke (1976) points out that the magnitude of the correlation between dissatisfaction and absenteeism is generally quite low, seldom surpassing $r = .40$ and typically much lower. Moreover, Nicholson *et al.* (1976), in their review of 29 such studies, concluded that "at best it seems that job satisfaction and absence from work are tenuously related [p. 734]." Nicholson *et al.* also observed that the strength of this relationship deteriorates as one moves from group-based studies to the more rigorous individual-based studies. Similar weak

[1]Much of the remainder of this chapter is based on earlier work of Steers and Rhodes (1978).

findings were reported earlier by Vroom (1964) and Porter and Steers (1973). Implicit in these modest findings is the probable existence of additional variables (both personal and organizational) that serve to moderate or enhance the satisfaction–attendance relationship in work organizations.

A second problem that is consistently found in much of the current work on absenteeism is the implicit assumption that employees are generally free to choose whether or not to come to work. Herman (1973) and others have demonstrated that such is often not the case. In a variety of studies, important situational constraints were found that influenced the attitude–behavior relationship (Herman, 1973; Ilgen & Hollenback, 1977; Morgan & Herman, 1976; F.J. Smith, 1977). Hence, there appear to be several factors (e.g., family responsibilities, poor health, transportation problems) that can interfere with free choice in an attendance decision. Thus, any comprehensive model of attendance must include not only job attitudes and other influences on attendance motivation but also situational constraints that inhibit a strong motivation–behavior relationship (Herman, 1973).

Because of the many narrowly focused studies of absenteeism and the lack of conceptual frameworks for integrating these findings, it is useful to identify the major sets of variables that influence attendance behavior and to suggest how such variables fit together in a general model of employee attendance. Toward this end, a model of employee attendance has been suggested by Steers and Rhodes (1978). This model incorporates both voluntary and involuntary absenteeism and was based on a review of over 100 studies of absenteeism (see Rhodes & Steers, 1978).

Briefly stated, the Steers and Rhodes (1978) model posits that employee attendance is largely a function of two important variables: (*a*) an employee's *motivation to attend* and (*b*) an employee's *ability to attend.* Both of these factors are included in the schematic diagram presented in Figure 4.3, and each is discussed separately as it relates to existing research, beginning with the proposed antecedents of attendance motivation.

Job Situation, Satisfaction, and Attendance Motivation

The model suggested here rests on a fundamental premise that an employee's motivation to come to work represents the primary influence on actual attendance, assuming he or she has the ability to attend (Herman, 1973). Given this premise, questions are logically raised concerning the major influences on attendance motivation. Available evidence indicates that such motivation is determined largely by a combination of (*a*) an

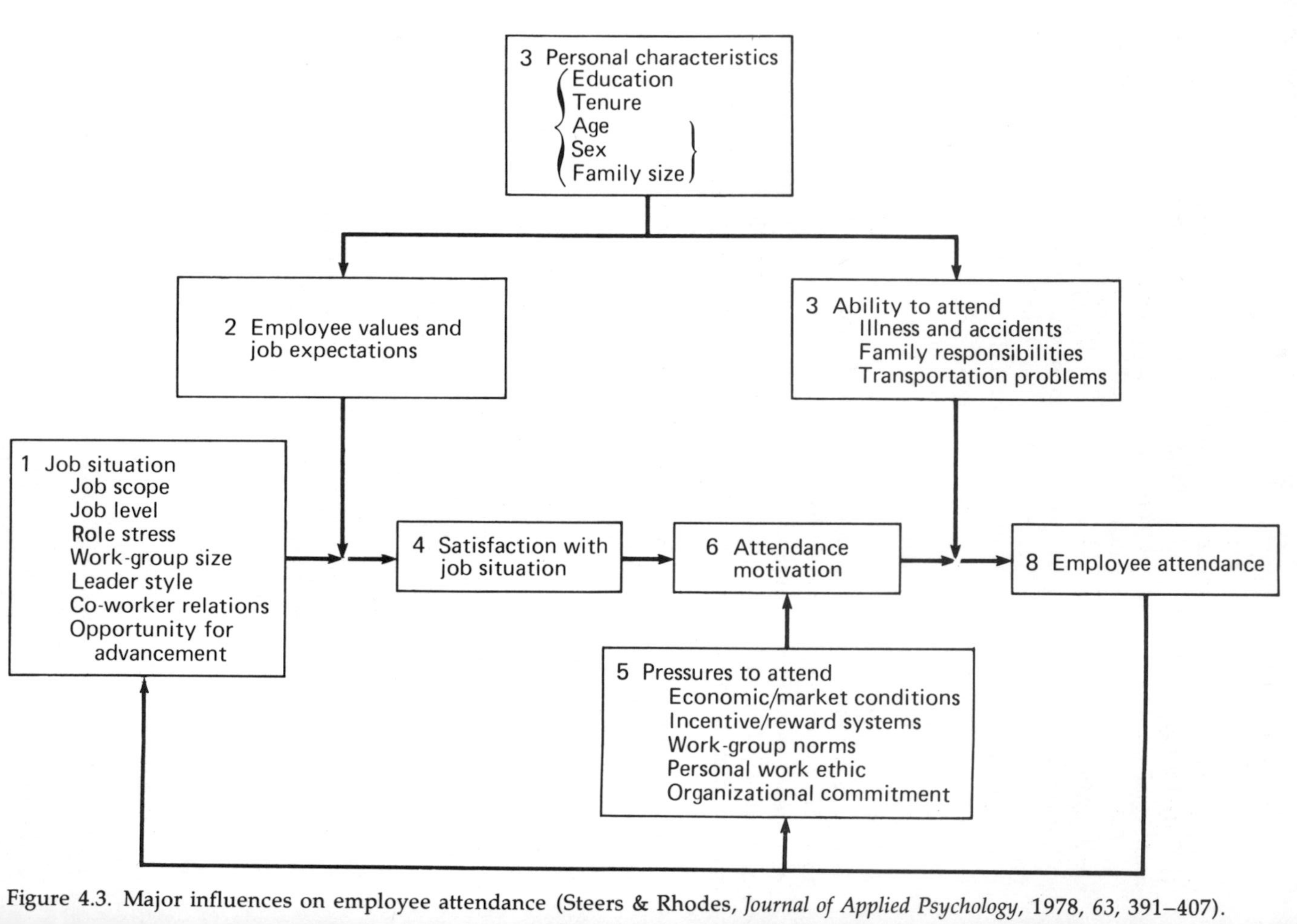

Figure 4.3. Major influences on employee attendance (Steers & Rhodes, *Journal of Applied Psychology*, 1978, 63, 391–407).

employee's *affective responses* to the job situation and (*b*) various internal and external *pressures to attend* (Hackman & Lawler, 1971; Locke, 1976; Porter & Lawler, 1968; Vroom, 1964). First, let us examine the relationship between an employee's satisfaction with the job situation and attendance motivation. Following this discussion, the second major influence on attendance motivation, pressures to atend, will be dealt with.

A major contention of the Steers and Rhodes (1978) model is that, other things being equal, when an employee enjoys the work environment and the tasks that characterize his or her job situation, we would expect that employee to have a strong desire to come to work (Hackman & Lawler, 1971; Lundquist, 1958; Newman, 1974; Porter & Steers, 1973; Terborg, Davis, Smith,& Turbin, 1980; Vroom, 1964). Under such circumstances, the work experience would be a pleasurable one. In view of this relationship, it is logical to consider the manner in which the job situation affects one's attendance motivation. The job situation (box 1 in Figure 4.3), as conceived here, consists of those variables that characterize the nature of the job and the surrounding work environment. Included in the job situation are such variables as: (*a*) job scope, (*b*) job level, (*c*) role stress, (*d*) work-group size, (*e*) leader style, (*f*) co-worker relations, and (*g*) opportunities for advancement. It must be emphasized that we are referring to the general work environment here, not simply to the nature of the required tasks. The influences of various aspects of the job situation on job attitudes and absenteeism are well documented, and they are briefly summarized here as they relate to the model.

JOB SCOPE

A review of the available research yields a fairly consistent if modest relationship between variations in job scope and absenteeism. In particular, absenteeism has been found to be inversely related to perceived measures of task identity (Hackman & Lawler, 1971), autonomy (Baumgartel & Sobel, 1959; Fried, Wertman, & Davis, 1972; Hackman & Lawler, 1971; Hackman & Oldham, 1976; Turner & Lawrence, 1965), variety (Hackman & Oldham, 1976), level of responsibility (Baumgartel & Sobol, 1959), participation in decisions affecting employees' immediate jobs (Nicholson, Wall, & Lischeron, 1977), sense of achievement (Waters & Roach, 1971, 1973), and job challenge (Johns, 1978; Spencer & Steers, 1980). In addition, Mowday and Spencer (1981) found a main effect for job scope and interactions between job scope and the needs for achievement and autonomy in relation to absenteeism. These findings are not entirely unanimous, however (Hackman & Oldham, 1976; Kilbridge, 1961).

Similarly, experimental interventions aimed at redesigning and improving the nature of the job typically lead to a reduction in absenteeism, although exceptions to this trend are found. That is, a wide variety of field experiments found that improving or enriching the nature of an employee's job substantially reduced absenteeism (Beer & Huse, 1972; Copenhaver, 1973; Ford, 1969; Hackman, Oldham, Janson, & Purdy, 1975; Hautaluoma & Gavin, 1975; Ketchum, 1972; Lawler, Hackman, & Kaufman, 1973; Locke, Sirota, & Wolfson, 1976; Oster, 1970; A.L. Smith, 1972; Spiegel, 1975; Trist, Higgins, Murry, & Pollack, 1965; World of Work Report, 1977). Four other industrial experiments among blue-and white-collar employees are summarized by Glaser (1976), and results consistently show a modest relationship between enriched jobs and reduced absenteeism. Several other studies did not find such a relationship, however (Davis & Valfer, 1966; Frank & Hackman, 1975; Gomez & Mussie, 1975; King, 1974; Malone, 1975).

In contrast to the perceptual studies, most experimental studies failed to report both the specific absence measure used and the significance level. Moreover, more than half of these studies failed to use control groups and instead simply reported pre- and posttests on the experimental group. Hence, we are left with largely hearsay evidence that job enrichment reduced absenteeism. This is unfortunate in view of the potential contribution such experimental studies could make to an understanding of absenteeism.

The question that remains concerns why increased job scope often leads to improved attendance. According to the model suggested here, the basic rationale behind such findings is that increasing job scope increases the challenge and responsibility experienced by an employee, which in turn leads to more positive job attitudes (Figure 4.3, box 4). These attitudes then become translated into an increased desire to participate in what are perceived to be more desirable work activities (Figure 4.3, box 6). Support for this interpretation can be found in Hackman and Oldham (1976), Indik (1965), and Porter and Lawler (1965).

JOB LEVEL

A second apparent factor influencing experienced satisfaction with the job situation and subsequent attendance is one's level in the organizational hierarchy. From the limited research available, it appears that people who hold higher-level jobs are more satisfied and less likely to be absent than those who hold lower-level positions (Baumgartel & Sobol, 1959; Hrebiniak & Roteman, 1973; Waters & Roach, 1971, 1973; Yolles *et al.*, 1975). However, caution is in order here in interpreting these results. Hrebiniak and Roteman noted that after satisfaction was partialed out of the job level–

absenteeism relationship, no significant correlation was found (see also Garrison & Muchinsky, 1977). Hence, it is possible that the more challenging nature of higher-level jobs leads to higher job satisfaction, which in turn leads to less absenteeism.

Parenthetically, it should be noted that several of the job situation variables shown in box 1 of Figure 4.3 may interact with one another. For instance, job scope may influence role stress, which then may affect experienced satisfaction. However, in the interest of brevity, these job-related variables have been grouped so primary emphasis can be placed on how such variables influence subsequent attendance motivation and behavior. Since attendance behavior is our primary concern here, these variables are relevant only as they jointly influence those factors affecting attendance.

ROLE STRESS

Studies on role theory have emphasized the importance of role stress and conflict as important variables in work behavior. Miles and Perreault (1976), for example, found substantial evidence that role conflict is associated with job-related tension and reduced job satisfaction (see also Ivancevich & Matteson, 1980). Moreover, Hedges (1973) found absenteeism rates to be higher on jobs charcterized by high levels of stress (e.g., assembly-line jobs). Finally, several studies have found manifest anxiety to be related to employee absenteeism (Bernardin, 1977; Melbin, 1961; Pocock, Sergean, & Taylor, 1972; Sinha, 1963). To the extent that such anxiety, tension, and subsequent dissatisfaction exist, individuals would probably be less likely to want to come to work and may indeed look for excuses not to come to work (e.g., psychosomatic illness). In any case, role stress should not be overlooked as a potential major cause of absenteeism.

WORK-GROUP SIZE

The relationship between variations in the size of the work group and absenteeism suggests a positive linear relationship between increases in work-group size and absenteeism among blue-collar employees (Acton Society Trust, 1953; Argyle, Gardner, & Cioffi, 1958; Baumgartel & Sobol, 1959; Covner, 1950; Hewitt & Parfitt, 1953; Indik, 1965; Indik & Seashore, 1961; Revans, 1958). Three investigations examined blue- and white-collar employees and found no relationship between work-group size and absenteeism (Baumgartel & Sobol, 1959; W. Kerr, G. Koppelmeier, & J. Sullivan, 1951; Metzner & Mann, 1953). Finally Ingham (1970) found that increases in the size of the total organization were also associated modestly with increased absenteeism.

A possible explanation for these findings is that increased work-group size leads to lower group cohesiveness, higher task specialization, and poorer communication (Indik, 1965; Porter & Lawler, 1965). As a result, it becomes more difficult to satisfy one's higher-order needs on the job and job attendance becomes less appealing. This explanation may be more relevant for blue-collar employees than for white-collar employees, since those in the latter group generally have more autonomy and control over their jobs and are in a better position to find alternative mechanisms for securing intrinsic rewards.

LEADER STYLE

Research on leader behavior reviewed by Stogdill (1974) generally confirms that a more considerate leader style facilitates job satisfaction, whereas a more task-oriented or structured leader style often inhibits satisfaction. However, the relationship between leader style and absenteeism is more tenuous. Only 4 studies out of 12 found a significant inverse relationship between satisfaction with supervisory style and absenteeism (Johns, 1978; Metzner & Mann, 1953; Schriesheim & von Glinow, 1980; F.J Smith, 1977). Eight other studies found no such relationship (Garrison & Muchinsky, 1977; Hackman & Lawler, 1971; Lundquist, 1958; Newman, 1974; Nicholson *et al.*, 1976; Nicholson, Wall, & Lischeron, 1977; Waters & Roach, 1971, 1973). In addition, Argyle *et al.* (1958) did find that democratic supervision was related to reduced absenteeism, although supervisory pressure for production did not influence absenteeism. Finally, evidence by Bragg and Andrews (1973), Revans (1958), and C.G. Smith and G. Jones (1968) suggests that more decentralized (i.e., participative) leader control was related to reduced absenteeism, although supervisory pressure for production did not influence absenteeism. When taken together, these findings indicate that leader behavior has a more immediate impact on affective reactions to the job situation than on absenteeism itself. Hence, it appears that satisfaction very likely represents an intermediate variable in the relationship between leader style and absenteeism.

CO-WORKER RELATIONS

A similar sequence of relationships appears to exist for co-worker relations. That is, little evidence exists of a strong or direct association between the nature of co-worker relations and absenteeism. Only two out of nine studies found a significant relationship between these two variables (Metzner & Mann, 1953; Nicholson, Wall, & Lischeron, 1977). Seven other studies did not find this relationship (Garrison & Muchinsky, 1977;

Lundquist, 1958; Newman, 1974; Nicholson *et al.* 1976; Schriesheim & von Glinow, 1980; Waters & Roach, 1971, 1973). However, co-worker relations have generally been found to be quite strongly related to general job satisfaction, which in turn has been found to be related to attendance (Rhodes & Steers, 1978; Vroom, 1964).

OPPORTUNITIES FOR ADVANCEMENT

Finally, little evidence exists suggesting a direct relationship between satsifaction with one's rate of promotion and attendance. Although Patchen (1960), F.J. Smith (1977), and Metzner and Mann (1953) did report a modest relationship, eight other studies among divergent samples did not (Garrison & Muchinsky, 1977; Hackman & Lawler, 1971; Metzner & Mann, 1953; Newman, 1974; Nicholson *et al.*, 1976; Nicholson, Wall, & Lischeron, 1977; Waters & Roach, 1971, 1973). However, research does support the contention that the rate of promotion influences employees' affective response to the general job situation (Hackman & Lawler, 1971). Hence it appears suitable to include opportunities for advancement as an antecendent variable to satisfaction with the job situation, which in turn influences attendance motivation.

In summary, when the findings concerning the various job situation variables are compared, it appears that variables relating largely to job *content* have a stronger influence on actual absenteeism than those relating to job *context.* That is, job content variables were generally found to be consistently related to both satisfaction and absenteeism. In contrast, job context variables, although they were consistently related to satisfaction, were seldom related to absenteeism. Hence, they would be expected to influence absenteeism only to the extent that they altered one's satisfaction with the job situation. It should be noted, however, that job context variables have been found to be fairly consistent predictors of employee turnover, if not absenteeism (Mobley *et al.*, 1979).

Role of Employee Values and Job Expectations

Available research indicates that the relationship between job situation variables and subsequent satisfaction and attendance motivation is not a direct one (Locke, 1976; Vroom, 1964). Instead, a major influence on the extent to which employees experience satisfaction with the job situation appears to be the values and expectations they have concerning the job (box 2, Figure 4.3). It has been noted previously that people come to work with differing values and job expectations; that is, they value different features in a job and expect these features to be present to a certain degree in order to maintain membership (Locke, 1976; Porter & Steers, 1973).

These values and expectations are, in turn, influenced by the personal characteristics and backgrounds of the employees (box 3, Figure 4.3). The pervasive influence of personal characteristics on employee absenteeism is evidenced not only by their effects on values and job expectations (box 2), but also on the ability to attend (box 7). For example, employees with higher educational levels (e.g., a college degree) may value and expect greater (or at least different) rewards from an organization than those having less education (e.g., a private office, a secretary, a higher salary, greater freedom of action). Support for this contention can be found in Hedges (1973). Moreover, older and more tenured employees often value and expect certain prerequisites because of their seniority (Baumgartel & Sobol, 1959; R. Cooper & R. Payne, 1965; J.M. Hill & E.L. Trist, 1955; J. Martin, 1971; Nicholson *et al.*, 1976; Nicholson, Brown, & Chadwick-Jones, 1977; Spencer & Steers, 1980). Whatever the values and expectations that individuals bring to the job situation, it may be important that these factors be largely met for the individuals to be satisfied.

In this regard, A.L. Smith (1972) found that realistic job previews created realistic job expectations among employees and led to a significant decline in absenteeism. In a related vein, Stockford (1944) found that absenteeism was higher among a sample of industrial workers whose previous training was not seen as relevant for their current positions than among a sample whose training was more closely aligned with the realities of the job situation (see also Weaver & Holmes, 1972). In contrast, Mowday (1980) reported that met expectations were unrelated to absenteeism incidents for a sample of employees during the first year or so of employment. Thus, based on the limited evidence that is available, it would appear that the extent to which an employee's values and expectations are met on the job may influence the desirability of going to work and subsequent attendance.

Pressures to Attend

Even though an employee's satisfaction with the job situation apparently represents a major influence on attendance motivation, the relationship is clearly not a perfect one. Other factors can be identified that enhance attendance motivation, probably in an additive fashion (Garrison & Muchinsky, 1977; Ilgen & Hollenback, 1977; Nicholson *et al.*, 1976; Terborg *et al.*, 1980). These variables are collectively termed *pressures to attend* and represent the second major influence on the desire to come to work. These pressures may be economic, social, or personal and are represented in Figure 4.3 by box 5. Specifically, at least five major pressures can be identified: (*a*) economic and market conditions; (*b*) incentive/reward system; (*c*) work-group norms; (*d*) personal work ethic; and (*e*) organizational commitment.

ECONOMIC AND MARKET CONDITIONS

Because the general state of the economy and the job market place constraints on one's ability to change jobs, in times of high unemployment there may be increased pressure to maintain a good attendance record for fear of losing one's job. Evidence suggests that there is a close inverse relationship between changes in unemployment levels within a given geographical region and subsequent absence rates (Behrend, 1951, 1953; Crowther, 1957). Moreover, as the threat of layoff becomes even greater (e.g., when an employee's own employer begins layoffs), there is an even stronger decrease in absenteeism (Behrend, 1951).

On the other hand, when an employee knows that he or she is to be laid off (as opposed to a knowledge that layoffs are taking place in general), the situation is somewhat different. Owens (1966) found that railway repair employees in a depressed industry who had been given notice of layoff because of shop closure had significantly higher absence rates prior to layoffs than a comparable group of employees who were not to be laid off. Owens suggests that in addition to its being a reflection of manifest anxiety, the increased absenteeism allowed employees time to find new positions. However, Hershey (1972) found no significant differences in absence rates between employees who were scheduled for layoffs and employees not so scheduled. Hershey argued that the subjects in his study were much in demand in the labor market and generally felt assured of finding suitable jobs. Improved unemployment compensation may also have been a factor in minimizing absenteeism among those to be laid off or terminated.

Thus, economic and market factors may be largely related to attendance motivation and subsequent attendance through their effects on one's ability to change jobs. When *general* economic conditions are deteriorating, employees may be less likely to be absent for fear of reprisal. However, when the *individual* employee is to be lid off, absence rates are apparently influenced by perceptions of one's ability to find alternative employment. When such alternatives are readily available, no effect of impending layoff on absenteeism is noted; when such alternatives are not readily available, however, absence rates can be expected to increase as employees seek employment elsewhere.

INCENTIVE/REWARD SYSTEM

Several aspects of the reward system used by organizations have been found to influence attendance behavior. To begin with, when perceptual measures of pay and pay satisfaction are used, mixed results are found between such measures and absenteeism. Specifically, three studies among various work samples found an inverse relationship between pay satisfaction or perceived pay equity and absenteeism (Dittrich & Carrell, 1976; Patchen, 1960; F.J. Smith, 1977); seven other studies did not find such a relationship (Garrison & Muchinsky, 1977; Hackman & Lawler, 1971; Lundquist, 1958; Newman, 1974; Nicholson *et al.*, 1976; Nicholson, Wall, & Lischeron, 1977; Schriescheim & von Glinow, 1980). Three other studies found mixed results (Metzner & Mann, 1953; Waters & Roach, 1971, 1973). In short, it is difficult to draw any firm conclusions about pay and absenteeism from these studies based on perceptual measures.

When actual wage rates or incentive systems have been studied, however, the results are somewhat more definitive. Beatty and Beatty (1975), Bernardin (1977), Fried *et al.* (1972), and Lundquist (1958), all found a direct inverse relationship between wage rate and absenteeism. The Bernardin study is particularly useful here because several potentially spurious variables (e.g., age and tenure) were partialed out of the analysis and because the results were cross-validated. Moreover, the Lundquist study employed multiple absence measures with similar results. Other studies cited in Yolles *et al.* (1975) point to the same conclusion. Studies by Fried *et al.* (1972) and Weaver and Homes (1972), both using the less rigorous "total days absent" measure of absenteeism, did not support this relationship, however. In view of the objective nature of actual wage rates as opposed to perceptual measures, it would appear that greater confidence can be placed in them than in the perceptual studies mentioned. Hence, we would expect increases in salary or wage rates to represent one source of pressure to attend, even when employees do not enjoy the job activities themselves.

Researchers in the area have emphasized that several factors must be kept in mind when considering the role of incentives or reward systems in attendance motivation. To begin with, the rewards offered by the organization must be seen as being both attainable and tied directly to attendance. As Lawler (1971) points out, many organizations create reward systems that, up to a point, reward *nonattendance*. For instance, the practice of providing 12 days "sick leave" that employees lose if they fail to use only encourages people to be "sick" 12 days a year (see also Morgan & Herman, 1976). In this regard, Garrison and Muchinsky (1977) found a negative relationship between job satisfaction and absenteeism for employees absent without pay but no such relationship for employees absent with pay. Hammer *et al.* (1980a) also found evidence that certain aspects of the work situation led workers to feel they deserved some time off. Hence, there must be an expectancy on the part of the employee that attendance (and not absenteeism) will lead to desirable rewards. Moreover, the employees must value the rewards available. If an employee would prefer a 3-day weekend to having additional pay, there is little reason to expect that employee to be motivated to attend. On the other hand, employees with a strong financial need (perhaps because of a large family) would be expected to attend if financial rewards were tied directly to attendance.

Among unionized or blue-collar employees, a major portion of an employee's income is often derived fom overtime work. Consequently, the effects of such overtime on absenteeism are important to note. Two studies found that the availability of overtime work among both male and female employees was *positively* related to absenteeism (Gowler, 1969; J. Martin, 1971). Two other studies found no such relationship (Buck & Shimmin, 1959; Flanagan, Strauss, & Ulman, 1974). One could argue here that the availability of overtime with premium pay can lead to an incentive system that rewards absenteeism, not attendance. That is, if an employee is absent during regular working hours (and possibly compensated for this by sick leave), he or she can then work overtime later in the week to make up for the production lost earlier due to absenteeism. Clearly, such a reward system would operate differently than it was intended to. However, in view of the fact that all four relevant studies used either weak absence measures or unduly small samples, the influence of overtime availability on absenteeism must remain in the realm of conjecture pending additional study.

In two studies, it has been found that when employees share ownership in the organization, absenteeism declines in general (Hammer *et al.*, 1980a; Rhodes & Steers, in press). Apparently, worker ownership increases the employee's psychological investment in the organization, thereby increasing the motivation to attend. Attempts have also been made to examine the effects of incentive or reward systems in work organizations using experimental methods. In one study, Lawler and Hackman (1969; Scheflen, Lawler, & Hackman, 1971) experimentally introduced a bonus incentive plan to reward group attendance among a sample of part-time blue-collar employees. Two important findings emerged. First, the employees working under the bonus plan were found to have better attendance records than those not working under the plan. Moreover, the group that was allowed to participate in developing the bonus plan had higher attendance rates than the other experimental group, which was given the bonus plan without an opportunity to participate in its design (see also Glaser, 1976). Hence, both the adoption of a bonus incentive system to reward attendance and employee participation in the development of such a system appear to represent important influences on an employee's decision to come to work.

Punitive sanctions by management in controlling absenteeism have also been studied by a few researchers. Results have been mixed. Two studies found that the use of stringent reporting and control procedures (e.g., keeping detailed attendance records, requiring medical verifications for reported illness, strict disciplinary measures) was related to lower absence rates (Baum & Youngblood, 1975; Seatter, 1961), whereas one found no such relationship (Rosen & Turner, 1971). Baum (1978) reports that such control policies serve to reduce absenteeism among chronic offenders but not among average employees. Similarly, Buzzard and Liddell (1958) and Nicholson (1976) found that such controls did not influence average attendance rates but did lead to fewer but longer absences.

Such contradictory results concerning the use of punitive sanctions suggest that more effective results may be achieved through more positive reward systems than through punishment. One such positive approach is the use of a lottery reward system, where daily attendance qualifies employees for an opportunity to win some prize or bonus. This approach is closely tied to the behavior modification approach to employee motivation (Hamner & Hamner, 1976). Six studies report that such lotteris can represent a successful vehicle for reducing absenteeism (Dittrich & Carrell, 1976; Johnson & Wallin, 1976; Nord, 1970; Pedalino & Gamboa, 1974; Stephens & Burroughs, 1978; Tjersland, 1972). However, in view of the small magnitude of the rewards available for good attendance, it is possible here that results were caused more by the "Hawthorne effect" than by the lottery itself. As Locke (1977) points out, in at least one of the lottery experiments (Pedalino & Gamboa, 1974), absenteeism in the experimental group declined even before anyone in the group had been, or could have been, reinforced. In addition, more conventional behavior modification techniques for reducing absenteeism, reviewed in Hamner and Hamner (1976), show only moderate results over short periods of time.

A final approach to using incentives to curb absenteeism is the modification of the traditional workweek. Golembiewski, Hilles, and Kagno (1974) and Robinson (1976), for instance, both reported a moderate decline in absenteeism following the introduction of "flexi-time," in which hours worked can be altered somewhat to meet employee needs. Moreover, although Nord and Costigan (1973) found favorable results implementing a 4-day (40 hour) workweek, Ivancevich (1974) did not. Since both of these studies used similar samples, it is difficult to draw meaningful conclusions about the utility of such programs for increasing attendance behavior.

WORK-GROUP NORMS

One's colleagues can also exert pressure for or against attendance in the form of work-group norms. The power of such norms is clearly established (Cartwright & Zander, 1968; Shaw, 1981). Where the norms of the group emphasize the importance of good attendance for the benefit of the group, increased attendance would be expected (Gibson, 1966). Findings by Ilgen and Hollenback (1977; see also Spencer & Steers, 1980) support such a conclusion. This relationship would be expected to be particularly strong in work groups having a high degree of cohesiveness (Whyte, 1969). In his job attractiveness model of employee motivation, Lawler (1971) points out that members of highly cohesive groups view coming to work to help one's coworkers as highly desirable; hence, job attendance is more attractive than absenteeism. In this regard, several uncontrolled field experiments (summarized by Glaser, 1976) found that the creation of "autonomous work groups" consistently led to increased work-group cohesiveness and reduced absenteeism. It should be remembered, however, that work-group norms can also have detrimental impact on attendance where they support periodic absenteeism and punish perfect attendance by employees.

PERSONAL WORK ETHIC

The personal value systems that individuals have can also influence attendance motivation (Rokeach, 1973). Research on the "work ethic" has shown considerable variation across employees in the extent to which they feel morally obligated to work. In particular, several investigations have noted a direct relationship between a strong work ethic and the propensity to come to work (Feldman, 1974; Goodale, 1973; Ilgen & Hollenback, 1977; Searls, Braucht, & Miskimins, 1974). Hence, tentative findings indicate that one pressure to attend is the belief by individuals that work activity is an important aspect of life, almost irrespective of the nature of the job itself. To the extent that employees hold such beliefs, we would expect them to make every effort to come to work.

ORGANIZATIONAL COMMITMENT

Finally, somewhat related to the notion of a personal work ethic is the concept of organizational commitment, discussed in detail in Chapters 2 and 3. If an employee firmly believes in what an organization is trying to achieve (that is, he or she is committed to the organization), he or she should be more motivated to attend and contribute to those objectives. This motivation may exist even if the employee does not enjoy the tasks required by the job. Support for this proposition can be found in Hammer,

Landau, and Stern (1980a), Mowday *et al.* (1979), F.J. Smith (1977), Steers (1977a) and Terborg *et al.* (1980), where commitment and attendance were found to be related for five separate samples of employees. On the other hand, if an employee's primary commitments are in other areas, such as family, home, a hobby, or sports, he or she would experience less internal pressure to attend (Morgan & Herman, 1976).

Ability to Attend

Much of the current research on absenteeism fails to take into account involuntary absenteeism in the study of absence behavior. This failure has led to many contradictions in the research literature that may be explained by measurement error alone. In fact, in a comparison of five absenteeism measures, Nicholson and Goodge (1976) found an average intercorrelation of .24 between measures, certainly not an encouraging figure. Thus, if we are serious about studying absenteeism, a clear distinction must be made between voluntary and involuntary attendance behavior, and both must be accounted for in efforts to develop suitable models.

There are many situations in which a person may want to come to work and has a high attendance motivation, but is unable to do so because of a lack of behavioral discretion or choice (Herman, 1973). At least three such unavoidable limitations on attendance behavior can be identified: (*a*) illness and accidents, (*b*) family responsibilities, and (*c*) transportation problems (box 7, Figure 4.3).

ILLNESS AND ACCIDENTS

One primary cause of absenteeism is clearly poor health or injury (Hedges, 1973; Hill & Trist, 1955). Both illness and accidents are often associated with increased age (Baumgartel & Sobol, 1959; R. Cooper & R. Payne, 1965; de la Mare & Sergean, 1961; J. Martin, 1971). This influence of personal characteristics on ability to attend is shown in box 3 of Figure 4.3. Included in this category of health-related absences would also be problems of alcoholism and drug abuse as they inhibit attendance behavior (Yolles *et al.*, 1975).

FAMILY RESPONSIBILITIES

A second constraint on attendance is often overlooked, namely, family responsibilities. As with health, this limitation as it relates to attendance is largely determined by the personal characteristics of the individual (sex, age, and family size). In general, women as a group are absent more frequently than men (Covner, 1950; Flanagan *et al.*, 1974; Hedges, 1973; Isambert-Jamati, 1962; Kerr *et al.*, 1951; Killbridge, 1961; Spencer & Steers,

1980; Yolles *et al.*, 1975). In fact, Johns (1978) noted that gender was the single most effective predictor of absenteeism. This finding is apparently linked not only to the different types of jobs women typically hold compared to men but also to the traditional family responsibilities assigned to women (that is, it is generally the wife or mother who cares for sick children). Support for this assumption comes from Beatty and Beatty (1975), Naylor and Vincent (1959), and Noland (1945). Hence, we would expect female absenteeism to increase with family size (Ilgen & Hollenback 1977; Isambert-Jamati, 1962; Nicholson & Goodge, 1976).

Along these lines, however, it is interesting to note that the absenteeism rate for many women declines throughout their work career (possibly because the family responsibilities associated with young children decline). For males, on the other hand, unavoidable absenteeism apparently increases with age (presumably because of health reasons), whereas avoidable absenteeism does not (Martin, 1971; Nicholson, Brown, & Chadwick-Jones, 1977; Yolles *et al.*, 1975). In any case, gender and family responsibilities do appear to place constraints on attendance behavior for some employees, particularly women.

TRANSPORTATION PROBLEMS

Difficulty in getting to work can also influence actual attendance. On occasion, this difficulty may take the form of travel distance from work (Isambert-Jamati, 1962; J. Martin, 1971; Stockford, 1944), travel time to and from work (Knox, 1961), or weather conditions that impede traffic (F.J. Smith, 1977). Exceptions to this trend have been noted by M. Hill (1967) and Nicholson and Goodge (1976), who found no relationship between travel distance or availability of public transportation and absence. In general, however, increased difficulty in getting to work due to transportation problems represents one possible impediment to attendance behavior for some employees, despite high attendance motivation.

Finally, as shown in Figure 4.3, the model as presented here is a process model. That is, the act of attendance or absenteeism often influences the subsequent job situation and subsequent pressures to attend in a cyclical fashion. For example, a superior attendance record is often used in organizations as one indicator of noteworthy job performance and readiness for promotion. Conversely, a high rate of absenteeism may adversely affect an employee's relationship with his or her supervisor and co-workers and result in changes in leadership style and co-worker relations. Also, widespread absenteeism may cause changes in company incentive/reward systems, including absence-control policies. Other outcomes could be mentioned. The point here is that the model, as suggested, is a dynamic one, with employee attendance or absenteeism often leading to changes in the job situation that, in turn, influence subsequent attendance motivation. This interrelationship among the major influences on such behavior is often overlooked by both managers and researchers on the topic.

Summary of the Steers and Rhodes Model

The research literature on employee absenteeism clearly reveals a multiplicity of influences on the decision and ability to come to work. These influences emerge both from the individuals themselves (e.g., personal work ethic, demographic factors) and from the work environment (e.g., the job situation, incentive/reward systems, work-group norms). Moreover, some of these influences are largely under the control of the employees (e.g., organizational commitment), whereas others are clearly beyond their control (e.g., health). The model suggested here has attempted to integrate the available evidence into a systematic conceptual model of attendance behavior. In essence, it is suggested that the nature of the job situation interacts with employee values and expectations to determine satisfaction with the job situation (Locke, 1976; Porter & Steers, 1973). This satisfaction combines in an additive fashion with various pressures to attend to determine an employee's level of attendance motivation. Moreover, it is noted that the relationship between attendance motivation and actual attendance is influenced by one's ability to attend, a situational constraint (Herman, 1973; F.J. Smith, 1977). Finally, the model notes that feedback from the results of actual attendance behavior can often influence subsequent perceptions of the job situation, pressures to attend and attendance motivation. Hence, the cyclical nature of the model is emphasized.

The relative importance of the various factors in the model would be expected to vary somewhat across employees. That is, certain factors may facilitate attendance for some employees but not for others. For instance, one employee may be intrinsically motivated to attend because of a challenging job; this individual may not feel any strong external pressures to attend because he or she likes the job itself. Another employee, however, may have a distasteful job (and not be intrinsically motivated) and yet may come to work because of other pressures (e.g., financial need). Both employees would probably attend, but for somewhat different reasons, and with perhaps different levels of job involvement.

This interaction effect raises the possibility of a substitution effect, up to a point, across the major influences. For instance, managers concerned with reducing absenteeism on monotonous jobs may change the incentive/reward system (that is, increase the attendance–reward contingencies) as a substitute for an unenriched work environment. In fact, it has been noted elsewhere that most successful applications of behavior modification (a manipulation of behavior–reward contingencies) have been carried out among employees holding unenriched jobs (Steers & Spencer, 1977). Support for this substitutability principle can be found in Ilgen and Hollenback (1977), who found some evidence that various factors influence attendance in an additive fashion, not a multiplicative one. Thus, the strength of attendance motivation would be expected to increase as more and more major influences, or pressures, emerged to focus the employee's attention on the need or desirability of coming to work.

Differences can also be expected in the manner in which the various influences on attendance affect such behavior. That is, a few of the major variables are apparently fairly *directly* related to desire to attend (if not actual attendance). For instance, highly satisfied employees would probably want strongly to attend, whereas highly dissatisfied employees would probably want strongly not to attend. On the other hand, certain other factors appear to serve a gatekeeper function and do not covary directly with attendance. The most prominent gatekeeper variable is one's health. Although sick employees typically do not come to work, it does not necessarily follow that healthy employees will attend. Instead, other factors (e.g., attendance motivation) apparently influence a healthy person's desire or intent to come to work on a particular day.

Partial Tests of the Model

To date, four attempts have been made to provide for a partial test of the model suggested here. The first, by Hammer *et al.* (1980a) measured several of the variables noted in the Steers and Rhodes model (including job satisfaction, organizational commitment, job involvement, financial incentives, and demographic variables) and compared their predictive power vis-à-vis employee absenteeism among 112 worker-owners in a small furniture cooperative. The results indicated that attitudinal variables predicted *voluntary* absenteeism better than individual or job characteristics. However, contrary to earlier findings in the literature, Hammer *et al.* found satisfaction and voluntary absenteeism to be *positively* related; that is the more satisfied the employee, the more likely he or she was to be absent.

Hammer and her colleages hypothesized that the less satisfied employees who were simultaneously more commited to the company felt compelled to come to work and try to improve the situation. Hence, commitment to the organization emerged as a more potent attitude in attendance than job satisfaction. Such findings indicate that job attitudes and various pressures to attend are indeed more important influences on attendance motivation than either job characteristics or individual differences. What remains to be explained in the study is the contraindicative job satisfaction–absenteeism relationship. Clearly, more work is in order concerning the interrelationship between satisfaction and commitment as they influence absence behavior.

A second study that attempted to provide for a partial test of the model was carried out by Terborg *et al.* (1980). This study was carried out among a sample of 259 retail employees. Several findings that emerged from this study are germane to the model. To begin with, variables thought to index employee ability to attend were not found to be related to unpaid absenteeism. The absence of such a predicted relationship was explained in part by a restriction-of-range problem with some of the study variables (e.g., family size and distance from work) and in part because ability to attend was not assessed directly. Only surrogate measures were used. Even so, whatever the reason, Terborg *et al.* failed to find support for the role of ability to attend in actual attendance.

On the other hand, in the Terborg *et al.* study, variables used to index pressures to attend were found to influence attendance, although the magnitudes of the relationships were modest. Organizational commitment, for example, as measured by the OCQ, was significantly and inversely related to absenteeism. Moreover, tenure with the organization (classified in this study as a pressure to attend) was also found to be inversely related to absenteeism. Overall, Terborg *et al.* (1980) concluded that "the results for variables used to index pressure to attend were consistent with past research [p. 15]."

The results with respect to job satisfaction were consistent with that segment of the Steers and Rhodes model. Satisfaction with work was negatively related to absenteeism. Finally, Terborg *et al.* found that different retail stores experienced different levels of absenteeism and were characterized by different mean demographic characteristics among their employees. Hence, an argument is made against ignoring situational differences in studying employee behaviors. In considering the effects of situational factors, Terborg *et al.* (1980) note:

> We concur with Muchinsky (1977) and Steers and Rhodes (1978) in their request for more broadly based designs that include a variety of situational variables in the study of absenteeism. Our results convince us of the potential effects of situational factors. Situational factors might moderate the relationship between attitudes and behavior through affecting a person's ability to engage in the behavior. Or, situational factors may affect absentee-

> ism directly. . . . [The] consequences of being absent in this organization probably were more negative compared to consequences in other organizations. Yet, our review of the literature on abenteeism shows that only in a few limited cases have researchers either considered personnel practices as a factor or mentioned it in the discussion of their results [p. 18].

In summary, then, the Terborg *et al.* (1980) study found some support for the various parts of the model, with the exception of the effect of ability to attend on actual attendance.

In the third study, Watson (1981) studied 116 production workers using a time-lost index. The general hypothesis of this study was that absenteeism was a joint function of personal characteristics, the job situation, and job satisfaction. It was not expected that this relationship would be overly strong, however. Indeed, the Steers and Rhodes (1978) model points to a number of other mitigating factors (e.g., pressures to attend, ability to attend) that would lead one not to expect a strong relationship. No attempt was made to test the entire model. Although significant findings emerged in the multiple regression results, the strengths of the relationships were not particularly great. Moreover, satisfaction was found to be unrelated to time-lost absence for this sample. Since no variables measured pressures to attend or ability to attend (except for number of children), it is not possible to speculate about the extent to which these additional model-based variables would combine with the existing study variables to predict absenteeism.

The final study focused on 81 manufacturing employees (Frechette, 1981). Five personal characteristics (age, sex, marital status, family size, and educational level) were measured, as well as job satisfaction and job expectations. Ability to attend was estimated from company records concerning the reasons for employee absences (e.g., illness, accidents, family responsibilities, transportation problems). Salary was the only pressure-to-attend variable used in the analysis. Multiple measures of absenteeism were taken.

The results showed a significant relationship between the predictor variable and a frequency-of-absence measure ($R^2 = .25$, $p < .02$). The personal characteristics and the pressure-to-attend variable accounted for more of the variance here than did the satisfaction measures. In addition, it was found that the absence model being tested was able to predict absence frequency better than time-lost absence, and was able to predict both voluntary and involuntary absence. In conclusion, Frechette (1981) concluded that "the model was able to predict absenteeism quite well [p. 9]."

When taken together, these initial studies using correlational designs provide some support for the utility of the model. However, additional comprehensive studies using experimental or longitudinal designs are clearly needed to examine further the extent to which the model is useful in explaining employee attendance or absenteeism. Moreover, further studies should add to our knowledge of this process by suggesting refinements or extensions of the current model. In this way, we can build upon past research in a systematic way that facilitates increased understanding for both researchers and managers.

Employee Absenteeism: A Future Research Agenda

As can be seen, our existing knowledge of employee absenteeism is derived from piecing together a variety of bivariate and rather disjunctive research findings to form a conceptual model based largely on induction. Hence, in many ways, the foregoing model may be considered as a series of hypotheses suitable for subsequent testing. If we are to make further progress toward explicating absence processes in organizations, much more remains to be accomplished. At least seven lines of research activity can be identified for a research agenda on absenteeism.

Agenda item 1. As we just noted, the foregoing conceptual model relies primarily on an integration of somewhat fragmentary research findings. Very few comprehensive multivariate studies of absenteeism are to be found, although this trend may be changing (see, for example, Hammer *et al.*, 1980a; Spencer & Steers, 1980). Moreover, very few studies have attempted to explore causal sequences among variables. An earlier review by Porter and Steers (1973) argued that more comprehensive process models of withdrawal behavior were needed, instead of the continued proliferation of bivariate correlational analyses. The conceptual model presented here represents one such attempt. However, there exists a significan need to test such a model and other models using longitudinal and experimental methods.

For instance, efforts should be made to examine the nature of the relationship between satisfaction and various pressures to attend as they jointly influence attendance motivation. Do such variables influence attendance motivation in an additive or multiplicative fashion? Research is also needed concerning the interaction of attendance motivation and ability to attend as they determine actual attendance. How important are the various constraints on one's ability to come to work in moderating the relationship between attendance motivation and actual attendance? Do additional constraints exist that have not been recognized in the model that impinge on one's ability to come to work? Finally, and perhaps most important, comprehensive research designs are needed to estimate the relative importance of the many variables identified in the model as each influences attendance. For example, is an organization's incentive/reward system more influential than prevailing economic conditions or than satisfaction? How much variance exists across individuals concerning the relative importance of these variables? Until we have answers to questions such as these, we must acknowledge a rather limited understanding of attendance processes in organizations.

Agenda item 2. Are there other variables that influence absenteeism but have yet to be studied systematically? One possible example is the problem of multiple commitments and possible conflicts among such commitments (Hall, 1976). That is, what effect does a strong commitment to one's family or to a hobby (instead of to the organization) have on attendance motivation? Similarly, what effect does psychosomatic illness, possibly brought on by role pressures, have on actual attendance? Work by Staw and Oldham (1978) has touched on this subject. However, more detailed investigation is necessary. Additional work is also in order concerning the sustained impact of behavior modification on employee attendance. The influence of habitual behavior as it relates to attendance should also be examined. Finally, considerably more could be learned about the manner in which extraorganizational factors (e.g., family responsibilities, pressures, and norms; friendship groups) influence the attendance decision (see Smulders, 1980).

Agenda item 3. Some effort must be focused on the operationalization and conceptualization of absenteeism measures. For example, there is some disagreement concerning the relative preference for measures of absenteeism or measures of attendance. Latham and Pursell (1975, 1977) argue that measuring employee attendance (instead of absenteeism) leads to more stable measures over time and that the concept of attendance behavior is more appealing theoretically. Both of these assertions have been questioned by Ilgen (1977), however.

Moreover, as noted by Nicholson and Goodge (1976), various measures of absenteeism (total days lost, number of instances of absences, medically sanctioned absences, etc.) do not covary. Available data suggest that a frequency measure is preferable to time-lost measures or other indicators (Hammer, Landau, & Stern, 1980b). In any case, serious problems of interpretation emerge in attempts to compare results across various absenteeism studies. This problem is compounded by the reluctance of some investigators to specify clearly how absenteeism was measured in their own studies. Certainly, additional effort is needed to ensure that future research employs comparable (or at least multiple) measures of absenteeism so that greater integration of the various findings is possible.

It would also be highly desirable if future studies reported the absence control policies and sanctions that exist in the organization under study (e.g., sick-leave policy, medical certification of absences). Such controls may have an important influence on study results that is often overlooked.

Agenda item 4. The reported test–retest reliabilities of various absence measures have typically been unduly low. Chadwick-Jones *et al.* (1971), for example, report reliabilities ranging from .00 to .43 for various measures of absenteeism. Muchinsky (1977) reports reliabilities ranging from .00 to .74, with a median of .38. At least two interpretations of these data exist. On the one hand, it can be argued that such low reliabilities clearly raise doubts as to the utility of the reported findings. On the other hand, it can also be argued that attendance behavior over time is simply not a reliable phenomenon. Indeed, the model proposed here suggests several reasons why such behavior should *not* be stable over time. Although low test–retest reliabilities of absence measures increase the difficulty of dealing with such behavor, from both an empirical and a managerial standpoint, such instability may in fact reflect a reality that must be dealt with in future studies on employee absenteeism.

Agenda item 5. There is a prevailing assumption throughout much of the literature on absenteeism that all absenteeism is detrimental to organizational well-being. It is possible, however, that some absenteeism may in fact be healthy for organizations in that such behavior can allow for temporary escape from stressful situations (perhaps through the provision of personal days off), thereby potentially contributing to the mental health of employees (see, for example, Ivancevich & Matteson, 1980). In fact, rigid efforts to ensure perfect attendance (such as through behavior modification) may lead to unintended and detrimental consequences on the job, such as reduced product quality, increased accidents, and so forth. Hence, it would be helpful if future studies could examine the extent to which changes in absence rates do or do not have adverse consequences for other aspects of organizational effectiveness. If reduced absenteeism is accomplished at the expense of product quality, accident rate, strike activity, or employee mental health, serious cost–benefit questions must be raised concerning the desirability of initiating efforts aimed at reducing such behavior.

Agenda item 6. In contrast to other areas of intellectual concern, it is not necessary here to argue for additional experimental (as opposed to correlational) studies. In point of fact, there have been a number of experimental studies of absenteeism, particularly as it relates to job redesign. However, many of these studies used multiple interventions simultaneously (Glaser, 1976), thus contaminating treatment effects. Moreover, the majority of experimental studies reviewed here failed to use matched control groups, and many failed to report the nature of the absence measures employed. Future experimental studies must therefore provide for a more rigorous test of the hypotheses by employing more stringent (and controlled) experimental designs, while clearly identifying and isolating the treatments. Confounding of variables remains a needless hallmark of studies of employee absenteeism.

Moreover, in view of the inconsistency (and possible instability) of most measures of absenteeism, it would be highly desirable to cross-validate results. Evidence by Garrison and Muchinsky (1977) and Waters and Roach (1973) amply demonstrates the possible misinterpretation of results that can easily occur in the absence of cross-validation or replication of results.

Agenda item 7. A characteristic attribute of absenteeism studies is their focus on blue-collar and clerical employees. Managerial personnel either have largely been ignored because of a lack of data or because absenteeism data that are available suggest that little problem exists with managers. However, in view of the increased autonomy that managers have, which makes short absences from work relatively easy, it may be useful to reexamine de facto absenteeism among such employees. This reexamination really suggests the need to consider the productivity of such employees. When an assembly-line worker is absent (or is present but not actually working), it is quite noticeable. However, when a manager is "in conference" or "working privately," questions must be raised concerning the extent to which he or she is really present on the job, psychologically as well as physically. Lenz (cited in Yolles *et al.*, 1975) argues that one of the prerogatives of managers is the right to be absent. "It is the right to sit around the office and talk, the right to take a slightly longer lunch 'hour' than anyone else, the right to run personal errands during the day while blue-collar workers must wait until Saturday [p. 17]." In short, it would be helpful to learn more about the active participation levels of managers (and other employees), perhaps employing somewhat different measures of absenteeism. Such efforts may eventually lead to a call for a redefinition of absenteeism to reflect productivity on the job rather than mere presence.

Summary

In summary, then, we have attempted in this chapter to make a case for the utility of studying employee absenteeism in its own right instead of as an analogue of turnover. Moreover, it was noted that the costs associated with absenteeism are probably higher than most managers would expect.

A model of major factors influencing employee attendance was presented that attempts to account for both voluntary and involuntary absenteeism. It is suggested in the model that actual attendance is largely influenced by a combination of attendance motivation and ability to attend. Attendance motivation, in turn, is thought to be influenced primarily by an employee's satisfaction with the job situation combined with a variety of pressures to attend.

The model as presented is meant to be illustrative of the major forces accounting for employee attendance or absenteeism. It was also presented to guide future research efforts in the area. To date, at least four tests of certain parts of the model provide partial support for the usefulness of the model. Even so, more work is clearly needed, as has been noted. In particular, more research focusing on systematic and comprehensive tests of the proposed model using longitudinal or experimental designs would be helpful. Moreover, more progress could be made toward a better understanding of the individual and organizational consequences of absenteeism (or forced attendance). Finally, some work is in order concerning our current conceptualization of absenteeism. As noted, it may be useful to expand our definition of absenteeism to include the notion of active participation on the job instead of mere presence. Through such efforts, we may be able to move the field forward sufficiently such that more meaningful recommendations for organizational actions can be suggested.

5

Determinants of Employee Turnover

Investigations into the causes of employee turnover abound in the literature on organizational behavior and industrial psychology. Beginning with the early studies of Bernays (1910) and Crabb (1912) and continuing to the present, well over 1000 studies on the subject have been carried out. This is 10 times the number of studies carried out on absenteeism. Over the last 25 years, moreover, at least 13 review articles on turnover have been published (Brayfield & Crockett, 1955; Forrest, Cummings, & Johnson, 1977; Herzberg, Mausner, Peterson, & Capwell, 1957; Lefkowitz, 1971; March & Simon, 1958; Mobley *et al.*, 1979; Muchinsky & Tuttle, 1979; Pettman, 1973; Porter & Steers, 1973; Price, 1977, Schuh, 1967; Stoikov & Raimon, 1968; Vroom, 1964). Hence, the subject of employee turnover has clearly not been ignored by organizational scholars.

However, what do appear to have been neglected in the literature are serious, comprehensive efforts to construct useful models of the turnover process. Although several models exist (e.g., March & Simon, 1958; Mobley 1977; Price, 1977), their eloquence does not seem to match our current level of understanding in the area, perhaps because of the sheer amount of information available. In our efforts at parsimony, we have a natural tendency to simplify, often resulting in propositions for which contradictory data exist. This is not the fault of the researchers but rather a simple statement of reality in dealing with organizational problems.

Because of the numerous turnover studies and reviews of turnover studies it would be redundant to publish another review. Instead, a far more fruitful area of endeavor would be to venture further into the morass of turnover modeling and to attempt to extend our theoretical knowledge of the processes by which individuals decide whether to stay or leave an organization. Such an attempt is made here. Instead of a review, an attempt will be made to piece together the available data and summarize earlier modeling attempts into a fairly comprehensive process model of employee turnover.

Extent of Turnover

Before considering such a model, however, it is helpful to examine briefly the extent of the problem and the costs associated with turnover. There are several ways to gain a clearer understanding as to the extent of the problem. One can, for example, examine trends in turnover statistics across years and months of the year. Such data are presented in Figure 5.1. Among other facts, it will be noted that overall turnover rates increase dramatically toward the end of summer, reflecting the return of students to school. Moreover, as shown in Figure 5.2, turnover rates are lowest in the largest organizations, in contrast to absenteeism rates (see previous chapter). Turnover rates are also lower in the manufacturing sector of the economy, which typically pays higher wages. Turnover is also somewhat higher in the western region of the United States.

A second way to appreciate the extent and diversity of the problem is to consider longevity or tenure rates of employees in various industries. These data are shown in Table 5.1, which indicates median years on the job for employees in various occupations and industries. Again, it becomes readily apparent that certain sectors of the economy (e.g., railroads, agriculture, postal service) have significantly lower turnover rates on the average than other sectors (e.g., wholesale and retail trade, entertainment and recreation, construction, medical and health services). The implications of such findings for organizational effectiveness and managerial action will be discussed in the next chapter as we consider the consequences of turnover.

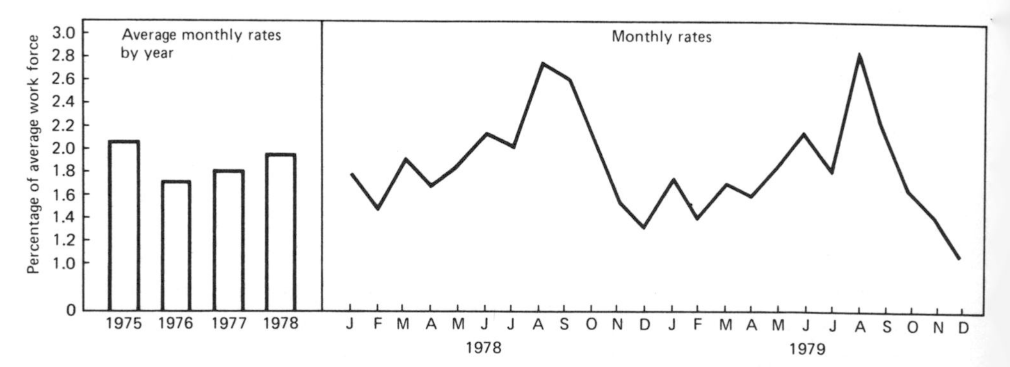

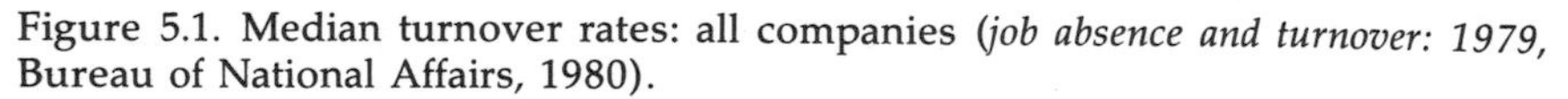

Figure 5.1. Median turnover rates: all companies (*job absence and turnover: 1979*, Bureau of National Affairs, 1980).

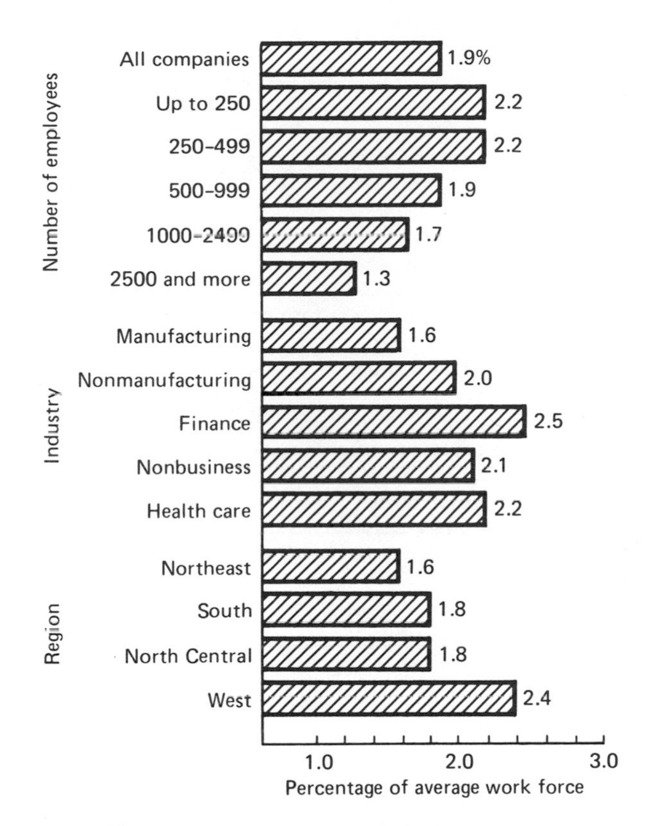

Figure 5.2. Average monthly turnover rates, 1979 (*job absence and turnover: 1979,* Bureau of National Affairs, 1980).

Measuring Employee Turnover

As with employee absenteeism, there exist various methods for calculating employee turnover rates. The most comprehensive description of these methods can be found in Price (1977). He identifies seven general methods:

1. Average length of service—sum of the length of service for each member divided by the number of members
2. Accession rate—number of new members added during the period divided by the average number of members during the period
3. Separation rate—number of members who left during the period divided by the average number of members during the period
4. Stability rate—number of beginning members who remain during the

Table 5.1
Median Years on the Job for Male Workers in Selected Industries

Industry	Median years on job
Railroads and railway express	19.6
Agriculture	11.5
Postal service	10.3
Federal public administration	7.6
Automobile manufacturing	7.0
Chemical and allied products manufacturing	6.8
Mining	6.4
Electrical machinery manufacturing	5.7
Communications	5.2
Instrument manufacturing	5.1
Food and kindred products manufacturing	5.1
Finance, insurance, and real estate	4.0
Rubber and plastics manufacturing	4.0
Medical and other health services	2.8
Construction	2.7
Wholesale and retail trade	2.6
Entertainment and recreation services	1.9
All durable goods manufacturing	5.7
All nondurable goods manufacturing	5.3

Source: Bureau of Labor Statistics (1975, p. A-13).

period divided by the number of members at the beginning of the period

5. Instability rate—number of beginning members who leave during the period divided by the number of members at the beginning of the period
6. Survival rate—number of new members who remain during the period divided by the number of new members
7. Wastage rate—number of new members who leave during the period divided by the number of new members

On the whole, it seems as though the most prevalent approach in organizations to turnover measurement is the separation rate (3). This measure reflects a general tendency to leave the organization regardless of employee tenure. As such, it perhaps provides the broadest indication of a turnover problem.

Previous Research on Employee Turnover

One way to trace our progress toward a better understanding of employee turnover in organizations is to examine the various reviews that have appeared over time. A careful reading of these reviews reveals that, although some progress has been made, much remains to be learned about the major causes of employee turnover.

The first formal reviews of the field appeared in the mid-1950s, with the work of Brayfield and Crockett (1955) and Herzberg *et al.* (1957). Both reviews found evidence of a significant relationship between employee dissatisfaction and subsequent turnover. However, it was noted that many of the studies to that date exhibited serious methodological problems (e.g., a failure to obtain independent measures, the use of poorly validated or ambiguous research instruments). In fact, these problems were so numerous that Brayfield and Crockett (1955) questioned whether methodological changes alone would substantially change the nature of the relationship. Hence, although not rejecting the hypothesis that dissatisfaction causes turnover, these reviewers argued that much more rigorous measurement techniques were in order if we were to advance our understanding of the topic.

Shortly after these reviews appeared, March and Simon (1958) published their now classic book *Organizations,* which presented a literature-based model of the "decision to participate." The model was based on the general postulate (after Barnard, 1938) that "increases in the balance of inducement utilities over contribution utilities decrease the propensity of the individual participant to leave the organization, whereas decreases in that balance have an opposite effect [p. 93]." The inducements–contributions balance was posited to be influenced by two major components: (*a*) the perceived desirability of leaving the organization; and (*b*) the perceived ease of movement from the organization.

On the basis of this proposition, March and Simon (1958) went on to suggest further refinements of the model (see Figures 5.3 and 5.4). Perceived desirability of movement was thought to be influenced by an individual's level of job satisfaction plus the perceived possibility of intraorganizational transfer. The "primary factor influencing this motivation [to leave] is employee satisfaction with the job as defined by him [p. 94]." On the other hand, perceived ease of movement was thought to be influenced by the number of extraorganizational alternatives perceived, which in turn were influenced by the current level of business activity, the number of visible organizations, and the personal characteristics of the employees. This inducements–contributions model represented a significant theoretical advance in the field and forms the basis of much of our current theorizing on turnover to this day.

Several years later, the literature was reviewed by Vroom (1964). Across seven studies, Vroom found a fairly consistent, if modest, relationship between job dissatisfaction and turnover. Viewing these findings within an

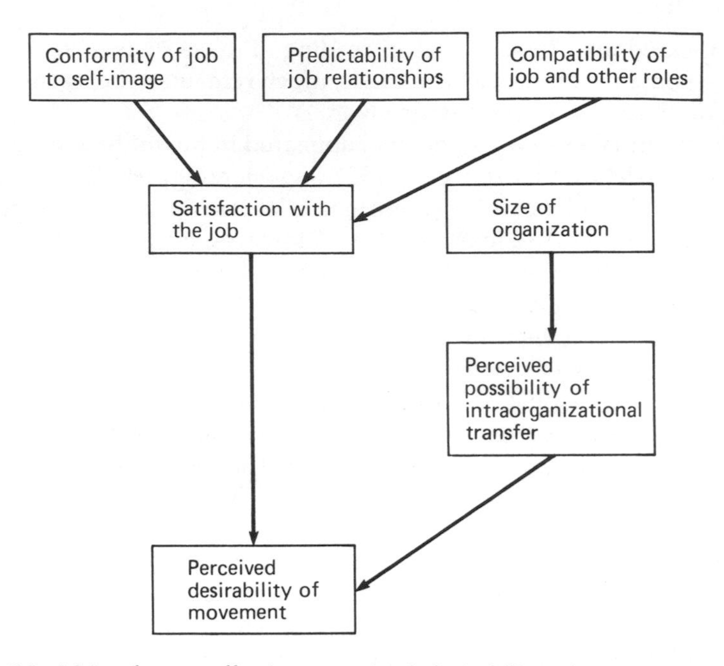

Figure 5.3. Major factors affecting perceived desirability of movement (Source: March & Simon, *Organizations*. New York: Wiley, 1958).

expectancy/valence theory framework, Vroom suggested that the probability of someone resigning was a function of the difference in strength between two opposing forces: those forces to remain and those forces to leave. The force to remain was assumed to be reflected in job satisfaction levels. The force to leave, on the other hand, was thought to be influenced by the valence of outcomes that an individual cannot attain without leaving his or her present position and by the expectancy that these other outcomes can in fact be attained elsewhere:

> It seems reasonable to assume that simultaneous measurements of the valence of one's present position (i.e., job satisfaction), the valence of other positions, and the expectancy that these other positions can be attained would yield a better prediction of the outcome of an individual's decision to stay or resign from his job than would measurements of job satisfaction alone [p. 178].

In 1967, a more limited review by Schuh focused on studies predicting turnover by means of personality and vocational inventories and biographical information. Schuh concluded that no consistent relationship

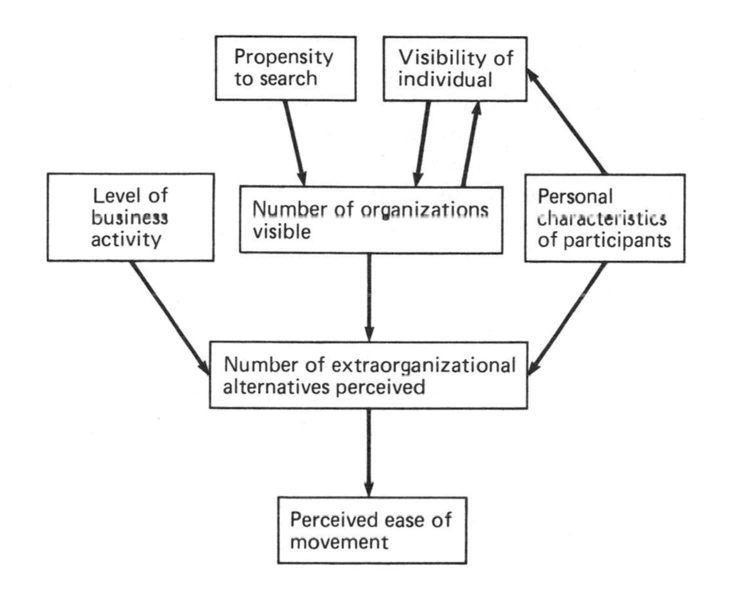

Figure 5.4. Major factors affecting perceived ease of movement (Source: March & Simon, *Organizations*. New York: Wiley, 1958).

existed between turnover and scores on intelligence, aptitude, or personality tests. Some evidence was found, however, that vocational interest inventories and scaled biographical information blanks could predict some turnover fairly accurately.

In contrast to earlier reviews that focused largely on psychological studies of turnover, Stoikov and Raimon (1968) examined the role of economic factors on turnover. Although not a review article per se, this paper is important because of the richness of detail concerning economic influence on withdrawal. The major finding emerging from this study was that when business conditions are good, monetary rewards have a sizable effect on turnover. "Coupled with Rice's findings to the effect that wage supplement expenditures vary systematically with money earnings, confidence is increased in the allocative role assigned to voluntary mobility by orthodox economic theory [p. 1289]." This conclusion is similar to the findings of Armknecht and Early (1972), that labor mobility increased in prosperous times and declined in less prosperous times.

Lefkowitz (1971) examined the literature from a clinical psychology perspective. His review, supporting earlier work, pointed to the following influences on turnover: (*a*) the employee's initial job expectations concerning the nature of the job; (*b*) job satisfaction; (*c*) the physical work environment; (*d*) financial compensation; (*e*) intrinsic aspects of the job; and (*f*) supervisory style and work-group dynamics.

In 1973, two reviews of the turnover literature appeared. In the first, by Porter and Steers (1973), over 60 studies of employee turnover were reviewed. In general, consistent support was found for the contention that job satisfaction represents an important influence on an individual's participation decision. Across 15 studies, the average correlation was $r = .25$, with a range from $r = .10$ to $r = .46$. Hence, although the relationship is consistent, the magnitude of the relationship clearly points to the existence of several additional variables that influence the participation decision.

In the review, job satisfaction was viewed as the sum of an individual's met expectations on the job. The more an individual's expectations are met, the greater the satisfaction. This interaction between employee expectations and available rewards is depicted in Figure 5.5. When the

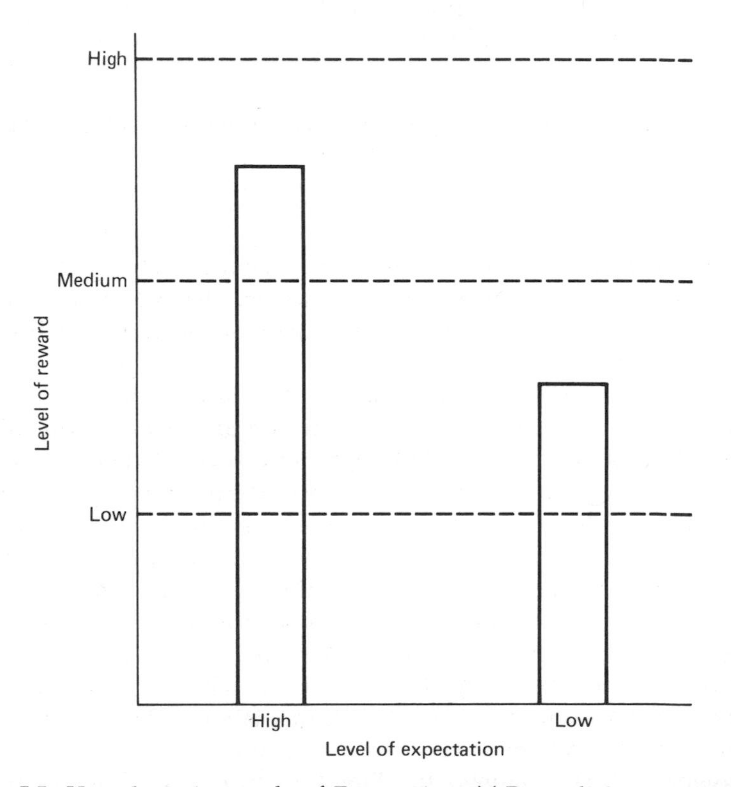

Figure 5.5. Hypothetical example of Expectations × Rewards interaction as they relate to the decision to withdraw (Source: Porter & Steers, *Psychological Bulletin*, 1973, *80*, 151–176).

level of rewards is relatively high, as shown by the left-hand bar, it becomes easier to meet the employee's expectation level, depicted by the horizontal dashed lines. Conversely, when the total rewards available to an employee are relatively low, as shown by the right-hand bar, meeting the employee's expectation level becomes more difficult.

When satisfaction is viewed in this fashion, questions are logically raised concerning which factors influence an employee's expectation set. Four general categories (or "levels" in organization) were suggested in which such factors could be found. As a result of the review, it was concluded that important influences on turnover could be found in each of the four categories. That is, influences on turnover could be found in the organization as a whole (e.g., pay and promotion policies), the immediate work environment (e.g., work-unit size, supervisory style, co-worker relations), the job itself (i.e., the nature of the job requirements), and the individual (e.g., age, tenure). "Based on these findings, the major roots of turnover appear to be fairly widespread throughout the various facets of organizational structure, as they interact with particular types of individuals [Porter & Steers, 1973, p. 169]."

Porter and Steers (1973) argued on the basis of their review that "much more emphasis should be placed in the future on the psychology of the withdrawal *process*. While correlational studies abound . . . which relate various factors to withdrawal, our understanding of the manner in which the actual decision is made is far from complete [p. 173]." Moreover, it was suggested that useful information could be obtained if researchers would direct some attention to the role of employee performance level in turnover. That is, it is possible that valued employees (i.e., high performers) may leave for quite different reasons than less valued employees. Hence, the role of job performance must be taken into account in any comprehensive model of employee turnover in work organizations.

Also published in 1973 was a review by Pettman (1973, 1975). Pettman reviewed available research specifically as it related to March and Simon's (1958) model. Support for some aspects of the model was found in studies published subsequent to March and Simon. However, many of the findings also showed "the equivocal nature of several other hypotheses [of March and Simon] [p. 56]." Pettman attributed many of the contradictory findings to poor methodology. In particular, he criticized the diverse methods of calculating turnover, the paucity of integration of disciplines, and the lack of a rigorous approach to study design. Such factors may have contributed to an inability to provide for a clear test of the March and Simon thesis.

The year 1977 was a banner year for research on turnover, with the publication of three important works. To begin with, viewing turnover largely from a sociological perspective, Price (1977) examined various ways in which turnover was defined and measured. Following this, correlates of turnover were considered and, on the basis of the review, Price suggested a conceptual model of the turnover process aimed at incorporating those variables shown to be more important in the review. The model suggests that five factors determine job satisfaction (pay, integration, instrumental communication, formal communication, and centralization), and that satisfaction in turn combines with opportunity to leave to determine actual employee turnover.

One of Price's (1977) signal contributions to the literature is his discussion of the impact of employee turnover on the organization. In a series of propositions, Price argued that successively higher amounts of turnover lead to (*a*) successively larger proportions of administrative staff relative to production workers; (*b*) successively higher amounts of formalization; (*c*) successively lower amounts of integration; (*d*) successively lower amounts of satisfaction; (*e*) successively higher amounts of innovation; and (*f*) successively lower amounts of centralization. Because of this, the net effect of turnover on organizational effectiveness is unclear, Price said. That is, turnover does facilitate effectiveness in some ways (e.g., increased innovation) but inhibits it in others (e.g., lower satisfaction, higher administrative costs). Dalton and Tudor (1979) also addressed this issue.

Also published in 1977 was a paper by Forrest *et al.* (1977), who suggested an expectancy/valence approach to understanding turnover that attempted to incorporate psychological and economic factors. The primary value of this work lies in its use of an expanded expectancy model beyond that originally proposed by Vroom (1964). Using this expanded model, Forrest *et al.* showed how various psychological and labor economic factors could potentially influence job attraction and subsequent employee willingness to maintain membership in the organization.

The third piece published in 1977 was a conceptual model by Mobley focusing on the intermediate linkages in the relationship between job satisfaction and employee turnover (see Figure 5.6). Rather than attempting a full model of the turnover process, Mobley concentrated on developing a better understanding of how satisfaction does (or does not) ultimately lead to turnover. Based on relevant literature, Mobley hypothesized that dissatisfaction leads to thinking of quitting, intention to search, intention to stay or leave, and finally, actual turnover. Support for this sequence of events can be found in Coverdale and Terborg (1980), Mobley, Horner, and Hollingsworth (1978), and Spencer, Steers, and Mowday (1980). In somewhat more stringent tests of the Mobley model, H.E. Miller, R. Katerberg, and C.L. Hulin (1979) reported cross-validation

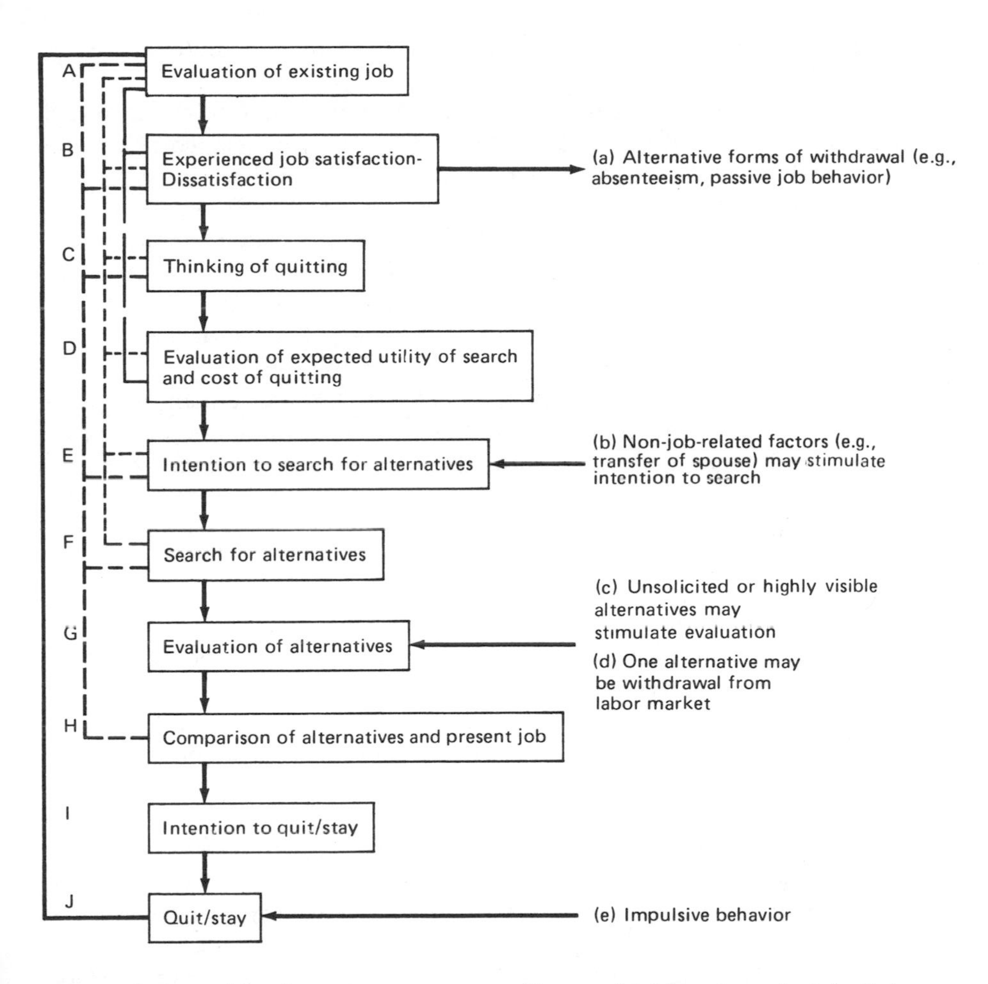

Figure 5.6. A model of employee turnover (Source: Mobley, *Journal of Applied Psychology*, 1977, *62*, 237–240).

of the model across two similar samples, whereas Mowday *et al.* (1980) were unable to cross-validate the model across two diverse samples.

A central point of Mobley's model is that, following Fishbein (1967), behavioral intention to leave represents the penultimate determinant of actual turnover and is more important in such a determination than is employee job satisfaction. In the Mobley *et al.* (1978) study, for example, behavioral intent was related to actual turnover at $r = .49$, whereas dissatisfaction and turnover were related at $r = .21$. As Mobley *et al.* (1978) conclude, "this finding . . . serves to reinforce and generalize the primacy of goals and intentions in models of specific organizational behaviors [p. 411]."

In a subsequent review of the literature, Mobley *et al.* (1979) concluded that supporting evidence could be found for the importance of several variables in determining turnover. These variables included age, tenure, overall satisfaction, job content, intention to stay, and organizational commitment. However, in the studies reviewed, it was generally found that less than 20% of the turnover variance was explained. Lack of a clear conceptual model, failure to consider alternatives available, insufficient multivariate research, and infrequent use of longitudinal studies were cited as possible reasons for our lack of progress on the topic.

On the basis of this review, Mobley *et al.* (1979) presented an expanded turnover model founded on the centrality of behavioral intentions to stay or leave. Though it included individual, organizational, and economic factors, the model explicitly recognizes the role of perceptions, expectations, and values as well as available job alternatives as factors in the turnover decision. In contrast to reviews by Porter and Steers (1973) and Muchinsky and Tuttle (1979), however, Mobley *et al.* felt that direct support for the hypothesized relationship between met expectations and turnover was weak. Rather, they proposed that expectations played a more complex role in the turnover decision process.

Finally, Muchinsky and Tuttle again reviewed the literature in 1979 on causes of employee turnover. Over 150 studies carried out over the preceding 50 years were grouped on the basis of common predictor variables into five general categories: (*a*) attitudinal factors, (*b*) biographical factors, (*c*) work-related factors, (*d*) personal factors, and (*e*) test-score factors. It was found that fairly consistent relationships between common predictor variables and employee turnover existed for each of the five categories except test-score predictors.

In addition, strong support was found for the importance of realistic job previews and of met expectations in reducing turnover. As Muchinsky and Tuttle (1979) note, "reductions in turnover have been achieved through the use of pre-employment booklets, job training, work sample measures, and orientation programs [p. 64]," all of which facilitate realistic job previews. Moreover, in examining the literature relating to Porter and Steers' (1973) hypothesis that employees are less likely to quit when their prior expectations have been met, Muchinsky and Tuttle (1979) conclude that "there appears to be substantial empirical evidence to support the Porter and Steers proposition for explaining individual employee turnover [p. 64]."

Perhaps the most significant contribution of the Muchinsky and Tuttle review lies in their consideration of methodological and interpretive sources of error in studies of employee turnover. These problems include a general lack of concern as to how turnover is measured, a failure to separate voluntary from involuntary turnover, a failure to separate criterion groups on the basis of sex or race for subgroup analyses, a general absence of cross-validated findings, and an implicit assumption in turnover research that all turnover is necessarily bad. As noted by Porter and Steers (1973) and Jeswald (1974), there are many circumstances under which some turnover may be healthy both for the individual and for the organization.

The major findings of these reviews are summarized in Table 5.2. As will be noted, several of these reviews point to the importance of job attitudes as a factor in turnover (Brayfield & Crockett, 1955; Herzberg *et al.*, 1957; Porter & Steers, 1973). In addition, evidence exists that personality and biodemographic data can predict turnover to some extent (Schuh, 1967). The importance of economic factors has also been shown (Stoikov & Raimon, 1968). Finally, several reviews point to the wide diversity of factors (e.g., personal factors, job characteristics, reward systems, supervisory and group relations) that combine to influence the decision to stay or leave (Lefkowitz, 1971; Porter & Steers, 1973; Price, 1977).

In addition to simply reviewing the literature, several researchers have attempted to propose conceptual models of the turnover process based on existing literature (March & Simon, 1958; Mobley, 1977; Price, 1977; Vroom, 1964). Although the details of the models differ, turnover is generally thought to be a function of negative job attitudes combined with an ability to secure employment elsewhere. Mobley (1977) goes further here in suggesting several intermediate linkages that intercede between attitudes and actual turnover, noting in particular the importance of behavioral intentions or actual behavior.

Despite this long tradition of empirical research on employee turnover, several issues remain unanswered. At least eight such shortcomings in many of the existing models can be identified that need to be addressed in any future models of voluntary employee turnover. These issues include the following:

1. Most of the existing models ignore the role of available information about one's job or prospective job in an individual's participation decision. Research on realistic job previews (Wanous, 1977) demonstrates how prior knowledge concerning the actual job environment can often affect turnover decisions.
2. The degree to which an employee's expectations and values surrounding a job are met by his or her organizational experiences has also been shown to be an important factor in turnover (Muchinsky &

Table 5.2
Summary of Empirical Reviews of Turnover Literature

Investigator(s)	Focus	Major findings	Formal model presented
Brayfield and Crockett (1955)	Effects of job satisfaction on turnover	Significant if modest relation between dissatisfaction and turnover	No
Herzberg *et al.* (1957)	Comprehensive review	Significant if modest relation between dissatisfaction and turnover	No
March and Simon (1958)	Comprehensive review	Turnover largely influenced by desirability of leaving plus ease of movement	Yes
Vroom (1964)	Limited review	Turnover influenced by force to remain versus force to leave	Yes
Schuh (1967)	Personality and biodemographic predictors of turnover	Modest evidence that vocational interest inventories and scaled biographical information blanks predicted some turnover	No
Stoikov and Raimon (1968)	Economic factors	Sizable influence of money and labor market factors on industry-wide turnover rates	No
Lefkowitz (1971)	Comprehensive review	Turnover influenced by job expectations, satisfaction, work environment, compensation, job itself, and supervisory style	No

Porter and Steers (1973)	Comprehensive review	Satisfaction modestly related to turnover; major influences on turnover found in person, job, work environment, and organization-wide factors, importance of met expectations	Partial
Pettman (1973, 1975)	Test of March and Simon model	Modest support for model based on review of literature	Yes
Price (1977)	Comprehensive review	Turnover influenced by dissatisfaction plus opportunity to leave; also considers organizational outcomes of turnover	Yes
Forrest *et al* (1977)	Effort to integrate psychological and economic influences on turnover	Based on Vroom model; both psychological and economic factors shown to influence turnover	Yes
Mobley (1977; Mobley *et al.*, 1979)	Comprehensive review	Model of intermediate linkages between satisfaction and actual turnover presented (1977); review of literature (1979) supports expanded version of model	Yes
Muchinsky and Tuttle (1979)	Comprehensive review	Major influences on turnover found in attitudes, person, work, and biographical sheets; support for met expectations proposition	No

Source: Steers and Mowday in L. Cummings and B. Staw (Eds.), *Research in Organizational Behavior* (Vol. 3). Greenwich, CT.: JAI Press, 1981.

Tuttle, 1979; Porter & Steers, 1973). This factor has been largely ignored in contemporary models of turnover.

3. Employee job performance level as a factor influencing desire or intent to leave has also been overlooked. High performers may experience heightened expectations concerning organizational rewards, whereas poor performers may experience lower attitudes concerning the intrinsic worth of the job (see, for example, Spencer & Steers, 1981). In both cases, performance must be recognized in the employee turnover decision.
4. Historically, models of employee turnover concentrate exclusively on one job attitude (namely, job satisfaction) and ignore other attitudes (like organizational commitment or job involvement) that may also be germane. In view of studies indicating that commitment may represent a better predictor of turnover than satisfaction (Hom *et al.*, 1979; Mowday, Steers, & Porter, 1979; Porter *et al.*, 1974), this almost exclusive focus on the single attitude variable of satisfaction appears unwarranted.
5. Nonwork influences on staying or leaving are consistently ignored. When a spouse is transferred—or when a spouse cannot transfer—the employee's mobility is affected. Moreover, family, church, and hobbies often play a major role in an employee's desire to leave.
6. Current models largely assume that once an employee has become dissatisfied with the job, the wheels are set in motion for subsequent termination. This assumption ignores the fact that employees may be able to change the current work situation (perhaps through bargaining with the supervisor, threats to quit, etc.). Ironically, March and Simon (1958) pointed to this factor over two decades ago, but most subsequent efforts have overlooked the point.
7. Furthermore, models of employee turnover should attempt to clarify the role of available alternative job opportunities, both in terms of which factors influence the perception of such availability and in terms of the consequences for employees of perceiving no such alternatives.
8. Contemporary turnover models typically assume a one-way flow process and ignore important feedback loops (e.g., attempts to change the work environment) that can enhance or ameliorate the desire to leave or the act of turnover.

As can be seen, there is a clear need for more comprehensive process models of employee turnover that take factors like these into account. One such model is presented in the next section, in the hopes that it will stimulate more comprehensive, multivariate efforts to study employee turnover and its outcomes. The model is largely inductive and has been developed from the existing literature on the topic.

A Model of Voluntary Employee Turnover

Building upon earlier theoretical and empirical work on turnover, it is possible to construct a largely cognitive model of employee turnover that focuses on the processes leading to the decision to participate or to withdraw.[1] The model proposed here was developed by Steers and Mowday (1981) to summarize and integrate earlier work and to extend such efforts by incorporating the points just mentioned. The model is schematically represented in Figure 5.7.

In order to clarify the dynamics of the model, it will be described in three sequential parts: (*a*) job expectations and job attitudes; (*b*) job attitudes and intent to leave; and (*c*) intent to leave, available alternatives, and actual turnover. Pertinent research will be noted as it relates to the model.

Job Expectations and Job Attitudes

JOB EXPECTATIONS AND VALUES

We could begin a model of employee turnover in many places, including the nature of the job or work environment, the job market and economic factors, and so forth. This model begins with the individual and his or her expectations and values, since it is the individual who must ultimately decide whether to stay or to leave. All individuals have expectations upon entering a new organization. These expectations may involve beliefs about the nature of the job, rewards for satisfactory performance, availability of interpersonal contacts and interactions, and so forth. It would be expected that each employee would have a somewhat different set of expectations depending on his or her own values and needs at any given time.

These expectations (shown in box 2 of Figure 5.7) are thought to be influenced by at least three factors: (*a*) individual characteristics; (*b*) available information about job and organization; and (*c*) alternative job opportunities. Several individual characteristics (see box 1) can influence job expectations and, ultimately, turnover. These include one's occupation, education, age, tenure, family responsibilities, family income level, personal work ethic, previous work experiences, and personality (Federico, Federico, & Lundquist, 1976; Hines, 1973; Mangione, 1973; Mobley *et al.*,

[1]This section is based on an earlier paper by Steers and Mowday (1981).

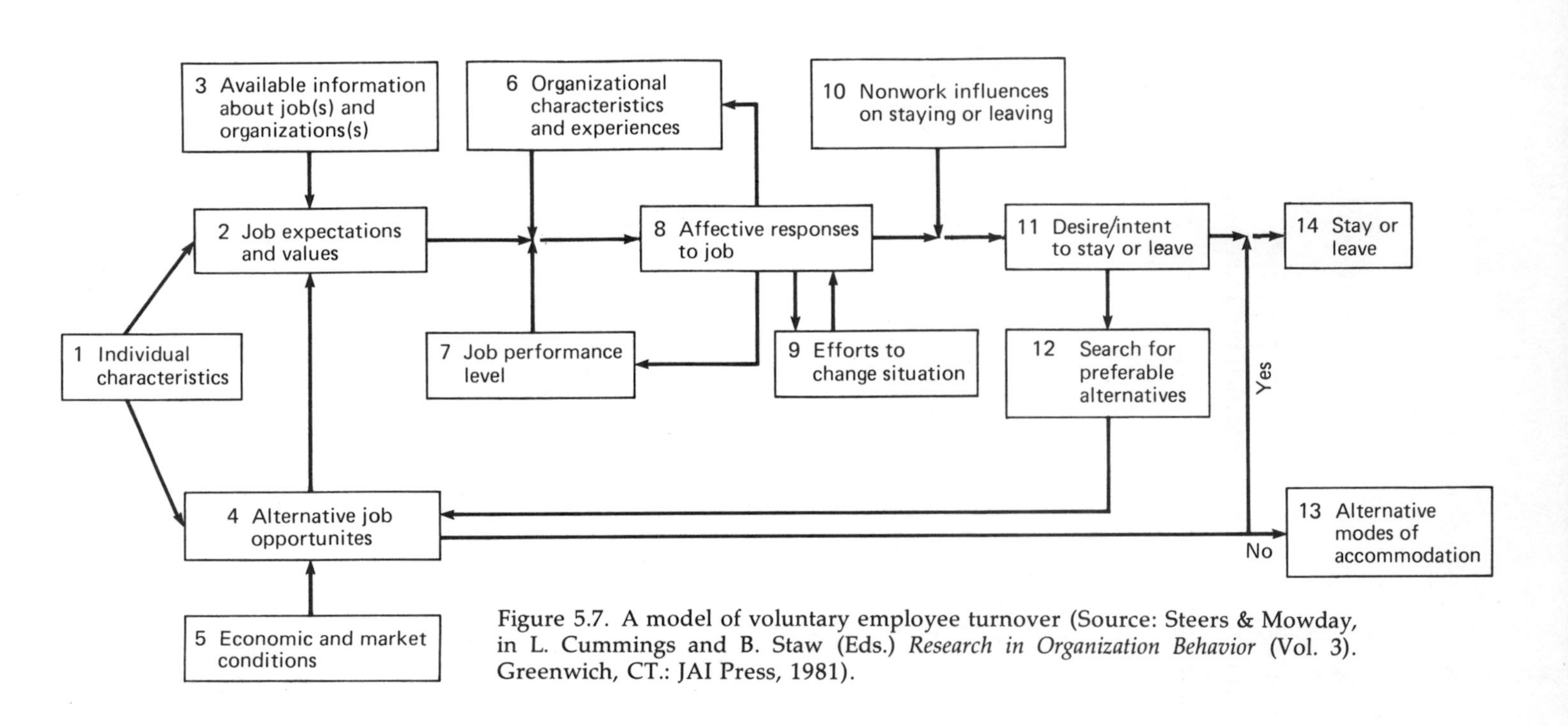

Figure 5.7. A model of voluntary employee turnover (Source: Steers & Mowday, in L. Cummings and B. Staw (Eds.) *Research in Organization Behavior* (Vol. 3). Greenwich, CT.: JAI Press, 1981).

1978; Mowday *et al.*, 1979; Porter & Steers, 1973; Waters, Roach, & Waters, 1976). As a result of such characteristics as these, individuals decide consciously or unconsciously what they expect from a job: what they feel they must have, what they would like to have, and what they can do without.

In addition, job expectations are influenced by the available information about the job and organization, both at the time of organizational choice and during reappraisal periods throughout one's career (box 3). The basic argument here follows from the literature on "realistic job previews" (Wanous, 1977). For instance, it has been found fairly consistently that when people are provided with more complete or more accurate information about prospective jobs, they are able to make more informed choices and, as a result, are more likely to develop realistic job expectations that are more easily met by the organization. Modest support for the ultimate impact of unmet expectations on turnover can be found in studies reviewed by Mobley *et al.* (1979), Muchinsky and Tuttle (1979), Porter and Steers (1973), and Wanous (1977).

Information about one's job or organization can also be important as one progresses through one's career. For example, if an accountant joins a major public accounting (CPA) firm in the hopes of eventually becoming a partner but later learns that the probability of attaining such status is minimal, the accountant may change his or her expectations and may decide to initiate a different course of action, such as corporate accounting.

The third major determinant of employee job expectations is the extent to which an individual has alternative job opportunies (box 4). Simply put, the greater the number of attractive job alternatives, the more demanding an individual may be when evaluating his or her current job or job offer. Pfeffer and Lawler (1980) found availability of alternative jobs to be negatively related to job attitudes among a large sample of university faculty. However, Mowday and McDade (1979) found that the mere availability of alternative jobs was a less important influence on job attitudes than the relative attractiveness of the alternatives. In addition, they found that the influence of attractive alternative jobs on attitudes changed over time. In a longitudinal analysis, attractiveness of alternative jobs was negatively related to organizational commitment on the first morning a new employee reported for work. After 1 month on the job, however, attractiveness of alternative job offers the individual did not take advantage of was positively related to organizational commitment.

Hence, on the first day at work, information about alternative jobs may be salient, since information about the chosen job is limited. After a period of time at work, however, the individual must justify his or her choice of the job and this may result in more positive attitudes for those who have given up an opportunity to take a relatively attractive alternative job. (This point is discussed in greater detail in chapter 3.) In view of the relevance of alternative jobs during the initial period of employment, it is not surprising to discover that expectation levels of employees are quite high at the point of organizational entry (Porter & Steers, 1973). After an employee has been on a given job for a period of time, however, expectations tend to become more realistic as the employee develops greater behavioral commitments that make it less attractive to go elsewhere (Salancik, 1977).

AFFECTIVE RESPONSES TO JOB

The next segment in the model relates job expectations and values to subsequent job attitudes (box 8). The literature on job attitudes suggests that affective responses (including job satisfaction and organizational commitment) result from the interaction of three factors: (*a*) job expectations; (*b*) organizational characteristics and experiences; and (*c*) job performance level. Of major concern here is the interaction between job expectations (box 2) and organizational characteristics and experiences (box 6). Again, following from the literature on realistic job previews (Wanous, 1977), the more one's experiences in the organization are congruent with what one expects, the greater the propensity for one to be satisfied and wish to remain with the organization (Muchinsky & Tuttle, 1979; Porter & Steers, 1973; Vroom, 1964). (Refer to Figure 5.5.) Such experiences have also been shown to be related to organizational commitment, as noted in Chapter 3.

Parenthetically, it is important to point out that the impact of expectations on subsequent job attitudes is open to dispute. It has been argued by Locke (1976) that when expectations are not met, the reaction by individuals is surprise, not dissatisfaction. He argues, instead, that it is the extent to which *valued* attributes (instead of expected attributes) are present in a job that influences satisfaction. Although values and expectations are conceptually distinct, available evidence suggests that they are highly related in practice. For instance, Bray *et al.* (1974) found the two to be correlated at $r = .87$. Hence, it is possible that employees develop higher expectations about those aspects of the job that are most highly valued and that both concepts may be related to subsequent attitudes.

In addition to organizational characteristics and experiences, other aspects of organizational life that could influence the extent to which one's expectations are met include an organization's pay and promotion policies, employees' actual job duties, co-worker relations, work-group size, supervisory style, organization structure and opportunities for participation in decision-making, geographic location, and organizational goals and values

(Dansereau, Cashman, & Graen, 1974; Ilgen & Dugoni, 1977; Koch & Steers, 1978; Krackhardt *et al.*, 1981; Marsh & Mannari, 1977; Waters *et al.*, 1976). Such variables, when taken together, constitute a form of experienced organizational reality that signals the individual as to whether his or her expectations are being (or are likely to be) met in the particular situation, or whether he or she is likely to find a more rewarding experience elsewhere.

Recent research also suggests that employee job performance may influence job attitudes and ultimate turnover (box 7). Poor performance has been shown to lead to poor attitudes about jobs, possibly in an attempt to rationalize the poor performance. ("This is a crummy job anyway.") Poor performance has also been shown to lead to increased anxiety and frustration (C. Cooper & R. Payne, 1978). Finally, three studies have shown that poor job performance represented an important influence on voluntary turnover (Marsh & Mannari, 1977; Spencer & Steers, 1981; Wanous, Stumpf & Bedrosian, 1978) although T. Martin, J. Price, and C. Mueller (1981) found job performance unrelated to turnover. In the Spencer and Steers (1981) study, for example, it was found that performance moderated the attitude–turnover relationship. That is, job satisfaction was found to be related to turnover for poor performers but not for good performers. It was suggested that organizations often find ways of enticing high performers to remain—even on dull jobs—but that no such efforts are typically made by organizations for poor performers.

The resulting employee attitudes, in turn, can be expected to influence several other aspects of behavior. First, attitudes can feed back and influence both organizational experiences (box 6) and job performance (box 7), as shown in Figure 5.7 (Forrest *et al.*, 1977). Poor job attitudes often color an employee's perceptions of organizational actions (e.g., promotion decisions, pay raises, supervisory behavior) as noted in attribution theory literature (Salancik & Pfeffer, 1978) and in studies of selective exposure to information (Janis & Mann, 1977).

Moreover, poor employee attitudes may lead managers to take certain punitive actions, which in turn lead to a further reduction in job attitudes. Likewise, negative affective responses to one's level of job performance can lead to further reductions in performance levels (a "who cares?" attitude). This degenerative, self-reinforcing cycle can significantly enhance an employee's desire or intent to leave the organization.

Poor job attitudes may also cause employees to engage in efforts to change the situation (box 9). It is logical to assume that before actually leaving, an individual would in many cases attempt to change or eliminate those aspects of the work situation that are compelling her or him to leave. Such efforts may take the form of attempted intraorganizational transfer

(March & Simon, 1958) or, alternatively, attempts to act on the work environment. Efforts to act on the environment can include attempts to restructure one's job or job responsibilities, changing the payoffs for continued participation, unionization efforts, threatening to leave, or forcing someone else to leave. Through mechanisms such as these, the work environment may become more tolerable to the employee, thereby improving his or her attitudes and desire to stay. However, when an employee finds it impossible to alter the situation, poor job attitudes would be expected to remain the same (or possibly intensify), thereby strengthening the resolve to leave. The potential effects of efforts to change the situation, whether successful or unsuccessful, on intent to leave and actual turnover represent a major topic area for further empirical investigation.

Job Attitudes and Intent to Leave

The second part of the model examines the relationship between one's job attitudes and one's desire and intent to stay or leave. Briefly, it is suggested that desire or intent to leave is influenced by (*a*) an employee's affective responses to the job; and (*b*) nonwork influences on staying or leaving.

Fishbein (1967) and others have suggested that one's affective responses to the job can lead to behavioral intentions and that these intentions govern behavior. In the case of employee turnover, we would expect reduced levels of job satisfaction and organizational commitment (box 8) to result in an increased desire or intent to leave (box 11; Mobley, 1977; Price, 1977; Steers, 1977a). Such a conclusion is common throughout the work on employee turnover.

However, what is often ignored in determining desire or intent to leave is a constellation of nonwork influences on staying or leaving (box 10). Many circumstances can be identified in which one may not like a particular job but still does not seek termination, including situations where (*a*) the employee tolerates an unpleasant job (e.g., an apprenticeship) because of its instrumentality for future career considerations (e.g., becoming a master craftsman); (*b*) a spouse is limited geographically to a certain region and alternative employment is scarce; (*c*) the employee's central life interests lie outside of work; and (*d*) family considerations (Dubin *et al.*, 1975; Schneider & Dachler, 1978). Following a review of relevant work, Sussman and Cogswell (1971) suggested that

> there is a direct relationship between the supply and demand of workers in any occupational system and the consideration of non-economic factors in job movement; the greater the demand for workers in any occupational

> system the greater is the consideration given to familial concerns such as work aspirations of spouses, special needs of children, community activities, linkages with kin, friends, and voluntary associations; physical and social environments [p. 485]."

Included here too as a nonwork influence on staying or leaving would be Fishbein's (1967) notion of subjective normative beliefs, or how those around an individual would feel about his or her leaving. These nonwork factors are often overlooked in turnover research but may, in fact, explain a greater proportion of the turnover variance than job attitudes.

Before considering the third part of the model, we should note that we have combined desire and intent to leave in our model. This has been done for the sake of parsimony and because of a wish to focus attention on the processes leading up to one's behavioral intentions. These early influences are perhaps the least understood segment of the participation decision. More elaborate distinctions between desire to leave and intent to leave are presented by Mobley (1977), Mobley *et al.*, (1978), and Fishbein (1967). Fishbein introduces the term "attitude toward the act," which is similar to our use of "desire to leave." Fishbein and others (e.g., Hom *et al.*, 1979) suggest that an employee's feelings toward the act of quitting (that is, desire) represent a more immediate determinant of intent to leave than feelings about the job itself.

Intent to Leave, Available Alternatives, and Actual Turnover

The third part of the model focuses on the link between behavioral intent to leave and actual turnover. Following from the earlier work of March and Simon (1958), it is argued that employee turnover is ultimately determined by a combination of behavioral intent to leave (box 11) and the availability of alternative job opportunities (box 4). Although research support for this contention is mixed, much of the discrepancy appears to result more from inadequate methodology than from any repudiation of the basic hypothesis (Dansereau *et al.*, 1974; Pettman, 1973; Schneider, 1976; Schwab & Dyer, 1974).

An employee's intent to leave can influence subsequent turnover in at least two ways. First, it may cause turnover fairly directly (Muchinsky & Tuttle, 1979). That is, some people decide to leave their jobs even when alternative jobs are not available. Changes in the social welfare system aimed at providing unemployed people with minimal support levels may enhance this direct relationship by providing an economic cushion to those who leave the organization. Second, an employee's intent to leave may further influence actual turnover indirectly by causing the employee to initiate search behavior for preferable alternative jobs (box 12). Research suggests that less satisfied people are more likely to be sensitive to job market changes than are more satisfied people (March & Simon, 1958). This search behavior often serves to open up to an employee a greater number of job possibilities, thereby increasing the likelihood of termination.

Furthermore, alternative job opportunities (box 4) are also influenced by individual characteristics (box 1) and economic and market conditions (box 5). Individual characteristics such as age, sex, and occupation often constrain one's opportunities for jobs (Porter & Steers, 1973). Moreover, economic and market conditions also influence the availability of jobs (Forrest *et al.*, 1977). If few alternative job opportunities exist, the employee would probably be less likely to leave the organization. Instead, however, he or she may engage in alternative forms of withdrawal or accommodation in order to reduce the anxiety or frustration that results from not being able to leave (box 13). These alternatives may include absenteeism, drug abuse or alcoholism, sabotage, slowdowns, and so forth. Or, alternatively, they may take the form of rationalizing why it is in one's best interest to remain, as we shall see in the next chapter. In any case, when an individual wishes to leave but is unable to do so, some form of accommodation process can be expected. When the individual wishes to leave and is able to do so, the probability of actual turnover (box 14) is markedly increased (Dansereau *et al.*, 1974; Mobley *et al.*, 1978; Woodward, 1975–1976).

We can see a further feedback loop in operation with regard to the availability of alternative job opportunities. Specifically, when an employee is presented with a new and attractive alternative position, perhaps because of changes in market conditions, his or her expectations on the current job are likely to be increased, making it more difficult for the organization to meet these expectations. As a result, job attitudes may suffer, which causes heightened desire and intent to leave. This, in turn, may sensitize the individual to the possibility of changing jobs. Again, this self-reinforcing cycle can ultimately hasten the employee's decision to leave the organization.

Relationship of the Steers and Mowday Model to Earlier Models

The model suggested here attempts to build upon much of the earlier theory concerning employee turnover. Though many aspects of the model have appeared earlier, other aspects are unique. To begin with, the role of available information about the prospective job and organization is explicitly recognized (box 3). Second, job performance level as a factor in affective responses to the job is also noted (box 7). Third, like the Mobley *et al.* (1979) model, but unlike others, several attitudes (not simply job satisfaction) are considered as they relate to turnover (box 8). Fourth, major emphasis is placed on a series of nonwork factors that have been shown to influence desire to leave and/or actual termination (box 10). Fifth, recognition is also given to the fact that when an employee is dissatisfied, he or she may engage in attempts to change the situation or work environment prior to deciding upon termination (box 9). Sixth, special recognition is given to the fact that employees who are unable to leave will ultimately discover some form of accommodation process to make the situation more palatable. In summary, the model suggested here does identify several new avenues for future research on the turnover decision that should aid in our understanding of the process.

Employee Turnover: A Future Research Agenda

Despite the rather large number of empirical studies that have been carried out with respect to employee turnover, our understanding of how employees decide whether to stay with or leave the organization is still fragmentary. It is apparent that the problem is not that the subject area has suffered from a lack of research attention. Rather, the problem can apparently be traced to the rather narrow range of issues associated with turnover that organizational researchers have chosen to examine and to the methodologies they have employed in such investigations.

In this regard, several important areas can be identified that together form a useful future research agenda on the topic. These areas include the following:

Agenda item 1. To begin with, much greater attention needs to be directed toward testing comprehensive models of the turnover process. Even though some research has begun to move in this direction, a need still exists to move beyond simple studies focusing on a limited number of variables or a limited perspective with respect to the turnover decision process. One effort toward this end is the model suggested by Steers and Mowday (1981). Such a model, based on an attempted integration of available piecemeal research, can be considered a series of hypotheses suitable for testing.

Agenda item 2. A need still remains for research on the role of employee performance level in the turnover decision. The model suggested here incorporates performance as one factor (see Wanous *et al.*, 1978), but more work is clearly needed. For example, do high performers leave for different reasons than poor performers? Initial exploratory analyses suggest that this may be the case (Spencer & Steers, 1981). What effect does poor performance have on subsequent job attitudes and on the employee's desire to remain? Moreover, do high performers raise their level of expectations, thereby increasing the difficulty to the organization in satisfying such expectations?

Agenda item 3. It was noted some time ago by March and Simon (1958) that dissatisfied employees can be expected to try to change the work situation and reduce or eliminate its less desirable aspects. Little has been done to verify this hypothesis, however. If employees do undertake such change efforts, what are some of the more common methods used in this regard? Under what conditions are such efforts likely to be more successful? Finally, when such efforts are unsuccessful, what is the effect (if any) on job attitudes?

Agenda item 4. The field is just beginning to recognize the existence of a series of nonwork factors that influence turnover decisions. Most of these influences appear to be related to matters of personal goals and values and to family considerations. Few studies have examined these factors systematically, however, (Sussman & Cogswell, 1971). Hence, the influence of nonwork factors on employee turnover remains perhaps one of the richest areas for future work.

Agenda item 5. Several of the existing models of employee turnover incorporate some notion of search behavior for preferable job alternatives. This notion often accompanies economic considerations or actual alternative job opportunities. However, a systematic examination of how people initiate search behavior is still lacking. Also lacking is an understanding about the quality of information collected in search behavior and how such information is processed in arriving at a decision. This topic is particularly well suited to laboratory study, a method of research not typically employed in turnover research.

Agenda item 6. Finally, some research on turnover suggests that some forms of withdrawal may at times act as a substitute for other forms (Muchinsky & Tuttle, 1979). For instance, when an employee is unable to leave a dissatisfying job, he or she may use absenteeism as a temporary form of escape. Alcoholism, drug abuse, sabotage, and work slowdowns also represent possible substitutes. Although pychiatrists have examined alcoholism and drug abuse and labor economists have studied sabotage and work slowdowns, few systematic attempts have been made by organizational psychologists to study the substitutability of these various forms of withdrawal for turnover. Thus, when an employee is unable to leave an undesirable job, how likely is he or she to use alternative modes of accommodation that are dysfunctional either to the employee or to the organization? Moreover, are certain types of employees more likely to use these accommodation techniques than others? Is there a generalizable sequence of accommodation techniques, perhaps beginning with increased absenteeism and then progressing to alcoholism and drug abuse, or do different individuals find different modes of accommodation without any particular pattern? Answers to questions such as these will go a long way toward helping us explicate turnover processes in organizations.

Summary

Based on the preceding discussion, several summary points can be made. To begin with, it was noted that turnover rates vary both by industry and by season. This variation is particularly prominent in Table 5.1, which shows significant differences in tenure rates by industry. Second, a review of the existing literature on employee turnover shows that several viable models exist. The topic of turnover has not suffered for lack of attention. Even so, it was argued that existing models, though making useful contributions, could be extended somewhat in the light of new research evidence.

In an attempt to do this, we have proposed a process model of turnover that attempts to incorporate many new features not found in most earlier models. For example, the model discussed here recognizes the influence of job expectations, employee performance level, ability to change the work situation, and nonwork factors on the decision to terminate. The turnover model is proposed in order to facilitate more systematic and comprehensive research on the topic. In this way, we hope to learn more about the *processes* leading to termination. With this information, we should be in a better position to propose improved theories of organizational behavior as well as more detailed implications for management practice.

6

Consequences of Employee Commitment, Turnover, and Absenteeism

Organizational researchers have historically been far more interested in predicting employee attitudes and behaviors than in understanding their consequences. This is particularly evident when employee turnover and absenteeism are considered. Reviews of the literature have identified a number of important antecedents of each behavior. Conspicuous by their absence, however, are systematic theoretical or empirical attempts to identify the consequences of these behaviors for individuals or organizations.

Somewhat more attention has been given to the consequences of employee commitment to organizations (see Chapter 2). However, the interest of researchers in commitment may be primarily the result of consistent relationships that have been found between this attitude and employee turnover and absenteeism. Although it appears clear that employee commitment predicts behaviors like turnover and absenteeism, we still have a poor understanding of the consequences of these behaviors. Moreover, there appear to be a number of additional consequences of employee commitment that have yet to receive research attention.

Because of the limited information available on this topic, the purpose of this chapter and the next is to begin systematically examining the consequences of employee attitudes and behaviors in organizations. In this chapter the consequences of employee commitment, turnover, and absenteeism will be considered. In the next chapter attention will be focused on the cognitive processes through which employees develop beliefs about the causes of turnover behavior and the implications of such beliefs for subsequent attitudes. Although these two topics will be discussed in separate chapters, they are clearly related. Many of the attitudinal consequences of turnover to be discussed in this chapter, for example, depend on the development of beliefs about the causes of turnover discussed in the next chapter. Although several attitudinal implications of turnover will be identified in this chapter, major discussion of this topic will be reserved for Chapter 7.

The discussion that follows will focus separately on the consequences of employee commitment, turnover, and absenteeism. Organizing the chapter in this fashion is convenient for purposes of discussion, but it should be apparent that these variables are interrelated and they may share common consequences. Although the causal nature of relationships among these variables is not yet entirely clear, it is possible that relationships exist in a sequential manner where one variable becomes a consequence of another. Turnover and absenteeism, for example, were identified in Chapter 2 as important correlates of employee commitment. One likely sequential pattern of relationships among these variables is one in which declining commitment leads to increased absenteeism, which leads to turnover. This pattern is consistent with situations in which declining commitment causes employees to think about leaving the organization. The process of job search may increase absenteeism and, once a satisfactory job is found, turnover may result. Alternatively, employees often submit their resignation but remain on the job for a period of time prior to actual termination. In this situation, the pattern of relationships may look quite different (e.g., turnover leads to declining commitment, which leads to absenteeism). Other patterns of relationships among these variables could also be described. At this point it is sufficient to recognize that the variables to be discussed separately in this chapter are in fact interrelated.

Three distinctions will be drawn in discussing the consequences of commitment, turnover, and absenteeism. First, consequences will be discussed at three levels of analysis. The discussion will focus separately on consequences for individuals, work groups, and organizations. In addition, a distinction will be drawn in the discussion of turnover and absenteeism at the individual level of analysis between consequences for the person performing the behavior (i.e., being absent or leaving) and for observers of these behaviors (i.e., co-workers and supervisors). Second, a distinction will be drawn between the positive and negative consequences of commitment, turnover, and absenteeism. Although previous theory and research have most often suggested that commitment has positive consequences and turnover and absenteeism have negative consequences, a more balanced view suggests that there may be positive and negative conseqences associated with each. Finally, an attempt will be made to identify the conditions under which a particular consequence is more or less likely to occur. These conditions will be discussed as moderators of the relationship between a particular attitude or behavior and its consequences. As will become clear in the forthcoming discussion, whether or not a particular consequence follows from a behavior depends largely on personal and situational variables. With the exception of Staw's (1980b) work on turnover, the consideration of moderating factors in these relationships has largely been ignored in previous work.

Though much of the discussion will focus on potential consequences that have yet to be empirically investigated, the discussion will draw upon existing research and theory where possible. Research on several consequences of employee commitment has already been presented in Chapter 2. In addition, several writers have attempted to identify possible consequences of employee turnover (Dalton & Tudor, 1979; Mobley, 1980; Price, 1977; Staw, 1980b; Steers & Mowday, 1981). The discussion that follows will summarize this previous literature and attempt to extend this work. Although there is less previous theory and research to draw upon in considering the consequences of employee absenteeism, it is clear that absence behavior has important implications that should be considered in future research.

Consequences of Employee Commitment

The consequences of a strong employee commitment to organization for individuals, work groups, and the overall organization are summarized in Table 6.1. The consequences will be discussed separately for each level of analysis.

Consequences for Individuals

At the individual level of analysis, employee commitment to the organization has been found to result in increased effort on the job and reduced absenteeism, turnover, and tardiness, as we saw in Chapter 2. Although this research has been carried out at the individual level of analysis, these outcomes might be considered consequences to the organization of high employee commitment. The primary concern of this research has been the implications of commitment for different organizationl effectiveness indicators (turnover and absenteeism). Thus, the positive consequences of commitment have been viewed as having fewer implications for individuals than for organizations. A number of potential consequences of high commitment more directly relevant to individual employees will be considered in this section.

POSITIVE CONSEQUENCES

High levels of commitment to an organization may be associated with such positive outcomes for individuals as enhanced feelings of belonging, security, efficacy, goals and purpose in life, and a positive self-image. It is

Table 6.1
Consequences of Organizational Commitment[a]

Level of analysis	Possible consequences: Positive	Possible consequences: Negative	Potential moderating variables
Individual	Feelings of belonging and attachment (1) Security (1) Goals and direction (1) Positive self-image (1) Organization rewards (2) Attractiveness to other potential employers (4)	Reduced mobility and career advancement (2) Reduced self-development and growth (2) Family strains/tension (1, 3) Stress (1, 3)	1. Nonwork commitments 2. Company policies on promotion and rewards 3. Job demands 4. Visibility of position
Work group	Membership stability (5) Group effectiveness (4) Cohesiveness (1, 2)	Groupthink (3) Lower creativity and adaptation (3) Intragroup conflict (2, 4)	1. Task interdependence 2. Distribution of commitment in group 3. Contacts with nongroup members 4. Group–organization goal congruence 5. organization transfer and promotion policies
Organization[b]	Increased effectiveness due to: Individual effort Reduced turnover Reduced absenteeism Reduced tardiness Attractiveness to nonorganization members	Decreased effectiveness due to: Reduced turnover Reduced absenteeism Lower innovation and adaptation	

[a]The numbers following each consequence refer to potential moderating variables thought to be closely associated with that consequence.
[b]See text for moderating variables relevant to the organizational level of analysis.

generally believed that most individuals desire more direction and purpose in their lives and the security that comes from attachments to stable institutions. Commitment to an organization can provide employees with stability and feelings of belonging. Moreover, a positive self-image may result from identification with and a contributing role in a recognized organization. Individuals may have other attachments, such as to family or church. To the extent such nonwork attachments are absent in a person's life, however, commitment to an organization may become even more important in shaping the self-image and feelings of belonging and contributing. The importance of commitment to an organization may be greatest for individuals with no family or social relationships outside of work. In addition, the more central and significant the job of the individual in the organization, the more likely it is that positive personal outcomes will be derived from organizational commitments.

Since loyalty and commitment are valued by many segments of our society, we would also expect employee commitment to lead to greater organizational rewards. Committed employees, depending on organizational reward policies, should be rewarded more highly than uncommitted employees for putting forth effort, continued membership, and loyalty. In addition, highly committed and loyal employees may be more attractive to alternative employers. Although commitment itself may make it more difficult to attract individuals away from an organization, it is likely that competing employers would be attracted to employees who exhibit high levels of commitment to their current organization. The more visible the committed individual's position in the organization, the more likely the individual is to be attractive to other organizations.

NEGATIVE CONSEQUENCES

The benefits that might accrue to individuals from commitment to an organization may not be without associated costs. Although organizational researchers have most often approached commitment in terms of its benefits to the organization, it is important to consider that commitment may have negative consequences for the individual. Highly committed individuals, for example, may reduce their opportunities for career advancement and mobility. In many occupations, career advancement is achieved by mobility among organizations. In addition, self-development and growth may result when individuals change jobs and assume new work-related challenges. Employees committed to a single organization, however, may forgo the possible benefits to be achieved by mobility. The extent to which committed employees reduce their opportunities for advancement and growth may depend on the promotion policies of their organization and opportunities for mobility within the organization. However, it appears likely that commitment to an organization may result in significant opportunity costs for many employees.

High levels of commitment to an organization may also result in stress and tension in family and social relationships. In extreme cases of commitment to work or a career, individuals may invest time and energy in the organization at the expense of family and other obligations. For some committed employees, meaningful family and social relationships may never be developed. For others, family ties and friendships may be threatened as individuals invest heavily in work-related activities. The potential for commitment to an organization to disrupt nonwork relationships may be greatest when the individual's job is highly demanding (e.g., professional positions that may require night and weekend work) and when the individual has family obligations (e.g., the individual is married and has children). The conflicting pressures from commitment to the organization and felt obligations to the family may be a source of high stress for the individual. A number of negative consequences may be associated with attempting to cope with conflicting demands from organization and family.

Consequences for Work Groups

Although work groups in organizations have been extensively studied as a source of attachment for employees (cf. Cartwright, 1968), the implications for groups of member commitment to the larger organization have been less extensively considered. The extent to which group members are committed to the organization, however, may have several important implications for group processes and effectiveness.

POSITIVE CONSEQUENCES

Groups that are composed of employees committed to the organization are likely to experience greater membership stability and effectiveness than groups having less committed members. Highly committed employees are less likely to be absent and to leave. Groups composed of committed members may thus be less likely to experience the disruptions associated with these behaviors, although membership instability may still occur as a result of normal transfers and promotions. In addition, the willingness of highly committed employees to exert effort on the job may result in greater work-group effectiveness. Mowday *et al.* (1974) found that the average level of commitment of employees in separate bank branches was related to the performance of those branches. Where groups tasks are highly interdependent, commitment to the organization may also result in higher levels of group cohesiveness. The expression of commitment in highy interdependent work groups may result in greater task interaction and social involvement, both of which may serve to strengthen the cohesiveness of the group. Moreover, the belief of members in the goals and values of the organization may provide the group with a common focus and group goal. The effects of commitment on work groups may be greatest when commitment is widely distributed among the members of the group rather than isolated among a few individuals.

NEGATIVE CONSEQUENCES

The potential negative consequences for the work group of high levels of commitment are often identified as reduced creativity and adaptation. Although he focused specifically on group cohesiveness, Janis' (1972) work on "groupthink" suggests that groups composed of highly committed members may be less open to new ideas or values that question existing goals of the organization. In addition, the stable membership characteristic of committed work groups may also be a barrier to creativity. The lowered levels of turnover among such groups suggest that they would be less likely to benefit from the new ideas and approaches brought to the group by new members. The extent to which high levels of commitment in groups result in reduced adaptation, however, may depend on other factors, such as frequent contact by group members with individuals outside the group, growth of the group that results in new members, and so forth.

It is also possible that higher levels of conflict may be found in groups where commitment is not widely shared by the members. When the goals of the work group and larger organization are viewed as incongruent by a majority of group members, the possession of high organization commitment by one or several members may be viewed as threatening to the group. Such highly committed members may be isolated by others in the group or subject to frequent attempts to influence their beliefs.

Consequences for Organizations

Several studies of employee commitment suggest that organizations composed of highly committed members are more likely to be effective. Increased organizational effectiveness is thought to result from the increased effort members put forth in pursuit of the organization's goals and lower levels of turnover, absenteeism, and tardiness (Angle & Perry, 1981). Although reduced levels of turnover and absenteeism may result in lower expenses for the organization, there is reason to question whether lower levels of these behaviors always lead to greater effectiveness (cf. Dalton & Tudor, 1979; Mobley, 1980; Staw, 1980b). The positive and negative consequences associated with turnover and absenteeism will be discussed at length in later sections. Since the consequences of commitment, such as turnover and absenteeism, can be viewed in both positive and negative terms depending on a number of situational variables, the discussion here will not focus separately on positive and negative consequences of high commitment for organizations. It is sufficient at this point to recognize that the outcomes commonly associated with high commitment may have both costs and benefits.

In addition to the outcomes mentioned previously, organizations composed of highly committed members may be more attractive to individuals outside the organization. Highly committed employees are likely to describe the organization in positive terms to nonmembers. This may enhance the organization's ability to recruit and hire high-quality employees. As with work groups, however, high levels of commitment may also result in lower levels of creativity and adaptation in organizations. Highly committed organization members may be less likely to question policies and recognize strategic opportunities that involve departures from past practices. This problem may be particularly evident when the executive ranks of the organization are characterized by high levels of commitment. John DeLorean's description of his experiences as an executive at General Motors (Wright, 1980), for example, suggests that overly high levels of commitment and loyalty at the top of the organization may stifle creativity and actually lead to decisions with disastrous consequences (e.g., failure to correct apparent safety defects in the design of cars).

Consequences of Employee Turnover

The consequences of employee turnover have received considerably more theoretical attention than the consequences of either commitment or absenteeism. Although most early writing on the consequences of turnover focused on the organizational level of analysis (Price, 1977), later writers have been concerned with the implications of turnover for individuals (Mobley, 1980; Staw, 1980b; Steers & Mowday, 1981). The consequences of turnover for work groups have received less attention than the consequences for individuals or organizations, although membership stability was a consideration in early research on groups (e.g., Ziller, 1965). In this section the consequences of turnover will be discussed at three levels of analysis: individual, work group, and organization. The discussion will attempt to summarize available research on this topic and extend previous research by suggesting several additional consequences that have not yet received consideration.

Consequences for Individuals

At the individual level of analysis it is possible to distinguish the consequences of turnover for individuals leaving the organization and individuals who remain. The latter group of individuals includes co-workers and supervisors of the person leaving who might be affected by the leaver's decision. Since the consequences of turnover are quite different for each group (actors versus observers), it is useful to examine each separately in the following discussion. The relationships discussed concerning the consequences of turnover for individuals are summarized in Table 6.2.

LEAVERS—POSITIVE CONSEQUENCES

For individuals deciding whether or not to leave an organization, there are often obvious advantages associated with turnover. A number of positive economic and job-related benefits may result from the turnover decision, although the likelihood that an individual will economically benefit from turnover may depend largely on conditions in the job market and the individual's skills and abilities. Many people who leave organizations are attracted to other jobs by higher salaries and better opportunities for career advancement. In many professions, mobility among organizations is commonly practiced by individuals seeking career advancement. Individuals with job skills and abilities that are in demand (e.g., engineers) are more likely to benefit from decisions to change jobs than individuals with fewer marketable skills.

In addition, turnover often provides the opportunity for individuals to improve their job situation in noneconomic ways. Turnover may result in a better fit between the individual and the job. Many people leave organizations to take jobs that better utilize their skills or that offer greater satisfaction and reduced stress. Mid-career job changes provide employees with the chance to undertake a new challenge or to develop entirely new job skills (Hall, 1976). The similarity between the old and new job may be a crucial determinant of the consequences that follow from turnover. Turnover is most likely to result in stimulation and challenge when the old and new jobs are dissmilar, although for some taking a similar job in a new organization may in itself be stimulating. When an individual moves to take the same job in a different organization the types of positive consequences that result from turnover are likely to differ from those that occur when the basic nature of the job changes.

Turnover may also be motivated by nonwork factors. Individuals may change jobs, for example, as a way to move to more desirable geographic locations or to be closer to (or farther away from) one's family. Whether

Table 6.2
Consequences of Turnover for Individuals[a]

Level of analysis	Possible consequences: Positive	Possible consequences: Negative	Potential moderating variables
Leavers	Increased earnings (2, 4) Career advancement (2, 4) Improved individual–job match (6) Increased challenge (6) Self-development (6) Nonwork benefits (e.g., geographic location (6) Increased family ties (3, 6) New social relationships (5) Enhanced commitment to new job and organization (6)	Loss of seniority (1) Loss of nonvested benefits (1) Unreimbursed moving costs (2, 6) Disruption of family (3, 6) Transition stress (3, 6) Loss of friendships (5) Decreased family ties (3, 6)	1. Tenure 2. Labor market 3. Family status 4. Job skills/abilities 5. Social involvement in work 6. Characteristics of old versus new job
Stayers	Opportunities for promotion (8, 9) More positive job attitudes (1, 4, 7, 9) Increased performance (3, 5) Stimulation at work (2, 9) Initiation of search that results in better job (1, 6, 7)	Increased workload (3, 5, 6, 9) Decreased performance (3, 5, 6, 9) Stress and uncertainty (6, 9) Less positive job attitudes (1, 4) Loss of friendships (2)	1. Beliefs about why others leave 2. Social relationship to leavers 3. Task interdependence 4. Status of leaver 5. Performance of leaver 6. Job market conditions 7. Career orientation of stayer 8. Level in organization of leaver 9. Organization promotion policies

[a]The numbers following each consequence refer to potential moderating variables thought to be most closely associated with that consequence.

these "benefits" result from turnover will of course depend on the individual's family status and the locations of the old and new jobs. Individuals changing jobs may benefit from the opportunity to make new friends among their co-workers. Turnover provides the opportunity for new friends and social activities, particularly for individuals who are likely to develop social involvements at work.

Finally, one outcome associated with turnover may be the opportunity to develop new commitments and loyalties to the employing organization. A change in jobs is likely to result in a shifting of loyalties from the old job to the new one (Steers & Mowday, 1981). Many people may enjoy the identification and sense of involvement that follows from establishing new commitments. Depending on characteristics of the old and new jobs, individuals may develop a more positive self-image from new jobs that involve more significant roles in the organization or from the simple fact that they were attractive to another organization. Hence, the job market provides one objective test of an individual's attractiveness and value to others.

LEAVERS—NEGATIVE CONSEQUENCES

Although a number of positive consequences of turnover can be identified there may also be several costs associated with the decision to change jobs. For many individuals, turnover may involve the loss of seniority and nonvested benefits. The longer a person has worked in the old job, the greater the costs associated with turnover may be. In addition, turnover may result in unreimbursed moving expenses and an increased cost of living resulting from moves between different parts of the country. Depending on job market conditions and the skills of the individual involved, some employers may be willing to assume the extra costs associated with changing jobs. It is becoming increasingly common for organizations to offer mortgage assistance, for example, to induce highly attractive employees to change jobs.

One set of negative consequences associated with turnover, however, may be less easily compensated by organizations. Changing jobs may be a significant source of stress, particularly when it involves moving from one city to another. Families with school-age children in the home may find their lives particularly disrupted by the decision to change jobs. Ruch and Holmes (1971), for example, identified changes in line of work, residence, schools, recreation, church, and social activities as potential sources of stress. The amount of stress associated with changing jobs may be related to the similarity between the old job and the new and to the distance between the old and new employers.

The decision to change jobs may also threaten social relationships with previous co-workers and family ties. Even when turnover involves movement between jobs in the same location, social relationships with co-workers from the old job may become increasingly strained (Steers & Mowday, 1981). In addition, movement between jobs in different cities may increase distances between members of families. This may result in pressures from the family not to move or greater effort required to maintain family ties at previous levels.

STAYERS—POSITIVE CONSEQUENCES

Although perhaps less obvious, the decision by individuals to leave an organization may also have implications for those who remain. The impact of turnover on remaining employees represents an interesting but neglected area of study (Mowday, 1981; Steers & Mowday, 1981). One possible consequence of turnover for remaining employees is increased opportunities for advancement and promotion (Staw, 1980b). When superiors in the organization leave, openings are created that may be filled by lower-level employees. Organizations that follow policies of promotion from within may find that turnover is viewed positively by their employees, particularly by those who desire advancement in their career.

Increased opportunities for advancement alone may result in more positive attitudes among remaining employees following turnover. In addition, other factors associated with turnover may also serve to strengthen the attitudes of remaining employees. When the person leaving is not well respected or liked by remaining employees, the decision of the individual to leave may be a source of satisfaction. Even when the person leaving is respected, however, remaining employees may strengthen their positive attitudes following turnover as a result of attempts to justify their own decision to remain (see Chapter 7). The need to justify remaining in the organization may depend on the perceived reasons others leave. Mowday (1981) suggested that the decision to leave a job because it is dissatisfying may be most threatening to the employees who remain. When this occurs, remaining employees may either distort the reasons others leave or reevaluate the job and organization more positively to justify staying. Although evidence on these processes is limited, Mowday (1981) found that employees who were most highly committed to the organization were least likely to believe that others left because they found the job dissatisfying.

When the person leaving is a co-worker who is not particularly effective in performing his or her job, turnover may also lead to improved performance among remaining employees. The impact of turnover of performance of remaining employees is likely to be greatest in situations where tasks are highly interdependent. When organizations are effective in encouraging poor performers to leave, however, it is likely that remaining employees will benefit. Turnover may be of benefit to remaining employees in other ways. When open positions are filled by individuals outside the organization or from other departments, new employees may bring improved ideas about how to perform the job and increased levels of motivation. The introduction of new employees into a work group may be a source of stimulation for incumbent employees, both from new approaches to the job and from opportunities to develop friendships.

Turnover may have an additional benefit to individuals. For many employees, the decision to remain in an organization may result from a lack of information about available alternatives or simple motivation to search for better opportunities. Turnover by co-workers may serve as a stimulus to remaining employees to reconsider their employment. In some cases, turnover by co-workers provides information about alternative job opportunities that may stimulate job search. A search for alternative jobs may result in the decision to leave, which for the individual could mean higher salary, improved working conditions, or better career opportunities. Even when job search does not lead to eventual turnover, the process of considering alternatives may make salient the positive features of the current position. There may be a natural tendency to believe that opportunities are better elsewhere (e.g., the "greener grass" phenomenon). When these alternatives are actually explored, however, the individual may come to appreciate his or her current job even more.

STAYERS—NEGATIVE CONSEQUENCES

Some of the negative consequences of turnover for remaining employees follow from the previous discussion. Turnover may result in increased work loads for remaining employees, at least temporarily, and decreased performance, particularly where tasks are highly interdependent. It may take the organization some time to find a replacement for the individual who has left. During this period, the leaver's duties may have to be assumed by remaining employees. When leavers are key employees or high performers, the negative effects of turnover on remaining employees may be particularly severe. Remaining employees may experience increased work demands, stress, and uncertainty until the open position is filled. Even when a replacement is found, time may have to be devoted by employees to training the replacement or socializing the individual about group norms. On complex jobs, considerable time may be required before the new employee is able to perform his or her task effectively. This may increase demands on other employees to work harder until the replacement can effectively perform the job.

In addition to increased work demands and uncertainty, other factors may lead to less positive attitudes among remaining employees. When open positions are filled from outside the organization, for example, dissatisfaction may result among current employees who were not promoted. It was already suggested that turnover by co-workers may stimulate a reevaluation of the job and search for better alternatives among remaining employees. Negative features of the job may become salient if the leaving employee is vocal about his or her dissatisfaction with the job. Moreover, the search for better alternative jobs may result in increased dissatisfaction. The word that better-paying jobs or better working conditions are available in other organizations may spread quickly among remaining employees, resulting in general demoralization and feelings of inequity. Also, when the person leaving is a close friend, remaining employees may find co-worker relations on the job less satisfying. For individuals with strong social involvements at work, the loss of a close friend or colleague may be particularly traumatic.

Consequences for Work Groups

The consideration of work groups in organizations has been less prominent in the study of turnover than either individual or organizational concerns. Although several characteristics of work groups have been identified as predictors of turnover (e.g., group cohesiveness), the impact of employee turnover on the work group has not received systematic attention for many years. Several early programs of research on group processes examined the effects of membership instability (see Meister, [1976] and Ziller [1965] for a review of these studies). Later concern with the consequences of turnover in organizations, however, ignored the group dimension of analysis almost entirely. The importance of considering the consequences of turnover for groups is based on the important role work groups serve in organizations and the fact that turnover may have unique implications at the group level of analysis. The consequences of employee turnover for work groups to be discussed in this section are summarized in Table 6.3.

POSITIVE CONSEQUENCES

The composition of groups is a major determinant of group effectiveness (Hackman & Morris, 1975; Shaw, 1981). For many types of tasks, the performance of the group will be controlled by the most competent group member (Steiner, 1972). Changes in the composition of groups caused by member turnover are therefore likely to have an important influence on group effectiveness.

Turnover that results in new members being added to the group can

Table 6.3
Consequences of Turnover for Work Groups[a]

Level of analysis	Possible consequences: Positive	Possible consequences: Negative	Potential moderating variables
Work group	Increased effectiveness (3, 7)	Disruption of work (1, 3, 5–7)	1. Task interdependence
	New ideas and creativity (1, 3, 7)	Disruption of group processes (2–4, 7)	2. Group cohesiveness
	New performance strategies (1, 3, 7)	Decreased performance (1, 3, 5–7)	3. Characteristics of leaver
	New skills and abilities (3, 7)	Greater role specification (4, 5)	4. Size of group
	Reevaluation of group norms (2, 3, 7)	Structured relationships and communication channels (4, 5)	5. Predictability of turnover
	Increased cohesiveness (3, 7)	Efforts to socialize new member (2, 7)	6. Difficulty of replacement
	Decreased conflict (3)	Increased conflict (7)	7. Characteristics of replacement

[a] The numbers following each consequence refer to potential moderating variables thought to be closely associated with that consequence.

influence effectiveness in a number of ways. New members may bring creative ideas, new approaches to solving problems, and needed skills and abilities to the group. Moreover, new members may be more likely to question group norms and procedures that may impede effectiveness. Whether or not turnover in groups increases group effectiveness, however, may depend on a number of factors. First, the characteristics of the individuals leaving and joining the group are clearly important. Group effectiveness may be enhanced when the least proficient member leaves and the replacement brings needed skills and abilities to the group. Second, the extent to which turnover influences overall group effectiveness probably depends on the nature of the tasks performed by the group. The impact of member turnover may be greatest, for example, when tasks are interdependent rather than independent. Third, characteristics of the group itself may influence the impact of member turnover. The effects of member turnover on group effectiveness may be less important for large groups than for small. In addition, the cohesiveness of the group may influence the extent to which new members can question and influence group processes. The ability of new members to change operative norms of the group may be greater when the group is less cohesive.

Member turnover in groups may also influence the level of group cohesiveness. When the person leaving is an isolate or deviant member, cohesiveness among remaining group members may increase as a result of turnover. Moreover, conflict within groups may decrease when one of the parties to the conflict leaves. In this situation, group relations may become more harmonious following turnover (Staw, 1980b). The cohesiveness of work groups may also be influenced by turnover in another manner. When a group member leaves, his or her work may have to be divided among remaining groups members until a replacement is found. The burden of increased work loads shared by remaining group members may require higher levels of cooperation and coordination of efforts to ensure that the total effectiveness of the group is not threatened. The added burden shared by group members and the resulting cooperation required to ensure that the work gets done may bring the group closer together and thus increase cohesiveness.

NEGATIVE CONSEQUENCES

Although turnover may in some cases have positive implications for groups, it may also result in several problems that seriously threaten group effectiveness. Turnover in groups may disrupt both group processes and task performance, particularly when a key group member (e.g., a leader) or high performer leaves. As suggested earlier, the extent to which member turnover negatively influences group performance will depend on the characteristics of the person leaving, characteristics of the replacement, and nature of the task. In addition, turnover may be more disruptive in small groups and when turnover is a relatively rare rather than a predictable occurrence. Ziller (1965) suggested that groups with high membership instability cope by increasing the structure of group relations and role specification. In highly structured groups with formally prescribed roles, the dependence of the group on any particular member or informal understandings among members may be decreased.

There may be other costs to groups associated with member turnover. Unless replacements are quickly found, group members may be forced to take on the work load of the person leaving. The increased work load shared by members of the group may be a source of dissatisfaction and may decrease the overall effectiveness of the group. Groups may also have to expend considerable effort in socializing and training the new member. In highly cohesive groups, socializing new members about appropriate behavior may be considered particularly important by the group. When these socialization efforts are not entirely effective, conflict may result from adding a new member to the group. New members who do not consider existing group norms appropriate may generate considerable disagreement within the group and cause group members to devote substantial time to the task of "educating" the new member. Time spent by group members in training and socialization may come at the expense of time directed toward task accomplishment.

Consequences for Organizations

The consequences of turnover have most often been considered at the organizational level of analysis (Mobley, 1980; Price, 1977; Staw, 1980b). One possible reason for this is that the costs associated with turnover have rather clear and straightforward implications for overall organization effectiveness (Steers, 1977b). Although the amount of turnover in an organization has generally been viewed as negatively related to effectiveness, the discussion that follows will suggest that this is not always the case. Rather, in certain circumstances, turnover may prove beneficial to organizations (cf. Dalton & Tudor, 1979). Dalton, Krackhardt, and Porter (in press), for example, found that 42% of the voluntary leavers in a sample of bank employees could be classified as poor performers and thus, from the organization's perspective, as "functional" turnover. An even higher percentage of these leavers were viewed as easily replaced by the organization. The fact that turnover at the organizational level of analysis may have both costs and benefits has been widely recognized (Dalton & Tudor, 1979; Mobley, 1980; Staw, 1980b). The following discussion will attempt to summarize this literature and specify the conditions under which turnover may have negative or positive consequences. The relationships to be discussed in this section are summarized in Table 6.4.

POSITIVE CONSEQUENCES

The positive consequences of turnover for organizations may include increased innovation, employee motivation and morale, and overall effectiveness. For relatively stable organizations in which growth cannot be counted upon to create new positions, turnover may be one of the few ways to hire new employees. The addition of new members, as suggested earlier, may be important to organizational innovation and adaptation (Staw (1980b). In comparison with longer-term employees, new members of the organization may be more likely to question existing practices and suggest new policies and procedures. This benefit of turnover may be lost, however, in organizations that fill vacancies by a rigid policy of promotion from inside. Organizations that fill vacancies by internal promotion may find that turnover results in increased employee morale and motivation due to promotional opportunities but not enhanced creativity or critical reappraisal of existing practices. When employees can only enter organizations at the lowest levels, new members may be in a poor position to influence organizational practices effectively. By the time such individuals are promoted into positions where influence is possible, they may have become so effectively socialized that little innovation is forthcoming (cf. Wright, 1980).

In evaluating the impact of turnover on organizations, it is critical to consider the internal labor pool of the organization and conditions in the external job market. Organizations with effective manpower planning systems may experience only minimal disruption from turnover. In addition, organizations operating in labor markets characterized by low demand relative to supply may also find that people who leave are easily replaced. In general, the impact of turnover on organizational functioning may be positively related to the level of the organization at which turnover takes place. Turnover among employees in entry-level positions is likely to pose fewer problems than turnover in the managerial or executive ranks.

Staw (1980b) also suggested another consideration in determining whether turnover might be beneficial to organizations. He argued that different jobs have characteristic tenure–performance curves. For many routine jobs, learning may take place quickly on the job. Individuals entering the organization may become proficient at the task and maintain constant levels of performance across a number of years. For certain

Table 6.4

Consequences of Turnover for Organizations[a]

Level of analysis	Possible consequences: Positive	Possible consequences: Negative	Potential moderating variables
Organization	Innovation and adaptation (3, 5)	Costs of turnover (1–5, 7)	1. Labor market conditions
	Increased employee morale and mobility (3, 5)	Selection and recruitment	2. Patterns of turnover
	Increased motivation (1, 3)	Training and development	3. Organization promotion policies
	Increased effectiveness (1, 4–7)	Administrative staff	4. Internal manpower pool
	Reduction in entrenched conflict (7)	Demoralization of employees (2, 7)	5. Growth of organization
		Negative public relations (7)	6. Job stress–role performance curve
		Operational disruption (2–4, 7)	7. Characteristics of leavers
		Decreased effectiveness (1, 2, 7)	
		Structural changes	
		Formalization (2)	
		Centralization (2)	
		Decreased employee social involvement at work (2)	

[a]The numbers following each consequence refer to potential moderating variables thought to be most closely associated with that consequence.

stressful and physically demanding jobs, however, the tenure–performance curve may take a different shape. In high-stress jobs such as social or police work, new employees may enter the organization with idealistic goals and high levels of motivation. As experience on the job increases, however, employees may become disillusioned and cynical about their ability to have a meaningful impact or about the goals they brought to the organization. For such employees, motivation may decrease as a function of tenure in the organization even though their experience has resulted in higher job skills and knowledge. In organizations characterized by stressful or physically demanding work, it may be beneficial to ensure a flow of new employees who are energetic and motivated. Turnover among older employees who have essentially "burned out" on the job may therefore actually contribute to overall organizational effectiveness. It should be apparent that this arguement is predicated on the assumption that older employees who leave are poorer performers, the job market allows easy replacement of leavers, and that new employees are capable and motivated. This may not always be the case, however.

Staw (1980b) also viewed turnovers as one way organizations can reduce entrenched conflict. Although the conflict-resolution literature most often focuses on such strategies as confrontation and accommodation, conflict can sometimes only be resolved by withdrawal from the organization of one of the parties. Conflicts at the executive level of the organization (e.g., between the CEO and president) for example, are frequently resolved in this fashion.

NEGATIVE CONSEQUENCES

The negative consequences of turnover for organizations have been discussed by a number of writers (e.g., Mobley, 1980; Price, 1977; Staw, 1980b). The most frequently mentioned negative consequences are the administrative costs associated with turnover. Turnover generally results in expenses for recruitment, selection, training, and development. Organizations with high levels of turnover may also have to maintain large personnel departments to handle the termination process for employees who leave and the hiring process for replacements. In addition, lost productivity until the new employee has mastered the job must be considered a cost of turnover. A complete discussion of the costs associated with turnover is beyond the scope of this chapter. Detailed discussions of costs can be found in Gaudet (1960) or Jeswald (1974).

Although procedures for identifying and calculating the costs associated with turnover have been less often considered, Staw (1980b) suggested that a number of situational factors would influence the overall administrative costs of turnover for organizations. First, conditions in the labor market are clearly important. In labor markets where there is an abundant supply of skilled labor, for example, recruiting costs may be low compared to those in labor markets in which demand exceeds supply. Second, patterns of turnover in the organization may be an important consideration. Patterns of turnover refer to both the level of the organization in which turnover most often takes place and the predictability of turnover. It is likely to be much costlier to replace managers, for example, than entry-level employees. Universities who are replacing a president may spend a year in the selection process and involve large numbers of people in the hiring decision. By comparison, replacing a clerical employee in the same university is likely to involve far fewer people and take a much shorter time. Whether or not turnover is predictable or rare also appears to be a factor. When turnover is predictable, routine procedures can be established for replacing employees. In cases where turnover is rare, however, replacing employees may require managers and others to drop projects to concentrate on hiring. Third, it was suggested earlier that organizations with policies of promoting from inside and with sufficient internal manpower pools may find it less difficult to replace leavers than organizations that typically recruit externally. Fourth, organizations undergoing rapid growth and development may also find that the costs associated with turnover are relatively small. Rapidly growing organizations are likely to maintain large personnel departments to hire people for newly created positions. The marginal costs associated with hiring replacements for employees who leave may be quite small in this situation. Finally, implicit in several of the things said earlier is the fact that costs of turnover are highly dependent on the characteristics of the people who leave. Holding the level of the organization constant, for example, it may be much more difficult to replace key employees with specialized skills than employees engaged in relatively routine tasks. In addition, replacing high-performing employees is likely to be much more difficult than replacing low performers without a decrease in overall performance.

In addition to the factors that have been mentioned, turnover has also been viewed as having a demoralizing effect on current employees and a negative effect on prospective employees. The extent to which turnover may have a demoralizing effect depends on several factors, including characteristics of the person leaving and patterns of turnover. The resignation of a high-level executive, for example, may raise more questions than turnover at lower levels in the organization, particularly if that individual is a popular and effective leader. In addition, the resignation of several high-level executives at one time may have a greater demoralizing effect than if each had resigned separately over an extended period of time. When turnover is among key personnel or groups of managers, the resignations may be a source of considerable speculation and rumors among remaining employees. Turnover may also have a negative impact on the organization's ability to recruit if dissatisfied employees who leave are vocal about their feelings toward the organization. Particularly in the case of high-level executives, negative publicity can result from the resignation of a highly dissatisfied employee.

Turnover in organizations may also disrupt operations and threaten the effectiveness of the overall organization. As with the other consequences of turnover, the possibility of disruption and decreased effectiveness may depend on a number of factors. In tight labor markets, turnover is likely to be most disruptive for organizations without policies for promoting current employees or where the supply of skilled replacements within the organization is limited. In general, the disruption that results from turnover, particularly among key personnel, will be positively related to the length of time required to find a replacement. Moreover, the timing of a decision to resign may influence the extent to which turnover is disruptive or decreases effectiveness. Turnover during slack work periods may have a limited impact on organizational operations. In contrast, the loss of personnel during peak periods may have very disruptive effects (e.g., the loss of a departmental secretary the week before the university is scheduled to begin the fall term). Although most organizations will ask employees to time their resignations to minimize any resulting disruption (e.g., stay on until a replacement is trained), this is not always possible.

Although they should not necessarily be considered negative consequences of turnover, Price (1977) also identified several structural characteristics that may be influenced by the level of turnover in organizations. Higher levels of formalization and centralization are likely to be found in organizations characterized by high rates of turnover. Price (1977) suggested that high levels of turnover, particularly among managerial personnel, may result in more formalized statements of rules, regulations, procedures, and policies. Whereas organizations with stable membership can rely on informal understandings about appropriate procedures, for example, organizations with high turnover must formalize statements of policy and procedures to aid in the transition of large numbers of new employees. High levels of turnover may also result in more centralized decision making. Centralization of decision making is one way organizations may attempt to minimize the disruption caused by turnover and ensure that important decisions are made by those with relevant experience and knowledge. Centralization of decision making also increases the importance of certain key personnel in the organization. When it is the key personnel who leave, however, centralization of decision making may actually increase the disruption caused by turnover.

Finally, Price (1977) suggested that high levels of turnover may decrease integration or the development of social relationships in the work place. As turnover increases, the development of close and continuing social relationships at work becomes more difficult. This may serve to decrease the general level of social involvement of employees in the organization.

Consequences of Employee Absenteeism

Absenteeism has often been studied as a secondary variable by researchers who were primarily interested in investigating turnover. The early literature on absenteeism often viewed absence as a less severe but conceptually similar form of withdrawal behavior to turnover. It was commonly assumed that turnover and absenteeism shared common antecedents. It has not been until recently that researchers have viewed absenteeism as a unique behavior deserving of separate research and theory (Steers & Rhodes, 1978). Since reviews of the turnover and absenteeism literature have shown that the two behaviors share only a few common antecedents (Porter & Steers, 1973), it is likely that absenteeism will have consequences that are different from those associated with turnover. This is evident from a consideration of the nature of absenteeism and turnover. Whereas turnover most often represents an irrevocable break between the individual and the organization, absenteeism is a temporary form of withdrawal that does not usually threaten the employment relationship. Turnover is most often viewed as motivated by either dissatisfaction with the current job or attraction to another job, whereas absenteeism may often occur for reasons that have little to do with the job (e.g, family responsibilities).

The purpose of this section is to identify a number of potential consequences of absenteeism for individuals, work groups, and organizations. Although some overlap will be evident between the consequences of turnover and absenteeism, particularly at the group and organizational levels of analysis, absenteeism has a number of unique consequences of research interest. Unfortunately, research on the consequences of absenteeism is limited and thus there is very little literature to draw upon in this discussion. The discussion that follows will be somewhat speculative as a result.

Consequences for Individuals

As was true of the consequences of turnover, at the individual level of analysis absenteeism has consequences for both the individual being absent and co-workers of the absentee. Moreover, these consequences can be considered both positive and negative from the perspective of the absentee or his or her work colleagues. The discussion in this section will be organized to reflect these differences. The relationships to be discussed in this section are summarized in Table 6.5.

ABSENTEES—POSITIVE CONSEQUENCES

Perhaps the most obvious consequence of absenteeism for the individual is the ability to recover from illness. Because absence occurs for reasons other than illness, however, it also has other consequences that may be more interesting from a research perspective. Absence from the organization, for example, is one way employees have to reduce stress or boredom associated with the job. The fact that periodic absences from stressful jobs are often sanctioned by company policy (e.g., paid sick leave) or work-group norms suggests that absenteeism may be a commonly accepted form of coping with the job. Absenteeism allows the employee to reduce job-related stress and thus maintain higher levels of motivation than might otherwise be possible. Individuals may return from an absence with renewed energy and motivation, although this will depend on the nature of the job and the individual.

Absence is also a way in which employees cope with nonwork demands. Numerous day-to-day tasks can only be accomplished between the hours of eight and five on weekdays (e.g., transacting business at a government office). We often neglect the fact that management employees have the discretion to take time away from work to perform these tasks without notice or penalty. For many rank-and-file employees, however, these nonwork demands can only be met by taking time off the job in the form of an absence. The importance of absenteeism in coping with nonwork demands is likely to differ among employees. Female employees with children in the home, for example, may be subject to greater pressures than other employees. It is important to recognize that absenteeism may be a response to either work-related or nonwork pressures and that the consequences of absenteeism for that individual will differ depending on the factors motivating the absence.

ABSENTEES—NEGATIVE CONSEQUENCES

Depending on the absence policies of the organization, absenteeism may result in a loss of earnings for the employee. Many organizations have a paid sick-leave policy, however that only penalizes absences beyond some specified number.

Table 6.5
Consequences of Absenteeism for Individuals[a]

Level of analysis	Possible consequences: Positive	Possible consequences: Negative	Potential moderating variables
Absentees	Reduced stress and boredom (1–3) Renewed motivation toward the job (2) Ability to take care of nonwork responsibilities (1)	Loss of earnings (1) (3) Lowered performance evaluation (2, 4, 5) Resentment of co-workers (2, 4, 5) Work accumulates while absent (2, 4) Altered job attitudes or self-perceptions (5)	1. Absence policies of organization 2. Nature of the task 3. Employee norms about absence 4. Timing of absence 5. Perceived reason for absence
Co-workers	Increased job variety (1, 2) Skill development and training (1, 2) Opportunities for overtime (2–4) Visibility to supervisor (1–4)	Increased work load (1–4) Resentment toward absent co-worker (1–4)	1. Nature of task 2. Availability of replacements 3. Timing of absence 4. Production pressures

[a]The numbers following each consequence refer to potential moderating variables thought to be closely associated with that consequence.

In addition to loss of earnings, absences may also negatively influence the employee's performance evaluation by his or her supervisor. Frequent absences most often result in negative performance evaluations by supervisors. The extent to which this occurs, however, may be influenced by the importance of the job performed by the absent employee and the timing of the absence. Absences by employees on key jobs or during peak periods are likely to be most visible to supervisors. In addition, supervisors may make judgments about the legitimacy of an absence that can affect subsequent employee evaluations.

Absent employees may also be resented by co-workers when absence causes the work load of others to increase. Resentment of co-workers toward the absent employee may be the greatest when the reasons for the absence are not considered legitimate, when tasks are highly interdependent, or when the absence occurs during a period of heavy work demand or over an extended period.

When the work of an employee cannot easily be performed by others during an absence (e.g., the work of professional or managerial employees), work is likely to accumulate while the employee is absent. The employee returning from an absence may be faced with the difficult task of catching up on work that has accumulated in addition to meeting current job demands.

Although less tangible than the other consequences that have been discussed, absenteeism may have implications for the employee's self-perceptions or job attitudes (cf. Johns & Nicholson, in press). Employees who are absent may develop causal attributions about the reasons for the absence. When external justification for an absence (e.g., illness) is not readily apparent, employees may come to believe the absence was caused by something about themselves or the job. An employee who spontaneously decides not to come to work, for example, may justify the decision by viewing the job as stressful or dissatisfying. Alternatively, the employee may come to belive that he or she is particularly illness-prone. We currently know very little about the cognitive consequences of absence for the individual absentee. How individuals justify absence from work and the resulting implications of such justifications for attitudes and beliefs, however, represent an interesting area of inquiry.

INDIVIDUAL CO-WORKERS—POSITIVE CONSEQUENCES

For individual co-workers of the absent employee, absenteeism incidents may represent an opportunity to increase variety on the job or to develop job-related skills and abilities. Absenteeism may create work demands that require transferring employees temporarily to different jobs. This would increase variety at work and provide opportunities for employees to learn different tasks. Some organizations create positions that have as their major responsibility replacing absent employees. The job of utilityman or woman on the automobile assembly line, for example, is often found to be more satisfying than regular assembly jobs, since these employees perform many different tasks in replacing absent employees. When replacements for absent employees are not readily available, absenteeism may result in opportunities for overtime work and thus increased earnings. In addition, employees who carry an extra work load because a co-worker is absent may become highly visible to supervisors, particularly when absences occur during peak work periods. This high visibility may result in higher performance evaluations, since supervisors are likely to reward employees who make contributions at crucial times.

INDIVIDUAL CO-WORKERS—NEGATIVE CONSEQUENCES

Although the absence of a co-worker may create opportunities for other employees, absenteeism may increase the work load and thus the burden shared by other employees. The increase in work load may be viewed by many as a negative consequence of absenteeism rather than an opportunity. The exent to which absenteeism increases the work load of co-workers will depend on the availability of replacements for the absent employee, the nature of the tasks performed, the timing of the absence, and pressures for production. The greatest increase in work load may occur, for example, when replacements are not available, tasks are interdependent, and the absence occurs during a period in which there are heavy pressures for production. In this situation, it is likely that resentment will be generated for the absent employee, particularly when the reason for absence is not viewed as legitimate. Absenteeism may therefore threaten interpersonal relationships among employees.

Consequences for Work Groups

As suggested in the preceding discussion, absenteeism may have important implications for employees in the organization other than the person who is absent. Although these implications can be discussed at the individual level of analysis, it is also important to consider the consequences of absenteeism for work-group functioning. In this section several consequences of absenteeism for work groups will be identified. The relationships to be discussed are summarized in Table 6.6.

POSITIVE CONSEQUENCES

There may be at least two positive consequences for work groups associated with absenteeism of group members. First, the absent employee

Table 6.6
Consequences of Absenteeism for Work Groups[a]

Level of analysis	Possible consequences		Potential moderating variables
	Positive	Negative	
Work group	Increased motivation from absent member (2) Mutual support and greater cohesiveness (1, 2, 4)	Increased workload (2, 4) Decreased group effectiveness (2, 4) Intragroup conflict (e.g., sanctions directed toward absent member) (1–4)	1. Group norms about absenteeism 2. Task interdependence and characteristics 3. Group cohesiveness 4. Availability of temporary replacements

[a]The numbers following each consequence refer to potential moderating variables thought to be most closely associated with that consequence.

may return to work in the group with increased motivation and interest in the job. As suggested earlier, absenteeism is one way employees have to reduce boredom and stress associated with the job. Since continued work under stressful conditions may negatively influence employee motivation, time away from the job may allow employees to recover from the impacts of stress and return to work with renewed motivation. Increased motivation on the part of the employees returning from an absence may facilitate the work of the group, particularly when tasks are highly interdependent.

Second, absenteeism may contribute to the overall level of cohesiveness in the work group. Work groups may develop norms about absence that legitimate periodic time away from the job by group members. Groups may develop informal understandings about covering for the absent employee to ensure that the work of the group still gets completed. A system of mutual support in which group members cover for one another in the event of an absence may be most likely to develop when tasks are highly interdependent. The mutual support that results from group norms about absenteeism may increase the felt obligation of members to the group and thus contribute to overall group cohesiveness.

NEGATIVE CONSEQUENCES

When tasks are highly interdependent, absenteeism is likely to increase the work load of group members and may threaten overall group effectiveness. Group members may simply have to work harder when a coworker is absent. Although in some situations this may be tolerated or even encouraged by the group, when absenteeism by a member becomes excessive it may be a source of intragroup conflict. Absences that are excessive or not viewed as legitimate may violate the norms of the group and result in group sanctions against the offending member. This may involve either the refusal of group members to cover for the absent member or overt hostility being directed toward the person. Although little is currently known about group norms governing absence behavior (cf. Johns & Nicholson, in press), it is likely that groups will react negatively toward members who are frequently absent or who always seem to be absent at critical times. The conflict generated as a result of absenteeism may only be resolved by a change in behavior of the group member who violates the norms or his or her removal from the group.

Consequences for Organizations

At the organizational level of analysis, absenteeism may have several consequences that influence overall effectiveness. Several such consequences will be identified in this section. The discussion is summarized in Table 6.7.

POSITIVE CONSEQUENCES

Although absenteeism has most often been viewed as having negative consequences for organizations, it is also possible that a certain level of absenteeism has benefits as well. Perhaps the most obvious benefit is that sick employees do not come to work. Overly strict absenteeism policies or incentives for attendance may encourage employees who are truly ill to report to work. Sick employees are unlikely to perform their jobs effectively and they may spread illness among their co-workers. In addition, a certain level of absenteeism may also contribute to the development of a skilled internal manpower pool. If organizations have a policy of transferring employees among different jobs to replace absentees, this will result in greater training and development of job skills among employees. Some organizations maintain crews of employees solely for the purpose of covering the jobs of absent employees. This crew may become a pool of talent that organizations can draw upon when turnover creates vacancies in regular positions. Absenteeism therefore provides organizations with the opportunity to train employees to perform a number of different tasks.

NEGATIVE CONSEQUENCES

The costs associated with absenteeism are the most salient and tangible negative consequences at the organizational level of analysis. Jeswald (1974) identified a number of costs associated with absenteeism in organizations and thus they will not be discussed in depth here. It is important to recognize, however, that organizations may pay wages and fringe benefits for absent workers even though they are not making a productive contribution. The extent of such costs will depend on absence policies in the organization (e.g., costs may be greatest for organizations with paid sick-leave policies). Organizations must also include administrative expenses required to keep attendance records as a cost of absenteeism. In addition, organizations that hire extra employees to replace those who are absent also have higher payroll costs attributable to absenteeism. Organizations that must hire 110 employees to ensure that 100 employees are available for work on any given day, for example, pay a heavy price for absenteeism. Problems may even increase when all employees show up for work, since jobs may not be available for everyone.

The costs associated with absenteeism are likely to influence organizational effectiveness negatively. High levels of absenteeism will reduce the overall productivity of employees. Moreover, organizations may have to build slack into production schedules to compensate for anticipated

Table 6.7

Consequences of Absenteeism for Organizations[a]

Level of analysis	Possible consequences		Potential moderating variables
	Positive	Negative	
Organization	Increased effectiveness (1–4)	Costs of absenteeism (1–4)	1. Patterns of absence and predictability
	Training and development of work force (1–3)	Wages	2. Technological interdependence of tasks
		Fringe benefits	3. Capacity utilization
		Administrative staff	4. Absence policies
		Increased personnel	
		Decreased overall effectiveness (1–4)	

[a] The numbers following each consequence refer to potential moderating variables thought to be most closely associated with that consequence.

absences. Even when replacements are available for absent employees, effectiveness may be decreased because temporary employees may not have the job skills or the knowledge of the absent employees they replace. This may result in lower productivity and quality-control problems. The extent to which absenteeism negatively influences the effectivenss of the organization may depend on several factors, including the predictability of absences, technological interdependence of tasks, and capacity utilization of facilities. Decreased effectiveness resulting from absenteeism may be most likely when absences are among key employees in strategic production positions, when absences are difficult to predict, and when there is little slack in the system.

Consequences of Employee–Organization Linkages: A Future Research Agenda

A number of potential consequences of employee commitment, turnover, and absenteeism have been presented in this chapter. Moreover, an attempt was made to identify various individual and situational variables that may influence the likelihood that specific consequences will occur. Since this area has received relatively little research attention, each consequence represents an area for future research and thus an element of a larger research agenda. Rather than attempt to present a detailed research agenda summarizing the previous discussion, we will discuss several general conclusions about future research in this area.

Agenda item 1. It is important to recognize that employee commitment, turnover, and absenteeism have both positive and negative consequences. The previous literature on these topics has most often stressed the positive consequences of commitment and negative implications of turnover and absenteeism. Perhaps this is attributable to the fact that certain outcomes (e.g, costs of turnover) are more tangible and easily studied than others. The discussion in this chapter should make clear, however, that a more balanced approach is necessary in evaluating the consequences of these behaviors. Although some of the consequences discussed in this chapter are less tangible and more difficult to study (e.g., demoralization of employees due to turnover), they are important to consider in our research nonetheless.

Agenda item 2. Whether commitment, turnover, and absenteeism have positive or negative consequences may be influenced by a number of situational factors. The relationships discussed in this chapter are far from simple or direct. A number of moderating factors were identified that may influence the way we approach the consequences of behavior. The question is *not* whether commitment, turnover, and absenteeism have positive or negative consequences. Rather, what is important is to determine under what conditions the consequences of these behaviors will be most positive or negative. The administrative costs associated with turnover, for example, may be minimal in organizations undergoing rapid growth and development. In stable organizations, however, these same costs may be relatively large. Moreover, in rapidly growing organizations turnover may have a negative impact, if any, on the morale of employees. In stable organizations, however, turnover may create opportunities for promotion and thus increase the morale of employees. Failure to deal with the complexities of relationships between various consequences and commitment, turnover, and absenteeism may result in misunderstanding and organizational practices that have unintended consequences (e.g., attendance incentive programs that encourage sick employees to report for work).

Agenda item 3. The consequences of commitment, turnover, and absenteeism must be considered at multiple levels of analysis. The approach taken in this chapter was to consider consequences separately at the individual, work-group, and organizational levels of analysis. Moreover, a distinction was made at the individual level of analysis between those who engage in a behavior (e.g., absence or turnover) and others who may observe and be affected by the behavior. This is a departure from previous literature that has most often focused on one level of analysis in considering the consequences of behavior. However, greater progress is likely to be made in our research when problems are studied at multiple rather than single levels of analysis (Roberts, Hulin & Rousseau, 1978).

Summary

It should be apparent that consideration of the consequences of behavior is an important area of study but one that has to date received little attention. Relative to the antecedents of commitment, turnover, and absenteeism, the consequences of these behaviors have been virtually ignored. Although there are exceptions to this sweeping statement, the point is that researchers have in the past been far more interested in factors leading up to behavior than in consequences that follow from it. The imbalance in our research is ironic, since our interest in these behaviors is primarily because they are thought to have important consequences. Our willingness to study systematically the presumed consequences of turnover, absenteeism, and, to a lesser extent, commitment has been limited. Recognizing that these behaviors have important consequences raises a number of interesting research questions for the future. The intent of this chapter was not to develop comprehensive models of the consequences of these behaviors. Rather, the goal was to identify relationships and moderating conditions that may become the subject of future research. The discussion in this chapter should be considered tentative, given the limited research support for many of the relationships considered. Speculation on the consequences of commitment, turnover, and absenteeism, however, should encourage research in this area.

7

Accommodating the Participation–Withdrawal Decision: A Cognitive Analysis

In the previous chapter a number of consequences of turnover and absenteeism were discussed. A majority of the consequences highlighted in the previous discussion were tangible outcomes of behavior. For example, the decision to leave an organization was discussed in terms of its implications for wage levels, job duties, and administrative costs. It was also suggested that behaviors such as turnover and absenteeism may have more subtle, yet no less important, implications for the attitudes held by employees. Since the attitudinal consequences of behavior appear to depend on complex cognitive processes, a discussion of this topic was postponed until this chapter.

The general concern of this chapter will be how individuals cognitively accommodate participation or withdrawal decisions, both their own and those made by other employees.[1] Primary attention will be given to the decision to stay with or leave an organization, since turnover is likely to have the greatest long-range implications for both individuals and the organization. Many of the cognitive processes discussed in this chapter, however, could also be extended to understand how individuals accommodate the decision to be absent from work (cf. Johns & Nicholson, in press).

In earlier work on accommodation processes, Steers and Mowday (1981) identified three different classes of employees who may be affected by withdrawal decisions in organizations. First, the decision to stay with or leave an organization has clear implications for the attitudes held by the person making the decision. Research on job choice has shown that individuals who select among alternative job offers systematically re-

[1]The discussion in this chapter draws on an earlier paper by Steers and Mowday (1981).

evaluate both the chosen and unchosen jobs following their choice (Lawler *et al.*, 1975; Vroom & Deci, 1971). Additional research extended earlier findings by identifying several factors that must be present in the processes through which people make decisions for attitudes to change following decisions (O'Reilly & Caldwell, 1980b). From the perspective of the individual leaving the organization, the act of turnover and the processes through which this decision is made may have important implications for attitudes toward both the old job and the new.

Second, the decision by an employee to leave the organization is likely to have implications for the attitudes held by former co-workers who remain in the organization. Turnover by an employee can be viewed by former co-workers as a rejection of the job and as an implicit, if not explicit, indication that better job opportunities exist in other organizations (Mowday, 1981). Those who remain in the organization may have to reconcile their decision to stay with the knowledge that others have found the job undesirable. Turnover may therefore cause former co-workers to reevaluate their position in the organization and may lead to more negative attitudes and a search for better job opportunities.

Third, turnover by an employee may have implications for the attitudes and beliefs held by his or her former supervisor. The processes through which supervisory personnel accommodate the decision of employees to leave are particularly important for organizations. Supervisors often have the responsibility for assessing the reasons why employees leave for the purpose of taking action to prevent additional turnover in the future. The accuracy with which supervisors assess the causes of turnover has important implications for the effectiveness of any steps taken to reduce turnover rates in the organization. Moreover, supervisors may also view turnover by employees as a rejection of the job or organization and have difficulty reconciling this belief with their own attitudes. We currently know very little about the processes through which supervisors develop beliefs about the causes of employee turnover or the role of attitudes in this process.

In this chapter the implications of turnover for attitudes and beliefs will be discussed from the perspective of both the person leaving and observers of the decision (e.g., co-workers and supervisors). In the first section the attitudinal consequences of the decision to stay with or leave an organization will be considered. Since the attitudinal implications of turnover are highly dependent on beliefs about why others decide to stay or leave, a second section will be devoted to the cognitive processes through which such beliefs are developed. A theoretical model based on the work of Steers and Mowday (1981) will be presented in which a number of factors that may influence beliefs about the causes of behavior are identified. In addition, initial research on aspects of the cognitive processes used by supervisors to assess the reasons for employee turnover will be discussed.

Attitudinal Consequences of Decisions to Stay or Leave

The attitudinal consequences of the decision to remain with or leave an organization are considered in this section. Since somewhat different consequences and issues are highlighted depending on whether the perspective of the person making the decision or others observing the decision is taken, these two perspectives are discussed separately.

Consequences for People Making the Decision

From an analytical standpoint, the decision to stay on a job that is satsifying or leave one that is dissatisfying is of less interest with respect to its consequences than cases in which satisfied employees leave or dissatisfied employees stay (i.e., "off-quadrant" behavior). In cases where behavior is consistent with prior attitudes (e.g., a dissatisfied employee leaves), there would appear to be less need to change subsequent attitudes as a consequence of the decision. Although behavior that is consistent with prior attitudes may strengthen preexisting feelings about the job, it is unlikely that attitudes would dramatically change. When behavior is inconsistent with prior attitudes (e.g., a dissatisfied employee remains in the organization), however, there is reason to believe that a shift in attitudes may, under certain conditions, result from the decision.

Cognitive dissonance theory is relevant to understanding the consequences of behavior that is inconsistent with prior attitudes (Festinger, 1957; Wicklund & Brehm, 1976). Briefly stated, the theory suggests that dissonance is aroused whenever two cognitions psychologically stand in obverse relation to each other. The existence of dissonance is viewed as creating tension within the individual and motivating actions designed to reduce the dissonance (cf. Zanna & Cooper, 1976). The motivation to reduce dissonance is a function of the magnitude of the dissonance created; the greater the dissonance, the greater the motivation to reduce it.

Applied to the turnover decision, the theory clearly suggests that the decision to leave a job that is satisfying or remain on a job that is dissatisfying will, under certain conditions, create dissonant congnitions in the mind of the employee. In the first case, the "satisfied leaver" may hold the two dissonant cognitons "I am satisfied with my job" and "I am leaving my job." The "dissatisfied stayer," on the other hand, may hold the two dissonant cognitions "I am dissatisfied with my job" and "I am remaining on the job." When such dissonant cognitions exist, the theory predicts that individuals will be motivated to reduce dissonance through either behavioral or cognitive means (Brehm & Cohen, 1962; Festinger, 1957; Wicklund & Brehm, 1976). Because it is usually difficult to change or deny a decision once it has been made, this generally suggests that the individual will change his or her attitudes or perceptions to be more consistent with the choice.

Building on the earlier work of Aronson (1968, 1978, 1980), Staw (1980a) has suggested that there may be a more general need on the part of individuals to justify the decisions they make. The self-justification processes he describes have their origin in the desire of individuals to protect their self-concept. Most people like to believe, for example, that they are rational and effective decision makers. The employee who has turned down a job offer to remain in a position that is dissatisfying, however, may find his or her self-concept as a good decision maker threatened by this action. "If I am such a good decision maker, why did I decide to remain in this dissatisfying job?" In such cases individuals may seek ways to justify their decision to protect their self-concept. Although Staw (1980a) suggests that self-justification processes provide an alternative explanation for many of the research findings in dissonance theory, the two processes are likely to produce similar effects on attitudes. Whether attitude change following the decision to stay with or leave an organization results from self-justification or dissonance reduction (cognitive consistency) processes is not central to the concern of this section. Both processes highlight the potential importance of decisions in shaping subsequent attitudes and beliefs.

BOUNDARY CONDITIONS FOR INFLUENCE OF DECISIONS ON ATTITUDES

As suggested in the discussion of self-justification processes, the self-image of the individual as a decision maker may be a boundary condition for the influence of decisions on attitudes (Staw, 1980a). Unless the individual views himself or herself as a careful and competent decision maker, there may be little need to justify decisions that are made, particularly when they lead to negative consequences. Research in the field has identified a number of additional situational factors that appear important in determining the extent to which decisions have implications for subsequent attitudes. These factors are briefly reviewed in the paragraphs that follow.

1. *Explicit Choice That Is Difficult to Revoke.* The likelihood of attitude change following a decision increases when an explicit choice is made and the choice is difficult to change or revoke (Brehm & Cohen, 1962; Staw, 1974). Decisions that are explicit are more difficult for the individual to deny. In this regard, it is important to recognize that the decision to leave an organization is generally more explicit than the decision to stay. For most employees, the decision to remain is not consciously made on a day-to-day or week-to-week basis. Rather, the decision to remain may be implicit in the failure actively to seek alternative job opportunities. When employees receive formal job offers from other organizations, however, the decision to remain in the organization becomes quite explicit. In addition, turnover by co-workers may make current versus alternative employment opportunities more salient and thus the decision to remain more explicit. Employees who decide to quit their jobs or who turn down alternative job offers may also find their decision difficult to change or revoke. When decisions are made that cannot be easily revoked, individuals must live with the consequences and thus may feel a greater need to justify their choice.
2. *Importance of decision and consequences.* In general, the need to justify a decision will be positively related to the importance of the decision and its consequences for the individual (Festinger, 1957). Norms of rationality are more likely to surround decisions with important consequences and thus the need to justify such decisions will be enhanced (Staw, 1980a). In addition, individuals may take greater time and effort in making important decisions such as changing jobs. There is considerable research evidence to suggest that effort can lead to greater postdecision justification processes (Aronson, 1980).
3. *Perceived Freedom of Choice.* The attitudinal implications of decisions are likely to be greatest when people feel personally responsible for a decision and its consequences (Collins & Hoyt, 1972; Staw, 1974). The greater the perceived freedom an individual has in making a decision, the more likely he or she is to feel personally responsible for its consequences. Decisions in which individuals are placed under external demands to take one choice over another, for example, may reduce perceived freedom and thus felt responsibility (Steiner, 1970).
4. *Insufficient Justification.* The need to justify a decision increases when there are negative consequences associated with the choice and these consequences were foreseeable (Brehm & Cohen, 1962; Freedman, 1963; Staw, 1980a). Moreover, the lack of external inducement to

make a particular choice will increase the need to justify a decision that leads to some negative consequences. Insufficient justification can be associated with characteristics of both the old job and the new. Characteristics of an unchosen job that, if considered alone, would have led the individual to select the alternative, for example, can lead to feelings of insufficient justification. In addition, negative features of the chosen alternative that were foreseeable can also lead to such feelings. In general, the need to justify a decision should be greatest when the two alternatives are similar in overall attractiveness but differ in the attractiveness of different characteristics. For example, an individual may move from an unchallenging job in a desirable geographic location to a more challenging job in a less attractive place to live. This decision involves a clear trade-off between attractive and unattractive job features. Explicit trade-offs between features of alternative jobs may be common in most job change decision situations. Situations such as these may increase the need on the part of individuals to justify their decision.

The degree to which a particular decision is "justified" is primarily a subjective judgment on the part of the individual. For purposes of research, it is doubtful whether any "objective" standards could be identified for purposes of operationalizing the concept of insufficient justification. Early research on dissonance theory operationalized insufficient justification by inducing people to act in ways inconsistent with their stated beliefs or attitudes (cf. Staw, 1980a). However, Aronson (1968) has argued that dissonance really arises when people act in ways inconsistent with their self-concept, and Staw (1980a) has suggested that people have a general need to justify their choices and behaviors to protect their self-concept. Viewed more broadly, an individual's self-concept as well as anticipated reactions from others to the choice (which may threaten the self-concept) may be important in justification processes. It should be clear, however, that no objective standard exists that can be applied to determine whether or not a particular decision will require justification.

5. *Public Knowledge.* Several writers have suggested that the need to justify a decision will be greatest when the decision is publicly known (O'Reilly & Caldwell, 1980b; Salancik, 1977). Decisions that are widely known to others are more difficult to deny and may elicit more inquiries that provide an opportunity for justification. In addition, people may feel a greater need to offer justification for decisions when they are known to close friends and respected colleagues.

INDIVIDUAL AND SITUATIONAL DIFFERENCES CONCERNING CONSEQUENCES

The turnover decision (and, to a lesser extent, the decision to remain) often involves an explicit choice, is difficult to change or revoke, has important consequences, and generally becomes publicly known to friends and co-workers. We would therefore expect people to feel a general need to justify decisions about changing jobs. Decisions about staying with or leaving an organization, however, may vary in the extent to which there is perceived freedom of choice and sufficient justification for the decision. Thus, these two factors may be more critical in determining the extent to which self-justification processes and attitude change follow decisions about jobs. To simplify the discussion that follows, the presence or absence of perceived freedom of choices and insufficient justification will be viewed as the primary determinants of whether or not individuals attempt to justify their decisions by cognitive or other means. This is not meant to suggest that the other factors discussed may not be important in some decision situations. Rather, *most* decision situations involving quitting or staying will be characterized by high explicitness and irrevocability, will have important consequences, and will be publicly known. Perceived freedom of choice and insufficient justification may therefore be more crucial in the sense that they are more likely to vary across decision situations.

In a given decision situation there are often a number of different ways in which individuals can justify their decisions. Unfortunately, it is difficult to make precise predictions about how people will act. Some support has been found for Festinger's (1957) assertion that the method of dissonance reduction (self-justification) chosen will be sensitive to the "reality" of the situation (e.g., Walster, Bersheid, & Barclay, 1967). Considerable ambiguity still remains, however, about what specific method of justification people will use in a given situation. As a consequence, the discussion in this section remains somewhat speculative.

In considering the attitudinal consequences of turnover for the individual making the decision, a distinction will be drawn between (*a*) whether a person is a "satisfied leaver" or a "dissatisfied stayer"; and (*b*) whether or not the conditions leading to the need to justify the decision are present. To simplify the discussion, only decision situations in which *both* perceived freedom of choice and insufficient justification are present or where at least one or both of these factors are absent will be considered. When both conditions are present, it is assumed that individuals will feel a stronger need to justify their actions. If one or both of the conditions are absent, the need to justify the action taken should be less since external justification for the decision will exist in the situation (e.g., "I was forced to make this choice" or "It was clearly the best of the two alternatives"). This distinction results in the fourfold classification of cases adapted from Steers and Mowday (1981) and presented in Table 7.1.

Table 7.1
Possible Attitudinal and Behavioral Consequences of the Decision to Participate for the Decision Maker

Situational characteristics	Emergent condition	Satisfied leaver	Dissatisfied stayer
High personal responsibility and inadequate justification	High need for justification	1. Denial of responsibility for decision to change jobs 2. Systematic distortion of characteristics of old and new jobs 3. High organizational commitment and satisfaction on new job 4. Selective perception of new job 5. Reduced social contacts with former co-workers	1. Denial of responsibility for decision to remain 2. Systematic distortion of characteristics of current and alternative jobs 3. Shifting valence of inducements for membership in present organization 4. Increased satisfaction and commitment on present job 5. Deliberate increase in dissonance
Low personal responsibility and/or adequate justification	Low need for justification	6. Pleasant memories of old job 7. Willingness to maintain social contacts with former co-workers	1. Change job situation 2. Continued job search behavior 3. Lowered self-esteem and self-confidence 4. Alternative forms of withdrawal 5. Shifting central life interests

Source: Steers and Mowday In L. Cummings and B. Staw (Eds.). *Research in Organizational Behavior* (Vol. 3). Greenwich, CT: JAI Press, 1981.

1. *Satisfied leaver–need for justification present.* This situation describes the case in which an employee has voluntarily resigned from a job (i.e., high personal responsibility and choice) that he or she found satisfying. Inadequate justification may exist because a trade-off was made between attractive elements of the old and new jobs. In this situation, it is predicted that postdecision justification processes will result.

   Several alternative modes of justification would be available for the decision to leave, as shown in Table 7.1. First, justification may be provided by denying personal responsibility for the decision (Cooper, 1971). For example, the employee may cognitively distort the circumstances surrounding the decision. One way this might be done is to believe the organization was subtly urging him or her to leave. This strategy is equivalent to cognitively manipulating the attribution of the reason for leaving. (Attribution processes surrounding the turnover decisions are discussed in the next section.) The fact that people are more likely to attribute the causes of their own behavior to characteristics of the environment (Jones, 1976) suggests that this may be a common strategy. However, this belief may be difficult to reconcile with reality when the organization has made repeated attempts to retain the employee (e.g., promised pay raise or promotion).

   A second plausible method of justification is to cognitively distort the characteristics of the old and new jobs. This strategy can be seen in research on job choice, which has found that people systematically reevaluate the alternatives after a choice has been made (Lawler *et al.*, 1975; Vroom & Deci, 1971). This research suggests that people justify their choices by increasing the positive evaluation of the chosen (new) job while magnifying the negative aspects of the unchosen (old) job. In the turnover decision, this is likely to result in a third consequence, a rapid shifting of loyalties and commitment from the old job to the new. The generally high levels of commitment found among newly hired employees on the first day at work may be evidence of this phenomenon (Porter *et al.*, 1976; Van Maanen, 1975).

   Fourth, and consistent with the process of systematically reevaluating the old and new jobs, individuals may avoid information that is inconsistent with their choice and selectively seek information that confirms the choice (Festinger, 1957; Janis & Mann, 1977). This may result in selective perception of the new job environment. Finally, employees may reduce social contacts with co-workers on the previous job and develop new social relationships based on the chosen job, since association with previous co-workers may make salient information inconsistent with the choice. Caplow (1964) suggests that the termination of social relationships based on past organizational memberships is an important part of socialization into a new organization. This socialization requirement may in part serve to reconfirm the job choice of the individual.

2. *Dissatisfied stayer—need for justification present.* This situation may be characterized by an employee who voluntarily turns down a job offer to remain in a relatively dissatisfying position. Inadequate justification for the decision to remain may be perceived when the alternative job was at least in some respect more attractive than the current job. The decision to remain would be predicted to lead to postdecision justification processes.

One method of justifying the decision in this situation is to deny responsibility for the decision. In other words, the circumstances surrounding the choice can be cognitively distorted to eliminate the perceived voluntary nature of the decision (e.g., low perceived choice or personal responsibility). Employees may attribute the causes for their behavior to environmental factors beyond their control (e.g., "I can't leave while my children are still in school"). As noted earlier, there is a tendency to attribute the causes of our own behavior to environmental factors and thus this may be a common strategy (Jones, 1976). Moreover, it may be a successful strategy, since a large number of such environmental factors are likely to exist in any decision situation. If this strategy is followed, the individual may remain dissatisfied with the job and react in a manner described subsequently in case 4.

When it is impossible to deny personal responsibility for the choice, the employee may distort perceptions of the existing job to magnify its positive features. Individuals may reevaluate the inducements associated with the job and place a higher valence on those inducements previously considered unattractive (an employee may come to value aspects of the current job such as seniority, pension benefits, and job security more highly than before). The individual may also "discover" features of the job that cast it in a more favorable light. For example, the individual may perceive greater opportunities for promotion in the future than were previously thought to exist. Alternatively, the employee may cognitively redefine the nature of the job itself to make it more attractive and satisfying (Porter, Lawler, & Hackman, 1975).

In general, it is unlikely that dissatisfied stayers will remain dissatisfied for long. This condition can be viewed as unstable when perceived choice and insufficient justification are present. The process of justifying the decision to remain through a cognitive reevaluation of the job is thus likely to result in movement from a dissatisfied stayer to a satisfied stayer.

When dissatisfaction with the job is very high, Festinger (1957) suggested one additional method through which dissonance can be reduced. This involves the temporary increase in the level of dissonance associated with the decision to remain to a point greater than the resistance to changing jobs. Once the level of dissonance met or exceeded the resistance to change, the individual would be predicted to leave the organization (i.e., become a dissatisfied leaver). Initially increasing dissonance to a level that is intolerable may be a less common way to reduce dissonance. However, evidence of such a strategy may be found in situations where some employees never seem to find anything right on the job and continually express a high degree of dissatisfation with relatively minor irritations at work. These employees may be following a more or less deliberate, albeit unconscious, strategy designed to increase dissonance associated with remaining on a job to a point where they have little choice but to leave (or be asked to leave). The negative consequences of this strategy for the organization in terms of potential work disruptions, discipline incidents, and spreading low morale among employees are apparent.

3. *Satisfied leaver—need for justification absent.* Employees often have little control over the decision to leave a job. In other cases, the decision may be voluntary but clearly perceived to be the "right" choice (i.e., adequate justification). In these situations there is little reason to believe that the individual will experience dissonance or feel a need to justify the decision. Theoretically, it is doubtful that the individual will engage in the systematic cognitive distortion described in case 1, since there is less psychological need to justify the decision. The employee may, depending on the circumstances under which he or she left, retain positive attitudes toward the old job and speak well of the organization to others. In addition, the individual may desire to maintain active social involvement with former co-workers and take an active interest in their work-related affairs. From the perspective of the leaver's former co-workers, however, these social contacts may become increasingly less attractive, for reasons to be discussed later.

   When individuals voluntarily leave a job for what is clearly to them a more attractive alternative, however, it is possible to question whether the concept of a satisfied leaver is realistic. Even though an employee may be satisfied with his or her current job, information about an attractive alternative may cause the person to reevaluate his or her current position. Comparing the current job to the attractive alternative may result in dissatisfaction and thus the person would become a dissatisfied leaver. Although there may be little need for justification or dissonance associated with this situation, the dissatisfaction that results from comparing the current job with the alternative may appear to be the consequence of postdecision justification processes. In other words, the employee may express increasing dissatisfaction with the job he or she is leaving when conditions requiring justification are either present or absent. When the conditions requiring justification are absent, however, dissatisfaction should increase *prior* to the decision to leave the organization, since this is when comparisons are made between the present and alternative job. In contrast, dissatisfaction should theoretically *follow* the decision to leave when the conditions requiring justification are present. Although this distinction follows from theory, it may be difficult in practice to distinguish between these two conditions, since it is often impossible to determine when individuals have made the actual decision to leave an organization.

4. *Dissatisfied stayer—need for justification absent.* This situation describes employees who are dissatisfied with their jobs but who, for a number of possible reasons, find it impossible to leave (i.e., low perceived choice). These reasons may include economic constraints (e.g., investments in the pension system), family considerations (e.g., dual-career families), or the lack of available alternative jobs. In contrast to the situation where the conditions requiring justification are present, employees in this situation may more pose serious problems to the organization. In considering the possible actions of employees in this situation, it should be remembered that these actions are motivated by a desire to deal with the dissatisfying job situation and not by an attempt to justify or reduce dissonance associated with the decision to remain in the organization.

   First, as suggested in Chapter 4, employees may engage in attempts to change the job situation. Dissatisfied employees who must remain in the organization may be motivated to remove the source of dissatisfaction through such means as restructuring the job, making efforts to obtain a transfer within the organization, unionizing, and so forth. Although little is currently known about how employees accommodate dissatisfying jobs by attempting to restructure the work environment, it is likely that such attempts are made.

   Second, when attempts at changing the job are unsuccessful or when the reason for remaining in the organization is the lack of alternative jobs, employees may be likely to continue to engage in search behavior designed to find another position (March & Simon, 1958; Mobley, 1977). Dissatisfaction may remain high and the individual will continue to look for any reasonable way to leave the organization. From the perspective of reactance theory (Brehm, 1966), heightened and continued search behavior would be predicted as a way for employees to reassert their freedom of action.

When continued search activity remains unsuccessful, several potentially negative consequences may result (cf. Wortman & Brehm, 1976). Employees may experience decreased self-esteem and self-confidence as a result of their failure to find another job, which may ultimately influence performance on the job (Korman, 1977). Alternatively, the employees may engage in alternative forms of withdrawal behavior such as absenteeism and tardiness (Porter & Steers, 1973). Employees may also turn to more severe forms of withdrawal such as alcoholism or drugs when other means of withdrawal are unavailable (cf. Staw & Oldham, 1978). Several authors (e.g., Kornhauser, 1965) have suggested that job-related frustrations may be related to mental and physical illness as well as to other problems off the job. These individuals are likely to present severe problems for the organization and it may be useful for organizations to consider making available periodic forms of withdrawal (e.g., "mental health" days) as a method of countering these problems.

Finally, a somewhat less severe reaction under these circumstances has been suggested by the work of Dubin (1956). Research on the "central life interests" of employees suggests that many employees cope with dissatisfying jobs by shifting their central life interests away from work to nonwork areas of their lives. The employee may become highly involved, for example, in family activities, church, or civic groups. Employees with nonwork central life interests may have little psychological investment in the work place. Their orientation toward the job is likely to be of an instrumental nature in which work is seen as a means to the attainment of more highly valued outcomes off the job. It is important to recognize, however, that these employees may remain productive and contributing members of the work force, although their commitment to the organization and involvement in the job are likely to remain low (Dubin *et al.*, 1975).

Consequences for Observers of Another Person's Turnover

As suggested in the previous chapter, the consequences of turnover for other individuals in the organization may include increased work load until a replacement is found, opportunities for transfer and promotion, and changes in beliefs and attitudes. This last implication of turnover is of primary interest in this section. From an information-processing perspective, the consequences of turnover by another individual appear straightforward. The fact that another employee has left the organization may be a valuable source of information and serve as the stimulus for future action. Former co-workers of the person leaving, for example, may analyze the reasons why the individual resigned for purposes of reevaluating their own positions in the organization. Employees who were previously satisfied with their jobs may reassess their feelings when others in the organization leave for stated reasons related to negative aspects of the job itself. Moreover, turnover by a co-worker may provide valuable information about attractive alternative job opportunities that were previously unknown. The processes associated with reassessing their own feelings toward the job and learning about better opportunities in other organizations may result in more negative attitudes among employees who remain.

Similarly, employee turnover has information value for the supervisor of the person leaving. The supervisor may carefully analyze the reasons why an employee voluntarily resigned to determine whether factors in the work place are causing problems. When deficiencies are identified, changes can be made by the supervisor to prevent other valued employees from leaving for the same reasons. When employees leave to take advantage of an attractive job opportunity and not because of dissatisfaction with the old job, supervisors may also analyze the characteristics of the employee's new job to determine whether the organization is remaining competitive in the job market. News that an employee is taking a similar job at higher pay in another organization, for example, may suggest that changes need to be made in salary structure to remain competitive in the local job market.

Although the consequences of turnover for other individuals can be approached from an information-processing perspective, it is likely that a number of factors may influence the interpretation of why another person has left the organization and thus the attitudinal implications of this act. The dissonance reduction and self-justification processes discussed previously are also relevant to understanding how others may react to turnover. In the case of supervisors, for example, beliefs that employees leave because of dissatisfaction with the job may conflict with their self-image as a good manager. Rather than change this self-image or make changes in the work place, it may be easier for the supervisor to justify turnover by distorting the reasons why the individual resigned. This may involve distortion of the person's prior job behavior (e.g., "The individual was a chronic complainer"), reasons for leaving (e.g., "The person left because of limited advancement but I have no control over that"), or characteristics of the new job to which the individual is moving (e.g., "The new job provides a once in a lifetime opportunity"). Cognitively distorting reasons why employees leave may shift blame for turnover from the supervisor to other factors beyond his or her control. As a result, the supervisor may come to believe that changes in supervisory practices are unnecessary. Alternatively, supervisors may make changes designed to reduce turnover that do not address the real reasons why employees leave.

Co-workers may also find that the knowledge that another employee has left the organization because of dissatisfaction or to take a better position is a source of psychological discomfort. The fact that another employee found the same job dissatisfying may conflict with the person's own implicit decision to stay in the organization. Rather than reassess one's own feelings toward the job and decision to stay, it may be easier to cognitively distort the reasons why others leave. As with the case of supervisors, this may involve distorting information about the employee, his or her behavior before resigning, or characteristics of the new job. Changing perceptions about why others leave the organization may make the act of turnover less threatening to employees who remain and thus diminish the attitudinal consequences of the act.

Given the two very different reactions to turnover discussed in this section, it is important to consider under what conditions employees may be most likely to evaluate information "rationally" in this situation rather than cognitively distort the reasons why people leave. Several situational factors that may influence how individuals react to turnover can be identified. In general, the greater the potential threat associated with a turnover decision the more likely it is that remaining employees will engage in cognitive processes designed to justify their own decision to remain. Potential threat associated with turnover may be greatest, for example, when a respected and admired colleague leaves or when the person staying has passed up a similar opportunity to leave (e.g., he or she has turned down a job offer from another firm). Individuals may feel a greater need to justify their decision to stay when they have the same freedom to leave but choose not to do so. The frequency of turnover among co-workers may also be a factor in how individuals react. When turnover among co-workers is common, for example, rationales for remaining in the organization may be developed that reduce the need to attend to each specific instance of turnover. In contrast, when turnover is very rare it would be harder to ignore the decision of a co-worker to leave. In departments where few people quite, the decision of a co-worker to leave may be followed by intense speculation and rumors among remaining employees.

Beliefs about the reasons why an employee has left the organization have been found to play an important role in determining the attitudinal consequences of turnover. Little is currently known, however, concerning how such beliefs about the reasons for turnover are formed. In the next section the processes through which people develop beliefs about the causes of turnover will be considered.

Interpreting the Causes of Turnover Behavior

The manner in which people react to turnover behavior, whether their own or that of another employee, may largely depend on the reasons why they believe turnover took place. The question of how people develop beliefs about the causes of turnover in organizations has been examined by Steers and Mowday (1981). They approached this question from the perspective of attribution theories developed by social psychologists (Heider, 1958; Jones & Davis, 1965; Kelley, 1973).

Attribution theorists view people as "intuitive scientists" who observe events in their environment and attempt to provide explanations for these events by identifying their causes (Ross, 1977). Research on attribution processes has been greatly influenced by two important theories: the theory of correspondent inferences developed by Jones and Davis (1965) and the complementary theory of attribution processes developed by Kelley (1967, 1972, 1973). The former theory focuses on the question of how personal characteristics can be inferred from the consequences of behavior, and the latter approach examines how multiple occurrences of behavior are attributed to either characteristics of the person, the environment, or the circumstances surrounding the behavior.

Although the attribution theories of Jones and Davis (1965) and Kelley (1973) are related (cf. Jones & McGillis, 1976), they emphasize different sources of information that can be used to assess the causes of turnover behavior. On the one hand, inferences about the causes of behavior can be made from information about the consequences of behavior. If we assume that most people act in a purposeful fashion, then the consequences of behavior can be used to infer the goals that motivated the behavior. For example, if a person quits a job to take a similar position at higher pay we may conclude that higher earnings were the goal that motivated turnover. On the other hand, we can examine events and factors that covary with behavior to determine its cause. When a person consistently expresses dissatisfaction when assigned to one task but not to others, we may conclude that it is the particular task itself rather than anything about the person that is causing dissatisfaction. This belief would be strengthened if we also observed that other employees assigned to that same task expressed similar dissatisfaction.

In the sections that follow, the two major approaches to attribution processes will be presented within an overall conceptual framework. In addition, factors thay may serve to mediate attributions will be identified and the question of how and when individuals attend to different information sources will be discussed.

Attribution Processes Associated with Turnover

Steers and Mowday (1981) proposed a model of attribution processes associated with turnover that integrated the two major approaches to making inferences mentioned previously. Their model is presented in Figure 7.1. The model suggests that people perceive different types of causal agents (i.e., characteristics of the person, environment, or circumstances) as causing an individual to leave the organization, and that turnover results in certain unique effects or consequences for the individual. The causal process identified in the model is one that flows from causal agent to turnover behavior to consequences of turnover. It is important to recognize, however, that people are assumed to reason backwards from the observation of turnover and its consequences to an inference about the cause of turnover. The logical flow of an individual's cognitive processes is thus from turnover behavior to the causes of turnover.

Three broadly defined categories of possible causes of turnover are identified in the model (box 1): characteristics of the individual employee (e.g., traits and dispositions); characteristics of the environment, including both the job and the external environment; and the circumstances under which the behavior took place (e.g., interactions between characteristics of the employee and environmental influences). The model also attempts to identify several types of information people may use in making inferences about the reasons for turnover. First, following Jones and Davis (1965), beliefs about the causes of turnover can be developed from an analysis of the effects or consequences of turnover (box 7). These effects may include a number of different factors such as increased earnings, a more challenging job, different geographic location, and improved opportunities for advancement. Second, the causes of turnover may be inferred from an analysis of the individual's behavior on the job prior to the point of termination. This latter analysis is more closely related to the attributional framework described by Kelley (1973) and involves consideration of the behavioral cues of consistency, distinctiveness, and consensus (box 5). The extent to which either approach leads to identification of a specific cause of

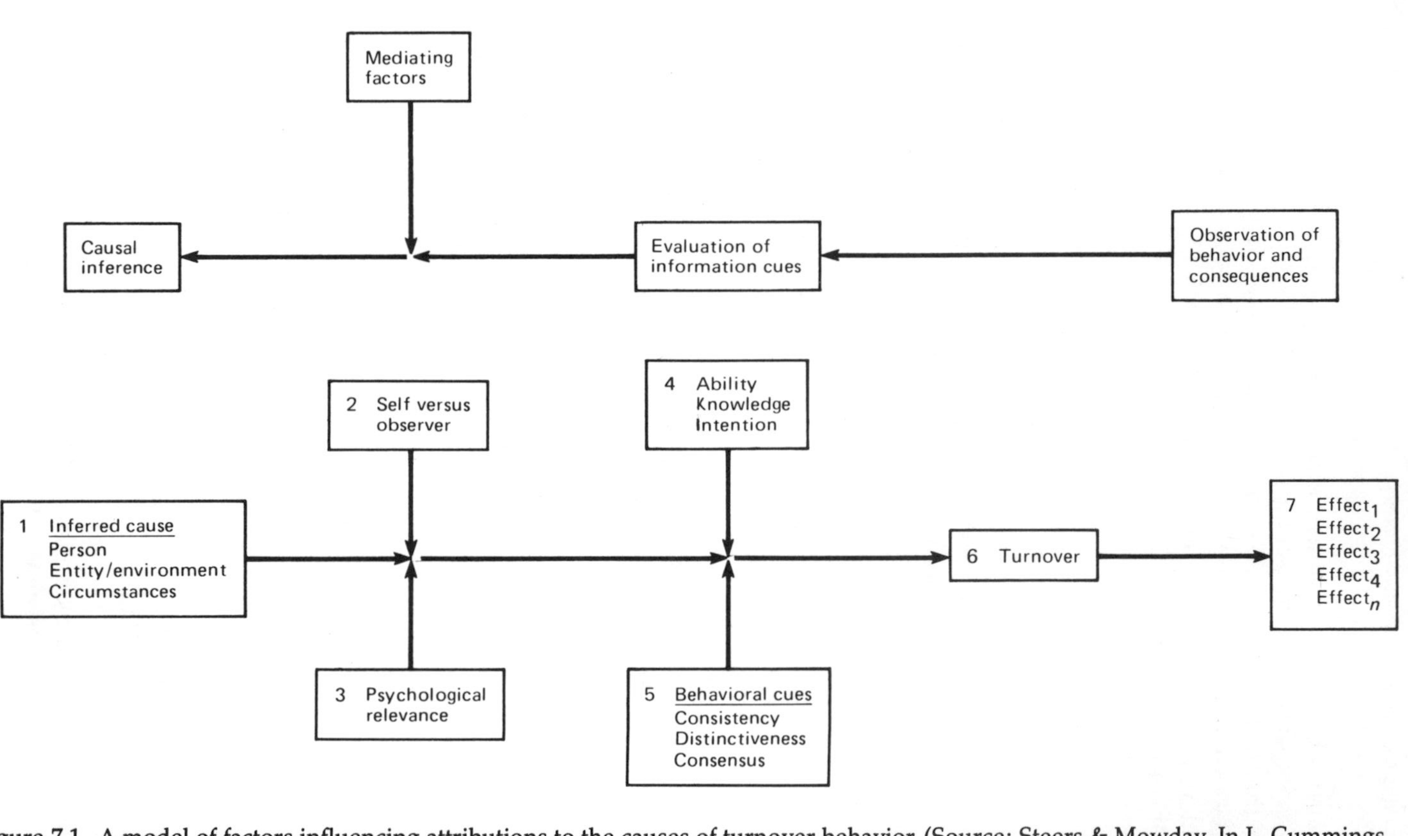

Figure 7.1. A model of factors influencing attributions to the causes of turnover behavior (Source: Steers & Mowday, In L. Cummings and B. Staw (Eds.), *Research in Organizational Behavior* (Vol. 3). Greenwich, CT: JAI Press, 1981).

turnover, however, is thought to depend on several mediating factors: whether an individal is analyzing his or her own behavior or that of another employee (box 2), the psychological relevance of the behavior for the person making the attribution (box 3), and beliefs about the ability, knowledge, and intentions of the person leaving to achieve the observed consequences of turnover (box 4).

Steers and Mowday (1981) suggested that it is useful to consider the two attribution approaches separately, since each implies the use of a somewhat different type of information in making inferences. It should be apparent, however, that the two types of information and thus the two attribution approaches are interdependent. This will be discussed in greater depth later in the chapter. The first two of the sections that follow describe these approaches to making attributions about the causes of turnover behavior.

ANALYSIS OF CONSEQUENCES

Jones and Davis' (1965) approach to attribution processes is based on the simple assumption that people with freedom of choice will attempt to achieve outcomes they positively value by their behavior. It follows from this assumption that a great deal can be learned about the reasons for an action by examining its effects or consequences.

The first step in such an attribution process involves comparing the characteristics of the job an individual has left with the characteristics of the new job he or she has taken. The characteristics that the two jobs share are separated from the characteristics that are unique to each job. Two hypothetical examples used by Steers and Mowday (1981) to highlight such comparisons are presented in Table 7.2.

In example A in Table 7.2, the old and new jobs are similar in pay, job security, and desirability of geographic location. The old and new jobs differ, however, in terms of the nature of the task (routine versus challenging). Few clues about the reasons why an individual left the job are contained in the characteristics the old and new jobs share. Information about the causes of turnover is therefore more likely to be found among characteristics of the jobs that differ. When there are a large number of unique effects, the task of determining which may have caused turnover is more difficult, if not impossible. When a large number of unique effects are present, we would have little confidence in asserting which particular effect was the actual reason for turnover since any one of them may have been a sufficient cause. This situation appears similar to Kelley's (1973) discussion of multiple sufficient causes and the discounting principle (i.e., the role of any particular cause of behavior will be discounted when other plausible causes for the behavior also exist in the situation).

Table 7.2

Inference Processes of the Causes of Turnover from an Analysis of Its Consequences

Example A		Example B	
Characteristics of old job	Characteristics of new job	Characteristics of old job	Characteristics of new job
Good pay	Good pay	Good pay	Good pay
Average job security	Average job security	Average job security	Average job security
Challenging and interesting job	Routine and uninteresting job	Routine and uninteresting job	Challenging and interesting job
Desirable geographic location	Desirable geographic location	Desirable geographic location	Desirable geographic location
Difference between jobs		*Difference between jobs*	
Challenging and interesting job	Routine and uninteresting job	Routine and uninteresting job	Challenging and interesting job
Inference		*Inference*	
Cause of turnover is related to characteristics of the person (e.g., cannot take demands associated with challenging task).		Cause of turnover is attractiveness of new job.	

Source: Steers and Mowday. In L. Cummings and B. Staw (Eds.), *Research in Organizational Behavior* (vol. 3). Greenwich, CT: JAI Press, 1981.

An attribution to characteristics of the person is most likely to occur when the unique effect associated with the new job is one that is not widely valued by most people or has some characteristic that would not have been expected to be valued by the person leaving (cf. Jones & McGillis, 1976). When an action such as turnover disconfirms our expectations about what the person was likely to do in that situation (i.e., leads to consequences we would not have expected the person to value), unique information is gained about the person. For instance, in example A in Table 7.2 the person is described as leaving an interesting and challenging job for one that is routine and uninteresting. Since we would assume that most people would want an interesting and challenging job, Jones and Davis (1965) suggest that this situation is more likely to lead to an attribution to the unique characteristics of the person as a cause for turnover. Although not explicitly considered in the theory, it also seems likely that the existence of undesirable unique effects associated with the new job would lead observers to continue to search for additional information until a more plausible explanation for turnover is found. In the absence of additional plausible explanations, however, undesirable effects associated with the new job are likely to be viewed as providing unique information about the individual and thus lead to an attribution to personal characteristics as the cause for turnover.

An attribution to environmental characteristics as the cause for turnover appears to be most likely when the effects achieved by turnover are ones that most people would be expected to value. In example B in Table 7.2 an individual has left a routine and uninteresting job for one that is challenging and interesting. Since most people would be assumed to desire an interesting job, the challenging nature of the new job provides a sufficient explanation for turnover. In this case, an environmental attribution to characteristics of the new job is likely to be made in explaining turnover.

Attribution processes can be complicated when the characteristics of the new job have both desirable and undesirable elements. For example, an individual may take a more challenging job in an undesirable geographic location. In this situation, the challenging nature of the new job still provides a sufficient explanation for turnver and thus the undesirable geographic location may be discounted as a potential cause. In fact, the undesirable geographic location may serve to strengthen the attribution to characteristics of the job itself, since the individual was willing to move even though there were costs involved (see Kelley's [1973] discussion of facilitating and inhibiting causes).

Some ambiguity may remain in this situation as to whether it was really the characteristics of the old job that "pushed" the individual out of the organization or the characteristics of the new job that exerted an attraction or "pull." How this ambiguity is resolved may depend on the knowledge possessed about the person's behavior on the old job (e.g., whether he or she frequently expressed dissatisfaction with the job). In addition, Newtson (1974) found that attributions are more highly influenced by characteristics of the chosen alternative (new job) than by characteristics of the alternative forgone (old job).

Jones and Davis (1965) identified several additional aspects of the situation that may be considered in making attributions about the causes of turnover from an analysis of its effects. First, the individual leaving must be assumed to have had freedom of choice in leaving the job. Second, the individual must be assumed to have had a knowledge of the effects of his or her action and the intention and ability to achieve these effects. When the effects of turnover are unknown to the individual at the time he or she left and/or the effects are unintended (e.g., lucky coincidence), it would be difficult to make attributions to characteristics of either the person or the environment as a cause of turnover.

ANALYSIS OF PRIOR JOB BEHAVIOR

The attribution theory suggested by Kelley (1973) provides a framework within which to understand how the causes of turnover can be inferred from knowledge about the leaver's *prior* job behavior. Since Kelley's theory is better known among organizational researchers than is the work of Jones and Davis (1965), it will be only briefly discussed here.

Kelley's approach is based on the principle of covariance. This principle states that a behavior will be attributed to a cause with which it covaries over time. Kelley (1973) identified three sources of information that are used to analyze covariation and make causal inferences about behavior: information from observations of people, of entities, and across time. These three sources of information provide specific types of information relevant to considering the cause of a behavior: the consensus, distinctiveness, and consistency of a response. Information from observations of people provides knowledge of consensus or the extent to which the individual behaves in a manner similar to that of other people in the same situation. Information from observations of entities provides clues about the distinctiveness of a response. Does the individual behave this way toward all entities or stimuli (e.g., supervisor, task, co-worker) or just one particular entity? Finally, information from observations across time provides clues about the consistency of a behavior or response. Does the individual respond this way to a particular entity each time it is encountered or was the response unique to just one occasion? Consistency information can also be over modality (i.e., whether the person responds to the entity in the same way regardless of the situation in which it is presented).

Consensus, consistency, and distinctiveness information are combined to make attributions about the cause of turnover. Kelley (1973) said this is done as if the different types of information are combined in the form of a $2 \times 2 \times 2$ analysis of variance framework. To simplify the analysis, each type of information is thought to take on either a high or low value (e.g., high or low consistency). This framework leads to eight cells or unique combinations of consensus, consistency, and distinctiveness information. Each unique combination or cell may lead to a specific attribution about the cause of a behavior.

On the basis of earlier work (Kelley, 1973; McArthur, 1972; Orvis, Cunningham, & Kelley, 1975), it is possible to predict attributions for various combinations of information. An attribution to characteristics of the person as the cause of behavior has been found to be most likely when consistency information is high and consensus and distinctiveness information are low. Attributions to an entity or stimulus are most likely when consensus, consistency, and distinctiveness information are high. Finally an attribution to the circumstances within which behavior took place is likely to occur when distinctiveness information is high and consensus and consistency information is low. The attributions resulting from other information combinations are less easily predicted on an intuitive basis and have empirically proven to be more complex. However, Orvis *et al.* (1975) found that people tend to limit their attributions to the three information combinations mentioned (i.e., to make attributions to characteristics of the person, entity or environment, or circumstances as the cause for an observed behavior). In fact, their research suggests that people look for information that is consistent with one of these three attributions and will fill in missing information to be consistent with one of these three combinations.

Applying Kelley's (1973) theory to the analysis of the causes of turnover behavior requires a less rigid interpretation of the covariance principle than originally implied by the theory. That is, attributions about the causes of turnover do not require that the behavioral cues of consensus, consistency, and distinctiveness occur at the *same* point in time as turnover. Rather, the individual's past job behavior that is consistent with the act of turnover is likely to be examined. For example, an entity attribution may result when the individual leaving consistently expressed dissatisfaction with a particular aspect of the job (e.g., the supervisor) in the past and other employees have also expressed dissatisfaction with this aspect.

McDade (1980) applied Kelley's (1973) attributional framework in a study that investigated how managers develop beliefs about the causes of employee turnover in organizations. The study involved presenting actual managers with descriptions of simulated turnover incidents in which consistency, consensus, and distinctiveness information was systematically manipulated. A major question addressed in the study was whether managers would analyze this information and draw conclusions about the reasons for turnover in a manner suggested by Kelley (1973). A portion of McDade's (1980) results are presented in Figure 7.2. The conclusions drawn by managers about the reasons for employee turnover were remarkably consistent with predictions of the model. Managers were more likely to make an attribution to characteristics of the person leaving as the cause for turnover when consistency information was high and distinctiveness and consensus information was low. In contrast, when distinctiveness, consensus, and consistency information was high, managers were more likely to make attributions to characteristics of the environment rather than the person as the cause for turnover. Moreover, McDade (1980) found that

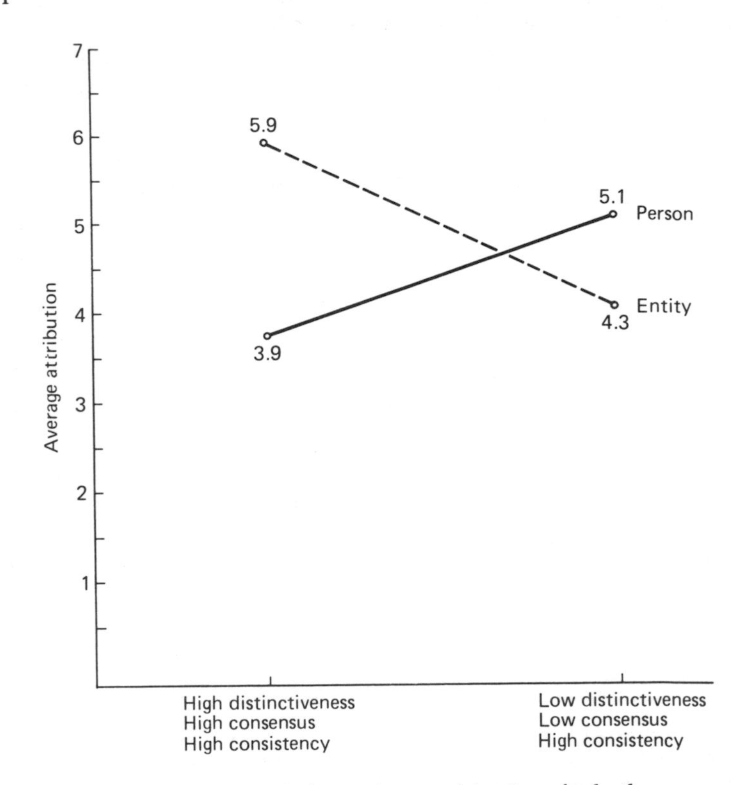

Figure 7.2. Contrasts between information combinations for both person and entity attributions (McDade, 1980).

managers in his sample relied most heavily on consensus information in making their judgments. This finding is particularly interesting in view of the fact that other studies have shown that people are relatively insensitive to baseline or consensus information in making judgments (Kahneman & Tversky, 1973).

Although McDade's (1980) study represents one of the few investigations of the attribution processes used by actual managers in dealing with organizationally relevant problems, it is important to recognize that his study was a simulation and thus may not reflect what actually happens in the work place. Whether or not managers actively seek out the types of information provided by McDade (1980) in making judgments about why employees leave, for example, is a question that cannot be answered from his study. When presented with information that Kelley (1973) suggested people should use in making causal inferences, however, managers did conform to the normative predictions of the model.

MEDIATING INFLUENCES ON ATTRIBUTIONS

The attribution theories discussed previously represent normative approaches to processing information rationally for purposes of making causal inferences. There is considerable research that suggests, however, that individuals will deviate from normative processes in some situations or that two individuals observing the same behavior may develop different causal beliefs. Several of these mediating factors need to be considered in making predictions about attribution processes.

First, Jones and Nisbett (1972) have suggested that actors and observers may develop quite different attributions about the same behavior. The fundamental attribution error was described by Jones (1976): "Whereas the actor sees his behavior primarily as a response to the situation in which he finds himself, the observer attributes the same behavior to the actor's dispositional characteristics [p. 300]." This error suggests that people who leave the organization may develop beliefs about the reasons for their decision that are quite different from those developed by co-workers and supervisors. Stated reasons for turnover may lack credibility as a result.

Second, individuals may be motivated to deviate from normatively correct attributions when such beliefs have negative consequences for the individual's self-image. Jones and Davis (1965) introduced the concept of "hedonic relevance" to refer to actions that may have relevance to the observer's values, beliefs, or goals. A commonly studied manifestation of hedonic relevance is the ego-defensive bias in attributions (Bradley, 1978; D.T. Miller & M. Ross, 1975; Ross, 1977; L. Stevens & E.E. Jones, 1976). Supervisors may be more likely to distort the reasons why employees leave, for example, in situations where their own behavior may have contributed to the action. Moreover, low-performing supervisors may be more likely to view factors beyond their control as reasons for turnover. McDade (1980) examined relationships between attributions of the causes of employee turnover and self-report measures of supervisory performance and found results consistent with such a prediction. His results are presented in Figure 7.3. Low-performing managers in his sample were more likely to view attributes of the person as the cause of turnover than were high-performing managers. The effect of self-reported performance level on attributions made by managers was significant, although a similar pattern of relationships found when the level of organizational commitment of the manager was examined failed to reach significance. McDade's (1980) findings with respect to performance are all the more remarkable since the potential threat inherent in the simulated turnover incidents he studied was low.

Finally, the egocentric or false-consensus bias in attribution processes suggests that people may use their own feelings or beliefs as a reference point in developing attributions about the behavior of others (Ross, 1977).

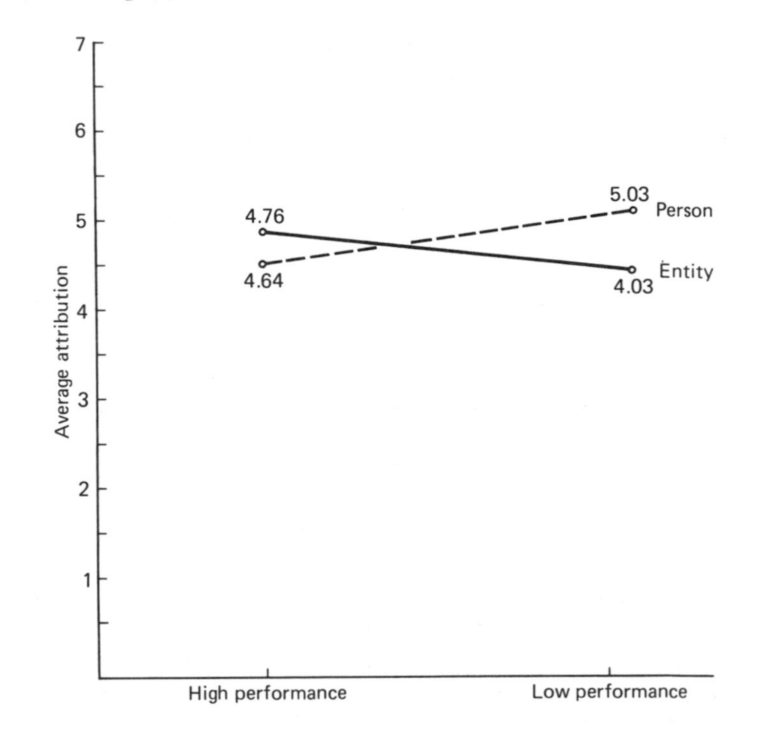

Figure 7.3. Person and entity attributions under high- and low-performance conditions (McDade, 1980).

This bias is based on a general tendency to view one's own feelings and attitudes as situationally appropriate and widely shared by others. For example, employees may view others as possessing job attitudes similar to their own and thus may interpret reasons for turnover behavior consistent with this assumption. Mowday (1981) found some support for this attributional bias in a study of employees in several government agencies. Employees were asked to indicate which of three reasons was the most important cause of turnover in their agency: (*a*) People left because they were dissatisfied; (*b*) people left to take advantage of a better opportunity but not because they were dissatisfied; (*c*) both reasons were equally important. Attributions of the general causes of turnover were related to employee attitudes. The results are presented in Table 7.3. Systematic relationships were found between employee attitudes and beliefs about why others left the organization. In general, the more positive an employee's attitudes (e.g., commitment and satisfaction), the less likely he or she was to believe that others left because they were dissatisfied. Although this finding is consistent with both the ego-defensive and egocentric biases, a close examination of the pattern of results led Mowday (1981) to conclude that the egocentric bias was more likely to be operating in this situation.

INFORMATION SOURCES AND ATTRIBUTIONS

The two attribution approaches incorporated in the model presented in Figure 7.1 suggest that different types of information may be used to make causal inferences about turnover. Attributions about the causes of turnover can be made from either an analysis of its consequences or an analysis of prior job behavior. In addition, a third source of information may be available in the person's stated reasons for leaving. The existence of several distinct sources of information that can be used in making inferences raises questions about which source is most likely to be used and under what circumstances.

The most direct source of information about why employees leave is available from stated reasons for turnover. Most people who leave organizations feel obligated to let others know the reasons for their decision. In many cases, organizations actively solicit such information through exit interviews. It is not entirely clear, however, whether personal statements about the reasons for leaving are viewed with much credibility by others in the organization (Steers & Mowday, 1981). Most personnel managers are probably aware of the research that suggests that exit interview data are often inaccurate. Other employees in the organization may also view stated reasons for leaving with skepticism, particularly if such statements are inconsistent with other information about the individual. Individuals who indicate that they are leaving because of dissatisfaction with pay, for

Table 7.3
Mean Attitudes and Behavioral Intentions for Employees Grouped According to Attributions of the Causes of Turnover

	Perceived reasons for turnover[a]			
	People leave because they are dissatisfied	Both reasons important	People do *not* leave because they are dissatisfied	Standardized discriminant weights
Organizational commitment	4.03 (1.15)	4.76 (.93)	5.04 (.87)	−.83
Job satisfaction	4.52 (1.76)	5.46 (1.39)	5.91 (.94)	−.41
Job involvement	3.40 (1.13)	3.73 (.99)	4.08 (.99)	.05
Desire to leave organization[b]	3.44 (1.97)	2.76 (1.60)	2.69 (1.68)	.01
Intent to leave organization[b]	3.81 (2.17)	2.91 (1.89)	2.67 (1.93)	.16
Perceived ease of mobility	3.67 (.55)	3.69 (.62)	3.71 (.54)	−.11
Tenure in the organization[c]	65.6 (68.8)	77.9 (88.6)	87.8 (91.8)	−.10
Sample size	166	291	83	

Source: Mowday *Journal of Applied Psychology*, 1981, *66*, 120–123.
[a]Standard deviations are presented in parentheses.
[b]Higher mean indicates greater desire or intent.
[c]Tenure measured in months.

example, may be viewed with more skepticism if they had never before expressed dissatisfaction with pay than if they frequently complained about wage levels. Even greater skepticism may result if it becomes known that the person has taken a job in another organization that pays about the same as the job he or she has left.

Employees who remain in the organization may check the veracity of stated reasons for leaving by a simple method of triangulation. In other words, employees may compare the stated reason for leaving with other information that is available. When the stated reason for leaving is consistent with other information about the leaver's prior job behavior or new job, the process may stop at this point. The stated reason for turnover would probably be considered a sufficient explanation. When information from different sources is inconsistent, however, employees may gather additional information. The particular approach adopted by an individual may depend on the type of information available. Job-related behaviors prior to turnover are likely to be most salient to the former supervisor and co-workers of the person leaving. In contrast, nonwork friends of the individual who leaves may only have information about the consequences of the action (e.g., information about the pay, security, and location of the old and new jobs). As a result, former supervisors and co-workers may be more likely to utilize the approach described by Kelley (1973), whereas nonwork friends may process information in a manner suggested by Jones and Davis (1965).

The type of information that becomes salient in making attributions about the causes of turnover may also be influenced by environmental considerations. For example, when economic conditions are good it may be more reasonable to believe that turnover was caused by a "pull" from an attractive job alternative. This would be more likely to lead to an analysis of the consequences of turnover for purposes of determining the specific cause. In contrast, when economic conditions are poor and few alternative jobs are available, it may be more reasonable to assume that turnover was caused by a "push" from the old job (e.g., dissatisfaction). In this situation, prior job-related behaviors may become more salient in trying to determine the reasons for turnover.

In addition, the concept of hedonic relevance or the ego-defensive bias suggests that individuals may be motivated to process information selectively in a manner that reinforces existing beliefs and attitudes. Employees who are highly satisfied and committed to the organization, for example, may be more likely to look to characteristics of the terminating employee's new job for an explanation for turnover. Believing that an employee left because of an attractive new job opportunity would be potentially less threatening than believing that the employee left because the old job was dissatisfying. Employees who are very dissatisfied and uncommitted may be more likely to look to prior job-related behaviors for evidence that the leaving employee had similar feelings. In general, the likelihood that remaining employees will use one of the several potential sources of information about the reasons for turnover may depend on the extent to which information is likely to be consistent with personal attitudes and beliefs.

The existence of several sources of information upon which to base attributions about the causes of turnover suggests that the beliefs resulting from different information sources may differ or be in conflict. It may not be surprising, for example, to discover that the employee who leaves, his or her former supervisor, and former co-workers all disagree on the "real" reason for turnover. Different people will not always have access to the same information or they may be motivated to interpret the same information in different ways. Even though the potential for conflict exists in making attributions about the causes of turnover, it is important to recognize that the approaches of Jones and Davis (1965) and Kelley (1973) overlap in terms of the information they use. The expectation that an individual intended to achieve a particular effect through turnover, for example, may be influenced by observations of prior job-related behavior. Also, we would expect some consistency between the stated reasons for turnover and information that is available to others in making attributions. The person leaving may be the only source of information about the consequences of turnover (e.g., characteristics of the new job). In addition, the person leaving may make salient to others certain job-related behaviors (e.g., "As you remember I was not very pleased after my last performance appraisal").

The extent to which conflicting beliefs may exist about the reasons why employees leave organizations is difficult to determine based on available research. Moreover, we currently know little about the conditions under which agreement or disagreement is most likely. These are questions that await further research before answers are known.

Cognitive Accommodation of the Participation Decision: A Future Research Agenda

There is little doubt that employees develop beliefs about the reasons why they or their co-workers leave the organization, are absent, or perform at certain levels. Moreover, these beliefs may have important implications for attitudes and behaviors. At present we know relatively little about the cognitive processes through which employees develop beliefs about the causes of behavior in the work place or the implications of these beliefs. Several important research agenda items for the future can be identified.

Agenda item 1. Attribution theories implicitly view people as incessant information processors. In other words, people observe events in their environment and seek explanations for the causes of these events by evaluating available information. It seems likely, however, that people may be more or less motivated to explain the events they observe depending on various situational factors. For example, in organizations where the turnover rate is particularly high we would not expect employees to cognitively evaluate each instance of turnover to determine its cause. Rather, employees may develop general explanations for turnover that can be applied in a number of specific cases (e.g., "People leave because the opportunities for promotion are limited"). Such general explanations reduce the cognitive task of explaining each instance of turnover, although at some sacrifice of accuracy in any particular case. In contrast, when turnover is relatively rare or a respected colleague leaves, employees may be motivated to analyze the event to determine its cause and assess its implications. The research question being raised here is whether the extensive information-processing activities associated with attribution processes are more likely to occur when the behavior observed is salient or unexpected. It is important to distinguish this question from the commonly reported finding that salient and unexpected behavior has greater information value about the person (cf. Jones, 1979). The two issues clearly differ in their focus. The question of whether extensive information processing will occur in response to a given behavioral observation is difficult to answer from previous research on attribution theory, since most tests of the theory have presented subjects with an explicit attributional task (i.e., subjects are given little choice about engaging in information processing). It seems likely, however, that attribution processes themselves and the extent to which people engage in extensive information search and processing may depend on the situation.

In general, it would be expected that the motivation to engage in the cognitive processes discussed in this chapter would be related to the salience of the turnover event. The salience of a particular turnover event is likely to be influenced by the frequency of turnover in the organization, the extent to which turnover by an individual is unexpected, the status or position of the leaver, and the closeness of the leaver to a particular individual. We currently know relatively little about the factors that may motivate people to cognitively evaluate actions such as turnover and thus this represents an interesting area for future research.

Agenda item 2. The attribution approaches presented in this chapter can be considered normative models in the sense that they describe a process individuals *should* use in making causal judgments. To a large extent these models have been tested in the psychology laboratory using relatively simple behaviors (e.g., McArthur, 1972; Orvis *et al.*, 1975). Whether or not managers and employees in complex organizational environments process information in ways consistent with the attribution models remains to be demonstrated. The best available evidence on this point is McDade's (1980) study of managerial attributions of the cause of employee turnover. Even though the managers in his study behaved in ways consistent with Kelley's (1973) attribution model, they were responding to simulated rather than actual turnover events. There are several reasons to believe that individuals may not process information in ways consistent with the normative predictions of attribution theory. First, the cognitive limitations of individuals as information processors have been well documented (Fischhoff, 1976; Kahneman & Tversky, 1973; Nisbett & Ross, 1980; Ross, 1977). Second, the informational environment of organizations is often much more complex than the research situations created when attribution theory has been studied. As suggested earlier, multiple sources of information may be available in making judgments about the causes of employee turnover. In addition to information relevant to making judgments about the causes of turnover, a great deal of information may also be present that is irrelevant to such judgments. We currently know very little about how managers sort through available information, determine what information is relevant and what is not, and then integrate information to make causal judgments. In addition, it is also possible that managers may be faced with a situation in which incomplete information is available. We do not know if managers will make judgments based on incomplete information or, if motivated to seek additional information, what types of information will be gathered. Faced with a complex environment in terms of information availability, managers could conceivably engage in an almost endless process of information search to improve the accuracy of their judgments. Alternatively, managers may only seek enough information to provide a reasonable and sufficient explanation for turnover while ignoring other available information (cf. Taylor & Fiske, 1978). Additional research is needed to examine how people in organizations actually acquire information and factors that influence the extent of information search.

Agenda item 3. A third area for future research concerns the influence of such factors as the individual's role and the type of problem being analyzed on cognitive processes. Attribution theory approaches generally assume that the cognitive processes underlying causal judgments are not influenced by the type of behavior being considered or the person making the judgment. Undergraduate students in psychology and managers in organizations, for example, are assumed to process information similarly whether they are dealing with the question of why Jane laughs at the comedian or why employees leave organizations. McDade's (1980) finding that managers placed much greater reliance on consensus information than on other types raises questions about this assumption. He argued that the nature of the managerial role and the problem being studied may have an impact on the importance attached to various types of information. The fact that managers must continually make comparative judgments about employees (e.g., performance appraisal and pay raise decision) may make them more sensitive than students to consensus information. In addition, judgments about turnover in organizations may make consensus information highly salient, since such judgments are made by managers to prevent other employees from leaving for similar reasons. This judgment task thus inherently focuses on the similarity of conditions leading one employee to leave and the conditions faced by other employees. Attribution theory has not fully explored the influence of individual roles and the types of judgments being made on attribution processes, although they would appear to be important. Another interesting question comes from the work of D. Miller and C. Porter (1980), who found that attributions may vary as a function of the time that has transpired between the behavior and the attribution. This suggests that attributions about the causes of turnover may differ depending on whether they are made immediately following the decision to leave or some time later.

Agenda item 4. Future research needs to examine relationships between cognitive judgments about the reasons for turnover and subsequent behaviors of the person making the judgment. It is implicitly assumed that managers assessing the reasons for employee turnover will take actions designed to reduce turnover that are consistent with their judgments. The linkage between causal inferences and the actual behavior of managers attempting to reduce turnover, however, has yet to be conclusively demonstrated. McDade (1980) found a complex pattern of results when he examined relationships between attributions and the actions managers said they would recommend to reduce turnover. Moreover, it would not be entirely surprising to find that attributions were only weakly related to action strategies in some situations. For example, even though managers may believe that characteristics of the employees are primarily causing turnover they may also feel that they have little control over who is hired by the organization. In this situation, managers may not take any actions to reduce employee turnover. Given the action-oriented nature of the manager's role, however, it is also possible that managers may feel compelled to take *some* action to reduce turnover. In this case, managers who believe that characteristics of employees cause turnover may make changes in the work environment, since this is an area in which they have some control. Alternatively, managers may actually distort the perceived reasons for employee turnover so that they are consistent with areas of the organization over which they have some control. It is important to recognize that environmental constraints may limit relationships between causal judgments and subsequent behaviors. The way in which the environment influences these relationships, however, is a question that will require further research.

The questions raised in this section do not exhaust the possibilities for future research on attribution processes associated with turnover in organizations. Other questions for future research could have been raised. The questions raised in this section, however, are sufficient to suggest that employee accommodation processes represent a potentially fertile area for future research in organizations.

Summary

This chapter represents an exploratory attempt to develop and refine our understanding of how individuals cognitively accommodate decisions concerning participation in organizations. Although research on turnover in organizations has extensively investigated individual and work-related factors leading up to the decision to stay or leave, much less research has focused on the consequences of these decisions, particularly consequences associated with the attitudes and beliefs of employees. There is little doubt that decisions to leave an organization are attended to and cognitively evaluated, both by those making the decision and by observers of the action. We currently know very little, however, about such cognitive accommodation processes or the factors thay may cause them to become initiated. Although the conceptual material presented in this chapter provides a rough framework for addressing this issue, more work of both a theoretical and an empirical nature will be required before we can answer some of the questions that have been raised. The intent of this chapter was not to provide definitive answers to issues concerning employee accommodation processes. Rather, our intent was to introduce the area and sketch a conceptual framework in sufficient detail to pique the interest of other researchers.

8

Conclusion: An Agenda for Managers

Throughout this book we have focused on the development and consequences of employee–organization linkages, both membership status and quality of membership linkages. We have attempted to provide an analysis of the issues, a review of the relevant literature, and several conceptual models to guide further thinking and research dealing with linkages. We have also tried to identify some of the crucial research problems that need additional investigation if increased understanding is to be obtained concerning how individuals become and remain connected, or not connected, to their employing organizations.

Nature of Employee–Organization Linkages

Here in this final chapter we will first draw some rather broad conclusions based on previous discussions in this book. This will be followed by an examination of linkages from an explicitly *organizational* perspective. Up to now we deliberately have not taken any single perspective—employee, organization, society—to explore the various aspects of linkages. Later in this chapter, however, we will consider the implications for management of the accumulated knowledge about linkages. This will be done in an attempt to see whether what has been learned could actually be applied by organizations (i.e., by those individuals in leadership and managerial positions within organizations).

Development of Linkages

In this section we will take stock—in a broad way—of what we have learned so far regarding linkages. First, what do we know about the *development* of membership status and quality—that is, the development of desires to stay with the organization, to not be absent, and to have an attitude of wanting to be identfied and involved with the organization? From the analyses and data provided in Chapters 3, 4, and 5 it is clear that the development of employee–organization linkages is an extremely complex process. It involves (*a*) many different factors or variables; (*b*) complex interactions among these factors or variables; and (*c*) changes in the importance of any given factor or set of factors across time.

The many factors affecting the development of linkages can be classified into a set of categories: the individual, the job (i.e., what the individual does at work), the immediate job situation (i.e., peer group and supervisor), the total organization situation, and off-the-job variables. Each of these categories can in turn be subdivided into many specific variables or dimensions. To take the first category, individuals, for example, one can consider demographic variables (age, education, etc.), personality factors, and job- and organization-specific expectations, among other variables. Similar subcategories could be developed for the other major factors. The point is that a multitude of factors have been found in previous research to be potentially influential in the development of linkages. For any given individual within a specific organizational context, and at a particular point in time, some factors will be important and others will be relatively insignificant. The task for researchers is to discover across many different samples of employees and different types of organizations and organizational settings which variables tend to have the most consistent and largest impacts on whether organizational linkages do or do not develop. We are a long way from that type of knowledge at the present time.

The fact that the variables affecting linkages interact adds an additional degree of complexity. It is highly unlikely that any given variable will have a completely consistent effect on linkages regardless of the other variables operating at a given time. A job that provides a large degree of discretion may be a major positive factor in developing strong linkages for a person with a high need for independence or autonomy. This same job may produce just the opposite reaction (a strong desire to leave or avoid the situation) for employees low in this need. Unfortunately, research investigating interactions between potential antecedents of commitment has been less common than research on the main effects of such antecedents on commitment. Although it is likely that numerous interactions exist in developing employee commitment, our present knowledge of such complex relationships is limited.

Finally, with respect to the development of linkages, there is the fact that different factors are differentially important across time. Nowhere is this better seen than in the issue of how behavioral acts and attitudes influence the development of *organizational* commitment. As repeatedly stressed in Chapter 3, a particular behavioral act (such as volunteering to take on an unpleasant task, or simply deciding to join a particular organization in the first place) at a given point in time may affect future attitudes, which then may affect the probability of future behavioral acts, and so on. Across time attitudes and behavioral acts appear to have a cyclical or reciprocal effect. The point here is that when we are considering linkages of individuals to organizations we cannot view linkages as static phenomena. They are constantly changing and what happens at time 1 influences what happens at time 2, and so on, and thus variables affecting linkage development vary in their importance across time.

Consequences of Linkages

The consequences of employee–organization linkages, as discussed in Chapters 1, 2, 6, and 7, are perhaps somewhat easier to analyze than the processes involved in their development. As was brought out in Chapters 1 and 6, the extent and strength of linkages have consequences for individual employees, for work groups, for organizations, and for society at large. Furthermore, as was repeatedly emphasized in those two chapters, strong linkages (and, hence, weak linkages) can have both positive and negative impacts on each of these groupings. Very strong linkages are not necessarily a blessing, as might be imagined at first glance, and weak linkages are not necessarily to be avoided. However, to reiterate, just because the more typically assumed effects of strong linkages are not always positive does not mean that the converse is true. Weak linkages are certainly not always good and can frequently create problems for individuals as well as for organizations and society. The important point to stress is that the state of linkages, whether strong or weak, is likely to influence individual employees, as well as work groups and the larger organization itself.

One other point about consequences of linkages that deserves emphasis is the fact that the linkages themselves interact in producing effects. That is, as was discussed in Chapters 2 and 6, for example, the level of organizational commitment among employees can affect their propensity to remain with the organization and their desire to come to work. Likewise, as analyzed in Chapter 7, acts of absenteeism or leaving an organization produce cognitive accommodations on the part of those who are absent and/or leave, those who come to work and/or stay, and those who supervise or manage within organizations. These cognitive reactions can thus influence organizational commitment, among other attitudes. Thus, linkages may act singly, collectively, simultaneously, and sequentially to produce consequences.

Given that the processes involved in the development of employee–organization linkages are of sufficient complexity to require systematic analysis of a large number of variables and additional research involving sophisticated designs, and given that particular strengths of linkages have multiple positive and negative consequences for individuals as well as for organizations and society, what kinds of applications of our existing knowledge could be made? As noted at the beginning of this chapter, we will attempt to respond to this question by deliberately taking the perspective of management.

Issues for Management

Organizations and managers seriously concerned about the status and quality of membership of employees may want to attempt to do something about these linkages in an effort to improve the situation. Before steps are taken, there is a set of issues or questions that need to be addressed. Some of the more important of these issues will be outlined below, utilizing the accompanying excerpted article (Figure 8.1) about an airline to illustrate several of the specific points.

1. *In what types of organizations are strong linkages most needed?* Although there is probably no conclusive answer to this question, it would appear that linkages, especially organizational commitment, would need to be strongest in those organizations that have a high percentage of jobs where the quality of performance is less tangible and more difficult to quantify. This is most likely to occur in service-type organizations, such as the airline described in Figure 8.1, where it is not as easy for the organization to identify inadequate job performance. Moreover, in service-type organizations close monitoring of employee performance may be more difficult but small differences in performance may have large impacts upon how the organization performs in the eyes of customers. In banking organizations, for example, it may be almost impossible to monitor the interaction of individual tellers with customers. In such competitive industries, however, customers may be very sensitive to subtle differences in treatment by employees who represent the organization (e.g., the difference between a teller who is correct but distant and a teller who is friendly and interested in establishing rapport with the customer).

BEIRUT, Lebanon—It is nearly dark, and the snipers are beginning their nightly frenzy of machine-gun fire. But overhead, with a roar that seems to defy the anarchy below, a Middle East Airlines jet is arriving on schedule from Europe. . . .

For the past five years, the Lebanese airline, known as MEA, has been operating in the midst of an intermittent civil war. . . .

Salim Salaam, the airline's general manager, ignores the sound of gunfire nearby as he recalls a much worse time, four years ago, when Beirut airport itself was a battleground. Braving daily shelling, Mr. Salaam slept at the airport for 144 straight days, guarding MEA's headquarters and its inventory of spare parts.

"All I wanted was to eat, to stay alive and to protect MEA," Mr. Salaam remembers. . . .

Most observers agree that the key to the airline's survival has been its ability to maintain the loyalty of its employes at a time when most other institutions in Lebanon were disintegrating. . . .

The company has fostered this employe loyalty through an old-fashioned paternalistic labor relations policy. Employes are never fired or laid off. Even when Beirut airport was closed for about five months in 1976, the local staff members contined to receive part of their salaries. The rest was paid out after the airport reopened and local flights resumed.

To add to the family atmosphere within MEA, all major management decisions are made at weekly staff meetings attended by representatives of each of the company's unions. There is also a generous profit-sharing plan that distributes 20% of each year's earnings to the staff. And if an employe's house is hit by a stray artillery shell, MEA provides money for a new home and furniture. . . .

MEA's staff has responded to this paternalistic labor policy with near-heroic dedication. During the worse days of the civil war, employes braved armed bands of kidnappers to get to work at the airport. Mr. Salaam estimates that as many as 500 employes were seized. But MEA negotiators managed to get them all released, and they kept coming to work.

When shelling finally closed the airport in 1976, more than 1,500 employes joined Mr. Salaam in guarding MEA's base of operations. The staff installed 82 showers for bathing. When all telex lines were cut, they rigged their own makeshift radio-communications system to keep in touch with the world outside. When the water supply became tainted, they dug their own wells.

Figure 8.1. Excerpt from *Wall Street Journal* (December 31, 1980).

In contrast, the quality of membership may be relatively unimportant in production organizations as long as the status of membership is adequate (i.e., acceptable levels of absenteeism and turnover). Because of the more tangible nature of job duties in the latter type of organization, it would often be easier to replace the temporarily or permanently absent employee, and the jobs are less likely to require extra-role behavior because of the clear boundary between acceptable and unacceptable performance.

2. *In what parts of the organization are the strongest linkages needed?* This issue raises the concept of the differentiated organization: strong linkages are probably not needed throughout the organization, but are particularly needed in certain parts of, or in certain positions

within the organization. One obvious answer to the question of "where?" would be: at the top. It is here that the key policy decisions are made that can have the widest impact. It is also here that behavior by example can have pronounced effects on all of the others within the organization. This was certainly the case with Middle East Airlines,where it seems clear that the general manager's extreme dedication to his organization had a pronounced impact on all other employees (see Figure 8.1).

The upper positions in the organization are not the only places where strong linkages would be especially important. Any positions that are critical to the success of the organization and where the occupants of the position are not easily replaced would also represent locations where organizations would need to pay close attention to linkages. Examples would be certain key technical positions that involve job duties that very few others in the organization could perform, where substitutes (whether from inside or outside the organization) would have a difficult time, and where there is a shortage of temporary or permanent replacements. As suggested earlier, in certain organizations, particularly those engaged in providing services, it may be important to have strong linkages among lower-level employees. Where lower-level employees interact with the primary consumers of the organization's services, strong linkages have potentially important influences on overall organizational effectiveness. Organizations in which strong linkages among lower-level employees may be crucial might include banks, hospitals, airlines, and educational institutions.

3. *For what types of employees are the strongest linkages needed?* This issue concerns not the position or location of the employee, but rather the type of employee in terms of performance in relation to any given position. As was stressed in Chapter 6, organizations often will want to do all that they can to encourage *some* employees to sever their membership ties. These would be employees who are performing poorly or who may be performing at a minimally adequate level but blocking the advancement of those who could perform better. It seems clear that high-performing or outstanding employees should be the target group for organizations to concentrate on in strengthening linkages, both commitment as well as the intent to remain and to come to work on a regular, consistent basis. High-performing employees, especially those in highly visible positions, may be more attractive to other organizations and thus have greater job opportunities than low-performing employees. Yet, it appears from both anecdotal and more systematic evidence that many organizations do

not distinguish between better-performing and worse-performing employees in the organization's attempts to reduce turnover and absenteeism and increase commitment.

Not only are strong linkages not usually necessary in all parts of organizations, they also are not usually necessary and in fact are sometimes negative in their effects if developed for all employees. Organizations need to recognize that low-performing employees with fewer alternative job possibilities may be most likely to become linked to the job, even though the nature of this linkage may not qualitatively be characterized as high commitment. Organizations that structure rewards in such a way as to encourage (rather than discourage) this continuing membership of poor employees while not providing sufficient inducements for high-performing employees to remain may have the worst of both worlds.

4. *When will organizations need strong linkages?* As a general rule it could probably be posited that the more critical or uncertain the circumstances facing the organization the greater the necessity for strong employee linkages. In very critical situations, in fact, organizations may not survive if linkages are not sufficiently strong. The Middle East Airlines story is a case in point, since one hesitates to imagine what might have happened to the airline if there had been excessive absenteeism or turnover at this time, or if employees had exhibited a significantly lower dedication to the welfare of the organization. Of course, this case is an extreme example, and most organizations will not often face crises of such a severe nature. Nevertheless, economic and other environmental circumstances for most organizations are not always smooth and there come times when an organization faces critical problems.

The importance of employee linkages may also be influenced by the organization's stage of development. In organizations experiencing rapid growth, demands may be placed on employees that call for performance above and beyond the normal call of duty. The strains placed on organizations by rapid growth and development may make particularly important the strength of employee linkages. In contrast, the strength of employee linkage may be less crucial in organizations that have become more stable or have ceased to grow altogether. In fact, stable organizations may find it desirable to maintain moderate turnover rates to ensure an influx of new people or opportunities for upward mobility for employees at lower levels.

The question of the degree or strength of linkages may thus become salient both when organizations are facing critical challenges and when they are characterized by relative stability. Of course, it must also be kept in mind that a serious drop-off in the strength of linkages (for whatever reason) may generate problems in many different types of organizations. Increasing rates of turnover, for example, may turn a relatively stable or benign situation into one with a whole host of problems. Moreover, increasing rates of turnover may increase the strains associated with rapid growth or critical challenges. Thus, it is possible that very low linkages paradoxically could eventually generate exactly the conditions where strong linkages are needed even more than normally. Conversely, if linkages are typically and consistently strong for an organization, it may never (or at least not frequently) get into the situation where especially strong connections with its employees are needed.

5. *Can organizations afford the costs of maintaining and/or increasing strong linkages?* Nothing comes without a price. As we have already indicated in Chapter 6, the existence of strong linkages can create its own set of unique problems (e.g., too many employees want to stay with the organization, thus blocking the way for younger, promising employees to move up at a rapid pace). Thus, as we have emphasized before, the existence of strong linkages has a number of potential advantages but also a number of costs. Aside from this, however, it may be very costly to the organization to develop or maintain strong linkages in the first place. Again, this is vividly demonstrated in the Middle East Airlines case where organization policies included generous profit-sharing plans and continued pay even when operations were disrupted. Most organizations probably have at least some capability to increase linkages if they are willing to pay the price, although this does not at all mean that they would have to adopt the "old-fashioned paternalistic labor relations policy" in the MEA example. It does mean, however, that strong linkages are unlikely to develop in the absence of efforts on the part of the organization and that whatever approaches are used—and we suggest a set of possible approaches in the next section—will have some sort of a cost factor involved. This places a premium on the organization's ability to diagnose what the level of linkages currently is, whether and where improvement is needed, and , if so, how to bring it about. It is to this last issue that we turn in the final section of this chapter.

Approaches Available to Managers to Strengthen Linkages

As we indicated at the opening of this chapter, we will conclude by describing some approaches that managers of organizations might consider taking *if* they desire to increase or maintain existing levels of linkages. If managers wish to reduce turnover and abenteeism and increase organizational commitment, then they might consider one or several of the following strategies.

1. *Select employees with the propensity to become linked.* Although not all organizations will have the "luxury" of being highly selective in whom they hire, managers might be able to utilize selection to strengthen the overall level of employee linkages. Even with a plentiful labor supply, however, it may not be feasible to choose employees based on this kind of selection criterion. Other employee characteristics may be much more important for the welfare of the organization, and hence they will predominate in any selection actions.

   If an organization does have enough job applicants from which to choose, and if other criteria for selection do not completely outweigh the desirability of strengthening linkages, then it might attempt the following.

   First, efforts can be made to determine the congruence between the individual's values and the organization's values. Of course, this assumes that the organization is explicit about its own value system such that it has a basis for comparing different prospective employees with respect to the mesh of their values with its own. This in no way implies that the individual need be a passive conformist like "the organization man," but it does suggest that it is possible to have a basic level of agreement between what the organization is undertaking to do and how it is going about it, on the one hand, and what the individual's fundamental priorities are with respect to an employing organization. Many examples abound on how organizations already frequently attempt to make this kind of judgment, but one will suffice: A research-oriented university often goes to great lengths to determine whether a prospective faculty member not only is capable of research but also values it and wants to be in an organizational setting that values it. When this judgment on the part of the prospective employee and/or the organization is off the mark, and an individual is hired who does not have a basic match with the organization's values, the results are often very painful for both parties.

   Second, the organization can attempt to determine whether an individual's goals will be attainable through attachment (attendance, continuing membership, and commitment) to the organization. Although this point is related to the first point discussed, it is somewhat different. It focuses on the question of whether the organization can determine in advance what objectives in a job situation are most important to the individual to achieve or accomplish and whether, therefore, the organization can make these contingent on strong attachment or linkage. If an individual's goal (e.g., learning a particular job skill that is easily transferable) can be obtained just as easily through relatively low attachment as through strong attachment, then this person is unlikely to contribute to an overall strengthened level of linkages. Of course, he or she may have other attributes that would result in selection regardless of the fact there will little connection between becoming linked to the organization and achieving personal goals.

Third, organizations can attempt to select those with strong beliefs in the value of work (and to whom work is central to their self-concept). Although there is some evidence (see Chapter 3) that those who value work highly and see work as very important to their own view of themselves do in fact show stronger commitment to organizations, this course of action may not be very feasible for an organization to follow. The reason is simply that in many instances it may be extremely difficult to differentiate among individuals with any degree of reliability and validity in this regard. However, the attempt to make these kinds of distinctions could potentially have payoffs for the organization, because it appears that individuals (across a sample) do differ rather markedly in their beliefs about the value of work.

Although the individual characteristics mentioned here may be desirable to consider in selection decisions if organizations wish to increase the commitment of employees, these criteria should not be considered to the exclusion of other factors. For both practical and legal reasons, organizations must be concerned about the relationship of selection criteria to ultimate performance on the job. The factors mentioned here may provide a better match between the new employee and the organization but additional criteria that perhaps better predict subsequent performance will have to be considered. In the first place, commitment has not been found to be highly related to performance, particularly at the individual level of analysis. Second, care must be taken in the selection process not to select those individuals who may become committed but who lack the skills or capabilities to perform the job.

2. *Create clear and realistic job and organization previews.* There is considerable literature (some of which was referred to in Chapter 3) that deals with the effects of providing "realistic job previews" for job applicants. Although the results of these studies are neither clear-cut

nor consistent, it seems safe to conclude that organizations are unlikely to be worse off if they provide prospective employees with candid information about both the positive and negative features of the job. Accurate information in advance about the organization has the potential for reducing turnover by creating a better match between the individual's goals and values and those of the organization. From a strictly social psychological perspective, realistic job previews may also help establish conditions whereby new employees become committed to their decision to join the organization. Realistic job previews, for example, may increase perceived freedom of choice, make potential negative consequences of the decision foreseeable, and generally increase the likelihood that individuals may feel a need to justify their decision. Although the effects of such behavioral commitment mechanisms may not be large or long-lasting, they may set the stage for new employees to become more strongly linked to the job by increasing the propensity to become committed.

3. *Improve the quality of early job experience.* By now it is a well-documented finding that a disproportionate amount of turnover occurs in the early period of an individual's association with an organization. Thus, the early experiences that an individual encounters, in relation to her or his expectations, have an especially important impact on how the individual feels about the work situation. These early feelings, in turn, will probably be crucial in determining whether the individual initiates search behavior (assuming he or she is free to leave) to change organizations and find another job. Improving the quality of early job experience involves a number of factors (mentioned in Chapter 3 and elsewhere in this book), such as competent and concerned supervision, congenial work-group members, and sufficient job scope. From the organization's perspective, the early employment period may be crucial in the development of employee commitment, if only because employees not attracted to remain in the job during the first year or so at work will not develop the long-term linkages that ensure continuing membership.
4. *Provide opportunities for committing acts.* This approach is based on the social psychological notion of behavioral commitment (see Salancik, 1977, and others referenced in Chapters 2 and 3). If employees have opportunities to perform behavioral acts on behalf of the organization, the potential exists for greater organizational commitment. Such acts—such as voluntarily working overtime or accepting assignment to an unfavorable location when not required—to be effective (from the organization's perspective) must meet the test of certain conditions or characteristics. They must be

—Explicit and unequivocal
—Difficult to revoke or change
—Observable (i.e., "public")
—Voluntarily engaged in

The last point is especially crucial. If the individual is assigned to overtime or to an undesirable geographic location, then the fact that he or she takes the assignment under these circumstances is unlikely to have much, if any, impact on commitment. In essence, the more there is an extrinsic reason (i.e., a reason from outside the person that requires or induces the act), the less the effect. Organizations would seem to have many opportunities to allow individuals the choice of engaging in work performance acts beyond the normal, routine job duties, but it is surprising how infrequently these opportunities are explicitly provided (where the individual retains the option to do it or not do it). Organizations might learn quite a bit by knowing more about certain parts of the social psychology literature.

5. *Provide jobs that maximize "felt responsibility" for what is happening in and to the organization.* Here we again draw feely on the ideas of Salancik (1977; see also Chapters 2 and 3, this volume), but with special reference to the question of commitment or attachment *to the organization.* If the individual is simply provided a job with a sense of "felt responsibility" for what is happening in that job, then he or she may be very committed to the job, but not necessarily to the organization. Therefore, what we are suggesting here, by analogy, is creating opportunities for the individual to experience "felt responsibility" for what is happening in and to the organization. This means that the individual, through job performance and other organizationally related activities (e.g., committees), needs to be provided with the means to see how what he or she does impacts the broader organization (and not just whether his or her own job has been performed well). Explicit prescriptions (for the organization) are not easy to generate, but they would appear to involve making as much information as possible available to the individual about his or her contributions to the larger organization and providing the circumstances that highlight the individual's feeling of being personally responsible for the quality or quantity of this organizational contribution. Reward systems that directly link individuals with the overall profitability of the firm, for example, may be one particularly successful method.
6. *Integrate employees into the social fabric of the organization.* Organizations are social entities and individuals are highly susceptible to social influence. Putting these two facts together leads us to the inescapable conclusion that employees' attitudes toward, and their actions in

regard to, their organizations will be strongly affected by what their fellow workers expect of them. If those communicated expectations involve notions of (in effect) "we depend on you," linkages are likely to be strengthened. To quote Salancik (1977) on this point,

> Commitment also derives from the relation of an employee's job to those of others in the organization. . . . Work integration can affect commitment by the fact that integrated jobs are likely to be associated with salient demands from others in the organization. If a person has a job which affects the work of others in the organization, it is likely that those others will communicate their expectations for performance of that job. Such expectations can be committing in that the other people inplicitly or explicitly hold the person accountable for what he does. . . . In general, we would expect that anything which contributes to creating definite expectations for a person's behavior would enhance his felt responsibility, and hence commitment. Integration may be one such contributor [p. 19].

Although Salancik was primarily addressing himself to the issue of commitment to one's job duties or responsibilities, the point is more general. If an employee is integrated into the social system of the organization, and if other employees hold high expectations for that person to make his or her contributions *to the organization,* then the employee's linkages to the organization are likely to be increased. Organizations need to give attention to the question of how each employee is provided the opportunities to become a part of the organization's social network. The design of tasks and reward systems that create greater interdependence between employees, for example, may serve to increase social involvement at work and thus strengthen the linkage of employees to the organization.

7. *Demonstrate a genuine concern for employees' welfare.* This was certainly the policy of Middle East Airlines as reported in Figure 8.1. It is also the policy, for example, of many Japanese firms. In both instances, commitment of employees has been reputed to be very high. However, before organizations leap to this approach to strengthening linkages, at least a couple of caveats should be pointed out. First, as previously mentioned, the costs of such a policy can be quite high. How any business firms in the Unied States, or any other country, for that matter, would be willing to enact a policy that employees are never fired or laid off? The point is clear: A comprehensive paternalistic policy requires very heavy investments by the organization. Whether such investments are worth the cost to the organization depends on many factors. A second caveat for the organization is that paternalism may bring many other problems (in addition to the direct

costs involved). The typical coal company in this country in the early decades was extremely paternalistic. Would very many modern organizations be willing to face up to running a company town, a company store, a company bank, and so on? Would the type of conditions created by the paternalistic coal companies of the 1920s and 1930s be acceptable to an organization today? Would they be acceptable to employees and to society, even if the organization were willing to live with the situation? The bottom line is that a paternalistic approach to increasing linkages is *possible*, but is it practical and is it desirable?

Summary

In the previous section several steps that organizations might take to strengthen employee linkages were identified. To place this discussion in perspective, however, several points need to be made clear. First, our approach throughout this book has been that strong employee linkages have both positive and negative implications for organizations. Although much of the literature in this area has implicitly assumed that employee commitment is positive and turnover and absenteeism are negative, this may be an overly simplistic view. Managers and organizations concerned about employee linkages need to make reasoned choices about policies designed to influence commitment, turnover, and absenteeism. At a minimum, decisions need to be made about where and when in the organization employee commitment may be most critical and whether the benefits associated with strengthening employee linkages outweigh the costs involved.

Second, research to date has focused primarily on different variables that correlate with commitment, turnover, and absenteeism. Our collective experience in making actual changes in organizations to see if we can influence employee linkages remains limited. This raises the question of whether organizations can actually have a substantial impact on these variables through changes in either the composition of the work force or the design of the job and work environment. A tentative answer to this question is yes. However, we recognize the importance of undertaking experiments in organizations designed to evaluate the extent to which specific changes do have an impact. It appears to be time to test our theories and conceptual models in actual organizational settings.

Even though the areas of employee commitment, turnover, and absenteeism have each received considerable, though separate, attention, the issue of employee linkages to organizations is likely to become more rather than less important in coming years. Current managerial concern about such issues as productivity and quality of working life suggests that concern about employee linkages and their impact upon organizations may increase. The research agendas identified at the end of Chapters 3–7 suggest a number of areas in which researchers may wish to direct investigation on questions related to employee linkages. In addition, the consequences of these linkages and implications of existing research for organizations have highlighted issues that may be of direct concern to managers. What appears most desirable at this point is to recognize that researchers and managers share common interests in the topic of employee linkages. Attempts in the future to coordinate more closely the efforts of researchers and the concerns of employees and organizations have greater potential to increase our understanding of this area and thus the practical significance of our research for organizations.

Appendix

The Measurement of Organizational Commitment

The conceptual richness and diversity found in the various approaches to defining organizational commitment (as noted in Chapter 2) necessarily lead to diversity in approaches to measuring the construct.[1] Although little effort has been made to develop suitable measures of behavioral commitment, several measures of commitment as an attitude can be identified in the literature. Most of these measures consist of from two- to four-item scales that are created on an a priori basis and for which little or no validity and reliability data are presented.

For example, Grusky's (1966) scale used four items, consisting of company seniority, identification with the company, attitudes toward company administrators, and general attitudes toward the company. The median intercorrelation between the items was $r = .15$. Hrebiniak and Alutto (1972) used a four-item scale that asked, in essence, what it would take for the employee to leave the organization. Spearman–Brown reliability was reported at .79 but no additional validity or reliability data were presented. Similar procedures were employed by Brown (1969), Buchanan (1974), Gouldner (1960), Hall *et al.* (1970), Hall and Schneider (1972), Lee (1971), and Sheldon (1971). Kanter (1968, 1977) used a 36-item scale but failed to report either validity or reliability data. Finally, Weiner and Gechman (1977) asked employees to keep diaries of voluntary work-related activities on personal time, using a decoding procedure to estimate commitment.

Hence, little evidence exists of any systematic or comprehensive efforts to determine the stability, consistency, or predictive powers of the various instruments. Researchers rely instead largely on face validity. If progress is to be made in explicating the commitment construct so that useful research

[1]This appendix is based on a previous article by Mowday, Steers, and Porter (1979).

about its nature and consequences can be carried out, there exists a need for an instrument that exhibits acceptable psychometric properties within the constraints of attitude measurement (Nunnally, 1967). One such effort was made by Porter and Smith (1970; Mowday, Steers, & Porter, 1979) in what was called the Organizational Commitment Questionnaire (OCQ).

The approach to instrument development that was taken by Porter and Smith (1970) was to identify 15 items that appeared to tap the three aspects of our definition of commitment. These items are shown in Table A.1. The response format employs a 7-point Likert scale with the following anchors: strongly disagree, moderately disagree, slightly disagree, neither agree nor disagree, slightly agree, moderately agree, strongly agree. Results are then summed and divided by 15 to arrive at a summary indicator of employee commitment. Several items were negatively phrased and reverse scored in an effort to reduce response bias. It was intended that the scale items, when taken together, would provide a fairly consistent indicator of employee commitment levels for most working populations.

In order to examine the psychometric properties of the instrument, a validation strategy was devised that included the use of multiple and diverse samples. It was felt that if a general measure of commitment was to be achieved, it was necessary to collect validity and reliability data for various types of employees in different work environments. Moreover, it was further necessary to cross-validate these results where possible. In order to provide such data, a series of empirical studies was initiated. The results of these studies suggest that the OCQ exhibits sufficient validity and reliability to support its use in research on organizational commitment. A detailed review of the psychometric properties of the instrument is presented elsewhere (Cook, Hepworth, Wall, & Warr, 1981; Mowday, Steers, & Porter, 1979); however, a summary of the findings may be useful here.

The Organizational Commitment Questionnaire (OCQ) was administered to 2563 employees working in a wide variety of jobs in nine different public and private work organizations. In all, the array of both job classifications and work organizations is thought to be sufficiently broad to tap a reasonably representative sample of the working population. A variety of analyses were carried out using the OCQ among these samples. In particular, interest focused on providing information pertinent to the following psychometric properties of the instrument: (*a*) means and standard deviations; (*b*) internal consistency reliability; (*c*) test–retest reliability; (*d*) convergent validity; (*e*) discriminant validity; and (*f*) norms. Evidence bearing on the predictive validity of the instrument was discussed in detail throughout Chapters 2 and 3. Although data from all

Table A.1
Organizational Commitment Questionnaire (OCQ)

Instructions

Listed below are a series of statements that represent possible feelings that individuals might have about the company or organization for which they work. With respect to your own feelings about the particular organization for which you are now working [company name] please indicate the degree of your agreement or disagreement with each statement by checking one of the seven alternatives below each statement.[a]

1. I am willing to put in a great deal of effort beyond that normally expected in order to help this organization be successful.
2. I talk up this organization to my friends as a great organization to work for.
3. I feel very little loyalty to this organization. (R)
4. I would accept almost any type of job assignment in order to keep working for this organization.
5. I find that my values and the organization's values are very similar.
6. I am proud to tell others that I am part of this organization.
7. I could just as well be working for a different organization as long as the type of work were similar. (R)
8. This organization really inspires the very best in me in the way of job performance.
9. It would take very little change in my present circumstances to cause me to leave this organization. (R)
10. I am extremely glad that I chose this organization to work for over others I was considering at the time I joined.
11. There's not too much to be gained by sticking with this organization indefinitely. (R)
12. Often, I find it difficult to agree with this organization's policies on important matters relating to its employees. (R)
13. I really care about the fate of this organization.
14. For me this is the best of all possible organizations for which to work.
15. Deciding to work for this organization was a definite mistake on my part. (R)

Source: Mowday, Steers, and Porter. *Journal of Vocational Behavior*, 1979, *14*, 224–247.

[a]Responses to each item are measured on a 7-point scale with scale point anchors labeled (1) strongly disagree; (2) moderately disagree; (3) slightly disagree; (4) neither disagree nor agree; (5) slightly agree; (6) moderately agree; (7) strongly agree. An *R* denotes a negatively phrased and reverse-scored item.

samples were not sufficient to carry out all analyses, results of those analyses that were possible are reported here.

Means and Standard Deviations

Initial attention was focused on the distribution properties of the OCQ across the nine samples. These results are shown in Table A-2. As can be seen from this table, the mean level of commitment ranges from a low of

Table A.2
Means, Standard Deviations, and Internal Consistencies for OCQ

Sample	*N*	Mean	*SD*	Coefficient alpha
Public employees	569	4.5	0.90	.90
Classified university employees	243	4.6	1.30	.90
Hospital employees	382	5.1	1.18	.88
Bank employees	411	5.2	1.07	.88
Telephone company employees	605	4.7	1.20	.90
Scientists and engineers	119	4.4	0.98	.84
Auto company managers	115	5.3	1.05	.90
Psychiatric technicians[a]	60	4.0/3.5	1.00/1.00	.82–.93
		4.3/3.5	1.10/0.91	
		4.3/3.3	0.96/0.88	
		4.0/3.0	1.10/0.98	
Retail-management trainees	59	6.1	0.64	NA[b]

Source: Mowday, Steers, and Porter. *Journal of Vocational Behavior*, 1979, *14*, 224–247.

[a]For this sample, means and standard deviations are reported separately for stayers and leavers across four time periods.

[b]NA = not available.

4.0 to a high of 6.1 across the nine samples. Mean scores are typically slightly above the midpoint on the 7-point Likert scale. Moreover, standard deviations indicate an acceptable distribution of responses within samples.

Internal Consistency Reliability

Estimates of internal consistency were calculated in three different ways: coefficient alpha, item analysis, and factor analysis. First, as shown in Table A-2, coefficient alpha is consistently high, ranging from .82 to .93, with a median of .90 (Cronbach, 1951). These results compare favorably with most attitude measures (cf. P.C. Smith *et al.*, 1969).

In addition, item analyses (correlations between each item of the commitment scale and the total score less the item) were also carried out. Results indicated that each item had a positive correlation with the total score for the OCQ, with the range of average correlations being from .36 to .72, and a median correlation of .64. In general, the negatively worded items correlate less highly with the total score than do the positively worded items, although this difference is not great. These results suggest the 15 items of the OCQ are relatively homogeneous with respect to the underlying attitude construct they measure.

Finally, to examine further the homogeneity of the OCQ items, factor analyses were performed and the results rotated to Kaiser's (1958) varimax solution. Results of these analyses for studies in which the 15-item scale was used are reported in Table A.3; results for studies using the 9-item short form, which omitted the negatively worded items, are reported in Table A.4. In each table factor loadings above .30, eigenvalues, and the percentage of common variance accounted for by each factor are presented. These analyses generally result in a single-factor solution and support the previously stated conclusion that the items are measuring a single common underlying construct. Where two factors emerged from an analysis, the eigenvalue associated with the second factor never exceeded 1.0. Furthermore, the percentage of common variance explained by the second factors ranged from 2.4 to 15.5, whereas the percentage of variance associated with the first factor ranged from 83.2 to 92.6. As would be expected, lower and more complex patterns of factor loadings were generally found for those items having a lower item–total score correlation (see Mowday *et al.*, 1979, for details).

Table A.3
Factor Analysis of Fifteen-Item Organizational Commitment Questionnaire

	Public employees ($N = 569$)		Bank employees ($N = 411$)		Telephone company employees ($N = 600$)	
Item	Factor 1	Factor 2	Factor 1	Factor 2	Factor 1	Factor 2
1		.76	.69		.67	
2	.43	.53	.72	.32	.72	.34
3	.45	.36		.53		.34
4					.39	
5	.40		.67		.66	
6	.50	.49	.75	.32	.75	.35
7	.35			.39		.40
8	.44	.41	.67		.55	.50
9	.60			.58		.54
10	.53	.38	.54	.46	.55	.55
11	.62		.38		.34	.63
12	.45			.50		.37
13		.60	.62	.38	.62	
14	.49	.36	.57	.36	.61	.45
15	.68	.37	.44	.49	.49	.58
Variance (%)	83.2	9.0	83.6	10.6	92.6	2.4
Eigenvalue	6.28	.68	5.99	.76	6.30	.50

Table A.4
Factor Analysis of Nine-Item Organizational Commitment Questionnaire

	Hospital employees ($N = 376$)	Scientist and engineers ($N = 119$)		Classified university employees ($N = 256$)
Item	Factor 1	Factor 1	Factor 2	Factor 1
1	.66		.78	.77
2	.82	.41	.57	.68
3	.33			.49
4	.68	.55	.45	.86
5	.83	.43	.57	.71
6	.73	.69		.65
7	.77	.66		.76
8	.68		.59	.74
9	.74	.73		.73
Variance (%)	100.0	84.5	15.5	100.0
Eigenvalue	4.5	3.6	.7	4.6

Test–Retest Reliability

In order to examine the stability of the OCQ over time, test–retest reliabilities were computed for those samples for which multiple data points were available. These test–retest reliabilities demonstrated acceptable levels (from $r = .53$ to $r = .75$) over periods ranging from 2 months to 4 months. These data compare favorably to other attitude measures (e.g., job satisfaction). For example, Smith *et al.*, (1969) reported test–retest reliabilities for the Job Descriptive Index from .45 to .75.

Evidence of Convergent Validity

It is difficult to establish convergent validity for a measure of organizational commitment in view of the absence of acceptable standards for comparison. Even so, it would appear that at least five lines of evidence can be identified that, when taken together, are suggestive of convergent validity. First, the OCQ should be related to other instruments designed to measure similar affective responses. In order to provide for such a comparison, the OCQ was correlated with the Sources of Organizational Attachment Questionnaire (Mowday *et al.*, 1974). This instrument seemed particularly relevant for a point of comparison since it differs structurally from the OCQ, thereby reducing common methods variance problems in the analysis. Convergent validities across six diverse samples ranged from .63 to .74, with a median of .70. In this case, then, consistent evidence of convergent validity for the OCQ was found.

The second step in determining convergent validity was to examine the extent to which the OCQ was related to employees' behavioral intentions to remain. Intent to remain is deeply imbedded in our conceptualization of commitment. In four studies, significant correlations were found between OCQ and intent to remain. Although the magnitude of three of the four correlations is not overly high, strong relationships would not be expected in view of the fact that intent to remain or leave represented only one of the three primary ingredients in the definition of commitment and a number of personal and environmental factors can be expected to influence intent to remain in addition to one's commitment to the organization. Moreover, in one study, the OCQ was found to be strongly related to employee's estimates of how long they would remain with the organization.

Third, following from the theory, organizational commitment should be related to motivational force to perform and intrinsic motivation. That is, highly committed employees are thought to be motivated to exert high levels of energy on behalf of the organization. Based on four studies where such data were available, some evidence emerged of a moderate relationship between the two variables (using two different measures of motivation), with correlations ranging from .35 to .45.

Fourth, Dubin *et al.*, (1975) found that organizational commitment was related to the central life interest of employees, defined in terms of an expressed orientation toward work or nonwork activities, in two diverse samples. The results indicated that employees with a work-oriented central life interest are more likely to be highly committed to the organization than employees expressing a nonwork interest. Moreover, non-work-oriented employees were more likely than work-oriented employees to express low levels of organizational commitment.

Fifth, in the study of retail employees, it was possible to secure independent ratings of employee commitment by the employees' superiors. Because of the narrow range of expressed commitment for this particular sample, the correlation between OCQ and supervisor ratings of commitment was calculated using the restriction of range formula (see Porter & Smith, 1970, for details). Using this procedure, the OCQ correlated at $r = .60$ with independent commitment ratings. In all, then, the pattern of findings does serve to provide some modest evidence of convergent validity for the OCQ.

Evidence of Discriminant Validity

Organizational commitment as an attitude would be expected to be related to other job-related attitudes. However, if we are to identify commitment as a unique variable in the study of organizational behavior, it must demonstrate acceptable levels of discriminant validity when compared to other attitudes. In order to investigate the extent of discriminant validity of the OCQ, it was compared with three other attitude measures: job involvement, career satisfaction, and job satisfaction. Several lines of evidence emerge from these data bearing on the question of discriminant validity of the OCQ.

To begin with, relationships between organizational commitment and Lodahl and Kejner's (1965) job involvement measure ranged from $r = .30$ to $r = .56$ across four samples. Second, correlations between organizational commitment and a three-item measure of career satisfaction were .39 and .40 for two samples. Finally, across four studies and 35 data points, correlations between organizational commitment and scales of the Job Descriptive Index ranged from .01 to .68, with a median correlation of .41. (These data include results from a study conducted independently by Brief and Aldag [1977].) The highest relationships were generally found between commitment and satisfaction with the work itself. In view of the typically high correlations found between various job attitudes measured at the same point in time, these correlations are sufficiently low as to provide some indication of an acceptable level of discriminant validity. The percentage of common variance shared by organizational commitment and the other measures did not exceed 50% and was generally less than 25% for most relationships.

Norms

Based on the results of the studies carried out to date, it is possible to provide a rough indication of how an employee's score on the OCQ compares in magnitude with other employees. Such information is shown in the normative data in Table A.5. This table shows the percentile conversions for raw scores on the OCQ for both males and females. Such data should facilitate more accurate comparative analyses of relative levels of employee commitment by indicating how a particular raw score on the OCQ compares against other scores for a broad sample of employees of the same gender.

Table A.5
OCQ Norms for Males and Females

OCQ score	Percentile score	
	Males ($N = 978$)	Females ($N = 1530$)
7.00	99.6	99.3
6.75	98.4	97.4
6.50	94.6	94.3
6.25	90.7	89.4
6.00	85.8	80.8
5.75	77.1	74.4
5.50	69.3	67.1
5.25	62.4	58.5
5.00	55.7	49.3
4.75	48.8	43.1
4.50	42.3	34.8
4.25	35.0	28.0
4.00	26.4	20.9
3.75	20.9	17.5
3.50	16.4	12.8
3.25	11.8	9.9
3.00	8.4	6.3
2.75	6.3	4.7
2.50	4.3	2.8
2.25	2.7	1.9
2.00	1.8	1.2
1.75	1.1	0.9
1.50	0.4	0.5
1.25	0.2	0.3
1.00	0.0	0.0

Source: Mowday, Steers, and Porter. *Journal of Vocational Behavior*, 1979, *14* 224–247.

Summary

Several conclusions can be drawn concerning the utility of the Organizational Commitment Questionnaire for research in organizations. Reasonably strong evidence was presented for the internal consistency and test–retest reliability of the OCQ. Compared with other measures, the items of the OCQ were found to be reasonably homogeneous and the results suggest that the overall measure of organizational commitment was relatively stable over short periods of time. Evidence also shows moderately acceptable levels of convergent, discriminant, and predictive validity (discussed in Chapter 2 and 3), particularly when compared against other similar attitude measures. The results of the analyses concerning the three types of validity require further comment, however, to place these findings in perspective.

Convergent validity for the OCQ was suggested by positive correlations found between organizational commitment and other measures of both similar attitude constructs (e.g., sources of organizational attachment) and one of the component parts of the definition of organizational commitment (e.g., motivational force to perform). Discriminant validity was assessed by examining the relationships between commitment and satisfaction with one's career and specific aspects of the job and work environment. Commitment was found, however, to be moderately correlated with several of these satisfaction measures, with the percentage of common variance shared by the measures about 15–25%. Although the correlations found for convergent validity are on the average larger than the correlations found for discriminant validity ($\bar{r} = .52$ versus .42), this difference is not as large as might be desired. Clearly, correlations of lower magnitude for discriminant validity would be more desirable to demonstrate conclusively that the OCQ is related more highly to similar constructs than to different constructs. What is perhaps most important in evaluating the validity of the OCQ, however, is the pattern of results across both analyses. The OCQ was generally found to be more highly related to measures of similar as opposed to different attitudes *and* the relationships found between commitment and satisfaction were not so high as to lead one to conclude they were measuring exactly the same attitude. Compared with the evidence for other measures, this pattern of results suggests the OCQ possesses acceptable, although clearly not perfect, levels of convergent and discriminant validity.

The predictive validity of the OCQ (see Chapters 2 and 3) is demonstrated by relatively consistent relationships in the predicted direction between commitment and measures of employee turnover, absenteeism, tenure in the organization, and, to a lesser extent, performance on the job. The magnitude of these relationships was frequently not high, however, suggesting that employee behavior in organizations is determined by a complex set of factors and not just commitment to the organization. Given the complexity of the determinants of such behaviors as turnover and absenteeism, it would be truly surprising to find any single attitude measure highly related to a particular behavior. The results presented here suggest that organizational commitment correlates as well, if not better than in some cases, with certain employee behaviors as most commonly used attitude measures (e.g., job satisfaction). Where comparisons were available between the relative predictive power of commitment and a well-developed measure of job satisfaction, commitment appeared to be a somewhat better and more stable predictor of turnover (Porter *et al.*, 1974) and group level performance (Mowday *et al.*, 1974). These results indicate that organizational commitment is an important construct to include among other determinants in modeling and researching employee behavior in organizations.

Experience to date with the OCQ suggests at least two possible cautions to potential users of the instrument. First, the OCQ is the type of instrument that respondents may easily dissemble, if they are so inclined. The intent of the items is not diguised in such a way as to make it difficult for respondents to manipulate their scores. In this regard, the results of any particular administration of the OCQ are likely to be somewhat dependent upon the circumstances of administration. Researchers interested in using the OCQ should be aware of the possibility that employees may distort their responses if they feel, for example, threatened by completing the questionnaire or if they are unsure how their responses will be used. It is important in using the OCQ, therefore, to exercise appropriate caution in administering the questionnaire.

Second, results of the reliability and item analyses suggest that the short form of the OCQ (i.e., using only the nine positively worded items) may be an acceptable substitute for the longer scale in situations where questionnaire length is a consideration. Even though the internal consistency for the nine-item scale is generally equal to that of the full instrument, care shoud be taken in constructing a short form since several of the negatively worded items that might be discarded were correlated more highly with the total score than several of the positively phrased items. Moreover, the negatively worded items were included to guard against the acquiescence response tendency and removal of these items may increase this tendency. The data presented here should allow individual researchers to make their own judgments concerning the appropriateness of a short form for their particular research situation. Where conditions permit, however, we recommend the use of the full instrument.

References

Acton Society Trust. *Size and morale.* London: Author, 1953.

Angle, H., & Perry, J. An empirical assessment of organizational commitment and organizational effectiveness. *Administrative Science Quarterly*, 1981, *26*, 1–14.

Argyle, M., Gardner, G., & Cioffi, I. Supervisory methods related to productivity, absenteeism and labor turnover. *Human Relations*, 1958, *11*, 23–40.

Armknecht, P. A., & Early, J. F. Quits in manufacturing: A study of their causes. *Monthly Labor Review*, 1972, *95*, 31–37.

Aronson, E. Dissonance theory: Progress and problems. In R. Abelson, E. Aronson, W. McGuire, T. Newcomb, M. Rosenberg, & P. Tannenbaum (Eds.), *Theories of cognitive consistency: A sourcebook.* Chicago: Rand McNally, 1968.

Aronson, E. The theory of cognitive dissonance: A current perspective. In L. Berkowitz (Ed.), *Cognitive theories in social psychology.* New York: Academic Press, 1978.

Aronson, E. *The social animal* (3rd ed.). San Francisco: W. H. Freeman, 1980.

Barnard, C. *Functions of the executive.* Boston: Harvard University Press, 1938.

Baum, J. F. Effectiveness of an attendance control policy in reducing chronic absenteeism. *Personnel Psychology*, 1978, *31*, 71–81.

Baum, J.F., & Youngblood, S. A. Impact of an organizational control policy on absenteeism, performance, and satisfaction. *Journal of Applied Psychology*, 1975, *60*, 688–694.

Baumgartel, H., & Sobol, R. Background and organizational factors in absenteeism. *Personnel Psychology*, 1959, *12*, 431–443.

Beatty, R. W., & Beatty, J. R. Longitudinal study of absenteeism of hardcore unemployed. *Psychological Reports*, 1975, *36*, 395–406.

Becker, H. S. Notes on the concept of commitment. *American Journal of Sociology*, 1960, *66*, 32–42.

Becker, H. Personal change in adult life. *Sociometry*, 1964, *27*, 40–53.

Beer, M., & Huse, E. F. A systems approach to organizational development. *Journal of Applied Behavioral Science*, 1972, *8*, 79–109.

Behrend, H. *Absence under full employment.* (Monograph A3, University of Birmingham Studies in Economics and Society.) Birmingham, England: University of Birmingham, 1951.

Behrend, H. Absence and labour turnover in a changing economic climate. *Occupational Psychology*, 1953, *27*, 69–79.

Berlew, D., & Hall, D. The socialization of managers: Effects of expectations on performance. *Administrative Science Quarterly*, 1966, *2*, 207–223.

Bernadin, H. J. The relationship of personality variables to organizational withdrawal. *Personnel Psychology*, 1977, *30*, 17–27.

Bernays, J. *Auslease und anpassung der arbeiterschaft der geschlossenen, grossindustri. Schriften des verein fur sozialpolitik*. Leipzig: Gerlag von Dunder und Humblot, 1910.

Bradley, G. W. Self-serving biases in the attibution process: A reexamination of the fact or fiction question. *Journal of Personality and Social Psychology*, 1978, *36*, 56–71.

Bragg, J. E., & Andrews, I. R. Participative decision-making: An experimental study in a hospital. *Journal of Applied Behavioral Science*, 1973, *9*, 727–736.

Bray, D. W., Campbell, R. J., & Grant, D. L. *Formative years in business*. New York: Wiley–Interscience, 1974.

Brayfield, A. H., & Crockett, W. H. Employee attitudes and employee performance. *Psychological Bulletin*, 1955, *52*, 396–424.

Brehm, J. W. *A theory of psychological reactance*. New York: Academic Press, 1966.

Brehm, J. W., & Cohen, A. R. *Explorations in cognitive dissonance*. New York: Wiley, 1962.

Brief, A. P., & Aldag, R. J. *Antecedents of organizational commitment among hospital nurses*. Working paper, University of Iowa, 1977.

Brief, A. P., Aldag, R. J., & Wallden, R. A. Correlates of supervisory style among policemen. *Criminal Justice and Behavior*, 1976, *3*, 263–271.

Brown, M. E. Identification and some conditions of organizational involvement. *Administrative Science Quarterly*, 1969, *14*, 346–355.

Buchanan, B. Building organizational commitment: The socialization of managers in work organizations. *Administrative Science Quarterly*, 1974, *19*, 533–546.

Buchanan, B. To walk an extra mile. *Organizational Dynamics*, 1975, *3*, 67–80.

Buck, L., & Shimmin, S. Overtime and financial responsibility. *Occupational Psychology*, 1959, *33*, 137–148.

Buzzard, R. B., & Liddell, F. D. E. *Coal miners' attendance at work*. NCB Medical Service, Medical Research Memorandum No. 3, 1958.

Caplow, T. *Principles of organization*. New York: Harcourt, Brace & World, 1964.

Card, J. J. Differences in the demographic and sociopsychological profile of ROTC vs. non-ROTC students. *Journal of Vocational Behavior*, 1978, *11*, 196–215.

Cartwright, D. The nature of group cohesiveness. In D. Cartwright & A. Zander (Eds.), *Group dynamics* (3rd ed.). New York: Harper & Row, 1968.

Cartwright, D., & Zander, A. *Group dynamics: Research and theory* (3rd ed.). New York: Harper & Row, 1968.

Catalano, R., & Dooley, D. Economic predictors of depressed mood and stressful life events. *Journal of Health and Social Behavior*, 1977, *18*, 293–307.

Chadwick-Jones, J. K., Brown, C. A., Nicholson, N., & Sheppard, C. Absence measures: Their reliability and stability in an industrial setting. *Personnel Psychology*, 1971, *24*, 463–470.

Collins, B. E., & Hoyt, M. F. Personal responsibility-for-consequences: An integration and extension of the "forced compliance" literature. *Journal of Experimental Social Psychology*, 1972, *8*, 558–593.

Cook, J., Hepworth, S., Wall, T., & Warr, P. *The experience of work: A compendium and review of 249 measures and their use*. London: Academic Press, 1981.

Cooper, C., & Payne, R. *Stress at work*. London: Wiley, 1978.

Cooper, R., & Payne, R. Age and Absence: A longitudinal study in three firms. *Occupational Psychology*, 1965, *39*, 31–43.

Cooper, J. Personal responsibility and dissonance: The role of unforeseen consequences. *Journal of Personality and Social Psychology*, 1971, *18*, 354–363.

Copenhaver, J. R. Training, job enrichment, reducing costs. *Hospitals*, 1973, *47*(3), 118, 122, 126.

Coverdale, S., & Terborg, J. R. *A reexamination of the Mobley, Horner, and Hollingsworth model of turnover: A useful replication*. Technical Report No. 80-4, University of Houston, 1980.

Covner, B. J. Management factors affecting absenteeism. *Harvard Business Review*, 1950, *28*, 42–48.

Crabb, J. T. Scientific hiring. *Efficiency Society Transactions*, 1912, *1*, 313–318.

Crampon, W., Mowday, R., Smith, F., & Porter, L. W. *Early attitudes predicting future behavior*. Paper presented at the 38th annual meeting of the Academy of Management, San Francisco, August 1978.

Cronbach, L. J. Coefficient alpha and the internal structure of tests. *Psychometrica*, 1951, *16*, 297–334.

Crowther, J. Absence and turnover in the divisions of one company: 1950–55. *Occupational Psychology*, 1957, *31*, 256–270.

Cummings, L. L., & Berger, C. J. Organization stucture: How does it influence attitudes and performance? *Organizational Dynamics*, 1976, *5*(2), 34–49.

Dalton, D., Krackhardt, D., & Porter, L. Functional turnover: An empirical investigation. *Journal of Applied Psychology*, in press.

Dalton, D., & Tudor, W. Turnover turned over: An expanded and positive perspective. *Academy of Management Review*, 1979, *4*, 225–235.

Dansereau, F., Cashman, J., & Graen, G. Expectancy as a moderator of the relationship between job attitudes and turnover. *Journal of Applied Psychology*, 1974, *59*, 228–229.

Davis, L. E., & Valfer, E. S. Studies in supervisory job design. *Human Relations*, 1966, *19*, 339–352.

de la Mare, G., & Sergean, R. Two methods of studying changes in absence with age. *Occupational Psychology*, 1961, *35*, 245–252.

Dittrich, J. E., & Carrell, M. R. *Dimensions of organizational fairness as predictors of job satisfaction, absence, and turnover*. Paper presented at the meeting of the Academy of Management, Kansas City, Missouri, August 1976.

Dubin, R. Industrial workers' worlds: A study of the "central life interests" of industrial workers. *Social Problems*, 1956, *3*, 131–142.

Dubin, R., Champoux, J. E. & Porter, L. W. Central life interests and organizational commitment of blue-collar and clerical workers. *Administrative Science Quarterly*, 1975, *20*, 411–421.

Etzioni, A. *A comparative analysis of complex organizations*. New York: Free Press, 1961.(a)

Etzioni, A. *Modern organizations*. Englewood Cliffs, N.J.: Prentice-Hall, 1961.(b)

Etzioni, A. Work in the American future: Reindustrialization or quality of life. In C. Kerr & J. M. Rostow (Eds.), *Work in America: The decade ahead*. New York: Van Nostrand, 1979.

Farr, J. L., O'Leary, B. S., & Bartlett, C. J. Ethnic group membership as a moderator of the prediction of job performance. *Personnel Psychology*, 1971, *24*, 609–636.

Farrell, D., & Rusbult, C. Exchange variables as predictors of job satisfaction, job commitment, and turnover: The impact of rewards, costs, alternatives, and investments. *Organizational Behavior and Human Performance*, in press.

Federico, J. M., Federico, P., & Lundquist, G. W. Predicting women's turnover as a function of extent of met salary expectations and biodemographic data. *Personnel Psychology*, 1976, *29*, 559–566.

Feldman, J. Race, economic class, and the intention to work: Some normative and attitudinal correlates. *Journal of Applied Psychology*, 1974, *59*, 179–186.

Festinger, L. *A theory of cognitive dissonance*. Evanston, Ill.: Row, Peterson, 1957.

Fischhoff, B. Attribution theory and judgement under uncertainty. In J. Harvey and W. Ickes (Eds.), *New directions in attibution research* (Vol. 1). Hillsdale, N.J. Lawrence Erlbaum, 1976.

Fishbein, M. Attitude and the prediction of behavior. In M. Fishbein (Ed.) *Reading in attitude theory and measurement*. New York: Wiley, 1967.

Flanagan, R. J., Strauss, G., & Ulman, L. Worker discontent and work place behavior. *Industrial Relations*, 1974, *13*, 101–123.

Ford, R. N. *Motivation through the work itself*. New York: American Management Association, 1969.

Forrest, C. R., Cummings, L. L., & Johnson, A. C. Organizational participation: A critique and model. *Academy of Management Review*, 1977, *2*, 586–601.

Frank, L. L., & Hackman, J. R. A failure of job enrichment: The case of the change that wasn't. *Journal of Applied Behavioral Science*, 1975, *11*, 413–436.

Frechette, H. *An investigation of the utility of Steers and Rhodes' process model of attendance behavior*. Paper presented at the 41st annual meeting of the Academy of Management, San Diego, August 1981.

Freedman, J. L. Attitudinal effects on inadequate justification. *Journal of Personality*, 1963, *31*, 371–385.

Fried, J., Wertman, M., & Davis, M. Man–machine interaction and absenteeism. *Journal of Applied Psychology*, 1972, *56*, 428–429.

Gandz, J., & Mikalachki, A. *Measuring absenteeism*. Working paper, University of Western Ontario, 1979.

Garrison, K. R., & Muchinsky, R. M. Attitudinal and biographical predictors of incidental absenteeism. *Journal of Vocational Behavior*, 1977, *10*, 221–230.

Gaudet, F. *Labor turnover: Calculation and cost*. New York: American Management Association, 1960.

Gibson, J. O. Toward a conceptualization of absence behavior of personnel in organizations. *Administrative Science Quarterly*, 1966, *11*, 107–133.

Glaser, E. M. *Productivity gains through worklife improvement*. New York: The Psychological Corporation, 1976.

Golembiewski, R. T., Hilles, R., & Kagno, M. S. A longitudinal study of flex-time effects: Some consequences of an OD structural intervention. *Journal of Applied Behavioral Science*, 1974, *10*, 503–532.

Gomez, L. R., & Mussie, S. J. An application of job enrichment in a civil service setting: A demonstration study. *Public Personnel Management*, 1975, *4*, 49–54.

Goodale, J. G. Effects of personal background and training on work values of the hard-core unemployed. *Journal of Applied Psychology*, 1973, *57*, 1–9.

Gould, S. *Correlates of organization identification and commitment*. Unpublished doctoral dissertation, Michigan State University, East Lansing, Michigan, 1975.

Gouldner, A. W. Cosmopolitans and locals: Toward an analysis of latent social roles: I. *Administrative Science Quarterly*, 1958, *62*, 444–480.

Gouldner, H. P. Dimensions of organizational commitment. *Administrative Science Quarterly*, 1960, *4*, 468–490.

Gowler, D. Determinants of the supply of labour to the firm. *Journal of Management Studies*, 1969, *6*, 73–95.

Grusky, O. Career mobility and organizational commitment. *Administrative Science Quarterly*, 1966, *10*, 488–503.

Hackman, J. R., & Lawler, E. E., III. Employee reactions to job characteristics. *Journal of Applied Psychology*, 1971, *55*, 259–286.

Hackman, J. R., & Morris, C. Group tasks, group interaction process, and group performance effectiveness: A review and proposed integration. In L. Berkowitz (Ed.), *Advances in experimental social psychology* (Vol. 8). New York: Academic Press, 1975.

Hackman, J. R. & Oldham, G. R. Motivation through the design of work: Test of a theory. *Organizational Behavior and Human Performance*, 1976, *16*, 250–279.

Hackman, J., Oldham, G., Janson, R., & Purdy, K. A new strategy for job enrichment. *California Management Review*, 1975, *17*, 57–71.

Hall, D. *Careers in organizations*. Santa Monica: Goodyear, 1976.

Hall, D. T. *Conflict and congruence among multiple career commitments as the career unfolds*. Paper presented at the Academy of Management Meeting, Orlando, Florida, August, 1977.

Hall, D. T., & Schneider, B. Correlates of organizational identification as a function of career pattern and organizational type. *Administrative Science Quarterly*, 1972, *17*, 340–350.

Hall, D. T., Schneider, B., & Nygren, H. T. Personal factors in organizational identification. *Administrative Science Quarterly*, 1970, *15*, 176–190.

Hammer, T., Landau, J., & Stern, R. *Absenteeism when workers have a voice: The case of employee ownership*. Working paper, Cornell University, 1980.(a)

Hammer, T., Landau, J., & Stern, R. *Methodological issues in the use of absenteeism data*. Working paper, Cornell University, 1980.(b)

Hamner, W. C., & Hamner, E. P. Behavior modification on the bottom line. *Organizational Dynamics*, 1976, *4*(4), 2–21.

Hautaluoma, J. E., & Gavin, J. F. Effects of organizational diagnosis and intervention on blue-collar "blues." *Journal of Applied Behavioral Science*, 1975, *11*, 475–498.

Hedges, J. N. Absence from work: A look at some national data. *Monthly Labor Review*, 1973, *96*, 24–31.

Heider, F. *The psychology of interpersonal relations*. New York: Wiley, 1958.

Herman, J. B. Are situational contingencies limiting job attitude–job performance relationships? *Organizational Behavior and Human Performance*, 1973, *10*, 208–224.

Hershey, R. Effects of anticipated job loss on employee behavior. *Journal of Applied Psychology*, 1972, *56*, 273–274.

Herzberg, F., Mausner, B., Peterson, R. O., & Capwell, R. *Job attitudes: Review of research and opinions*. Pittsburgh: Pittsburgh Psychological Services, 1957.

Hewitt, D., & Parfitt, J. A note on working morale and size of group. *Occupational Psychology*, 1953, *27*, 38–42.

Hill, J. M., & Trist, E. L. Changes in accidents and other absences with length of service. *Human Relations*, 1955, *8*, 121–152.

Hill, M. Who stays home? *New Society*, 1967, *9*, 459–460.

Hines, G. H. Achievement motivation, occupations, and labor turnover in New Zealand. *Journal of Applied Psychology*, 1973, *58*, 313–317.

Hom, P. W., Katerberg, R., & Hulin, C. L. Comparative examination of three approaches to the prediction of turnover. *Journal of Applied Psychology*, 1979, *64*, 280–290.

Hrebiniak, L. G. Effects of job level and participation on employee attitudes and perception of influence. *Academy of Management Journal*, 1974, *17*, 649–662.

Hrebiniak, L. G., & Alutto, J. A. Personal and role-related factors in the development of organizational commitment. *Administrative Science Quarterly*, 1972, *17*, 555–572.

Hrebiniak, L. G., & Roteman, M. R. A study of the relationship between need satisfaction and absenteeism among managerial personnel. *Journal of Applied Psychology*, 1973, *58*, 381–383.

Hulin, C. L., & Blood, M. I. Job enlargement, individual differences, and worker responses. *Psychological Bulletin*, 1968, *69*, 41–45.

Huse, E., & Taylor, E. The reliability of absence measures. *Journal of Applied Psychology*, 1962, *46*, 149–160.

Ilgen, D., & Dugoni, I. *Initial orientation to the organization: Its impact on psychological processes associated with the adjustment of new employees*. Paper presented at the National Meeting of the Academy of Management, Kissimee, Florida, August 1977.

Ilgen, D. R., & Hollenback, J. H. The role of job satisfaction in absence behavior. *Organizational*

Behavior and Human Performance, 1977, *19,* 148–161.

Indik, B. P. Organization size and member participation. *Human Relations,* 1965, *18,* 339–350.

Indik, B. P., & Seashore, S. *Effects of organization size on member attitudes and behavior.* Ann Arbor: University of Michigan, Survey Research Center of the Institute for Social Research, 1961.

Ingham, C. *Size of industrial organization and worker behavior.* Cambridge, England: Cambridge University Press, 1970.

Isambert-Jamati, V. Absenteeism among women workers in industry. *International Labour Review,* 1962, *85,* 248–261.

Ivancevich, J. M. Effects of the shorter workweek on selected satisfaction and performance measures. *Journal of Applied Psychology,* 1974, *59,* 717–721.

Ivancevich, J. M., & Matteson, T. *Stress at work.* Glenview, Ill.: Scott, Foresman, 1980.

Janis, I. *Victims of groupthink.* Boston: Houghton Mifflin, 1972.

Janis, I. L., & Mann, L. *Decision making.* New York: Free Press, 1977.

Jeswald, T. A. The cost of absenteeism and turnover in a large organization. In W. C. Hamner and G. L. Schmidt (Eds.) *Contemporary problems in personnel.* Chicago: St. Clair Press, 1974. pp.352–357.

Johns, G. Attitudinal and nonattitudinal predictors of two forms of absence from work. *Organizational Behavior and Human Performance,* 1978, *22,* 431–444.

Johns, G., & Nicholson, N. The meaning of absence: New strategies for theory and research. In B. Staw and L. Cummings (Eds.), *Research in organizational behavior.* Greenwich, CT: JAI Press, in press.

Johnson, R. D., & Wallin, J. A. *Employee attendance: An operant conditioning intervention in a field setting.* Paper presented at the meeting of the American Psychological Association, Washington, D.C., September 1976.

Jones, E. E. How do people perceive the causes of behavior? *American Scientist,* 1976, *64,* 300–305.

Jones, E. E. The rocky road from acts to dispositions. *American Psychologist,* 1979,

Jones, E. E., & Davis, K. E. From acts to dispositions: The attribution process in person perception. In L. Berkowitz (Ed.), *Advances in experimental social psychology.* New York: Academic Press, 1965.

Jones, E. E., & McGillis, D. Correspondent inferences and the attribution cube: A comparative reappraisal. In J. H. Harvey, W. J. Ickes, and R. F. Kidd (Eds.). *New directions in attribution theory* (Vol. 1). Hillsdale, N.J.: Lawrence Erlbaum, 1976.

Jones, E. E., & Nisbett, R. E. The actor and the observer: Divergent perceptions of the causes of behavior. In E. E. Jones, D. E. Kanouse, H. H. Kelley, R. E. Nisbett, S. Valins, and B. Weiner (Eds.), *Attribution: Perceiving the causes of behavior.* Morristown, N.J.: General Learning Press, 1972.

Kahneman, D., & Tversky, A. On the psychology of prediction. *Psychological Review,* 1973, *80,* 237–251.

Kaiser, H. F. The varimax criterion for analytic rotation in factor analysis. *Psychometrica,* 1958, *23,* 187–201.

Kanter, R. M. Commitment and social organization: A study of commitment mechanisms in utopian communities. *American Sociological Review,* 1968, *33,* 499–517.

Kanter, R. M. *Commitment and community: Communes and utopias in sociological perspective.* Cambridge: Harvard University Press, 1972.

Kanter, R. M. *Men and women of the corporation.* New York: Basic Books, 1977.

Katz, D. The motivational basis of organizational behavior. *Behavioral Science,* 1964, *9,* 131–146

Katzell, R. A. Changing attitudes toward work. In C. Kerr & J. M. Rostow (Eds.), *Work in America: The decade ahead.* New York: Van Nostrand, 1979.

Kelley, H. H. Attribution theory in social psychology. In D. Levine (Ed.), *Nebraska Symposium on Motivation*. Lincoln: University of Nebraska Press, 1967.

Kelley, H. H. Attribution in social interaction. In E. E. Jones, D. E. Kanouse, H. H. Kelley, R. E. Nisbett, S. Valins, and B. Weiner (Eds.), *Attribution: Perceiving the causes of behavior*. Morristown, N. J.: General Learning Press, 1972.

Kelley, H. H. The process of causal attribution. *American Psychologist*, 1973, *28*, 107–128.

Kerr, C. Introduction: Industrialism with a human face. In C. Kerr & J. M Rostow (Eds.), *Work in America: The decade ahead*. New York: Van Nostrand, 1979.

Kerr, W., Koppelmeier, G., & Sullivan, J. Absenteeism, turnover and morale in a metals fabrication factory. *Occupational Psychology*, 1951, *25*, 50–55.

Ketchum, L. D. Untitled paper presented at the American Association for the Advancement of Science Symposium on Humanizing of Work, Philadelphia, December 1972.

Kidron, A. Work values and organizational commitment. *Academy of Management Journal*, 1978, *21*, 239–247.

Kiesler, C. A. *The psychology of commitment: Experiments linking behavior to belief.* New York: Academic Press, 1971

Kilbridge, M. Turnover, absence, and transfer rates as indicators of employee dissatisfaction with repetitive work. *Industrial and Labor Relations Review*, 1961, *15*, 21–32.

King, A. S. Expectation effects in organizational change. *Administrative Science Quarterly*, 1974, *19*, 221–230.

Knox, J. B. Absenteeism and turnover in an Argentine factory. *American Sociological Review*, 1961, *26*, 424–428.

Koch, J. L. Need environment congruity and self-investment in organizational roles. *Sociology of Work and Occupations*, 1974, *1*, 175–196.

Koch, J. L., & Steers, R. M. Job attachment, satisfaction, and turnover among public employees. *Journal of Vocational Behavior*, 1978, *12*, 119–128.

Korman, A. *Organizational behavior*. Englewood Cliffs, N. J.: Prentice-Hall, 1977.

Kornhauser, A. *Mental health of the industrial worker*. New York: Wiley, 1965.

Krackhardt, D., McKenna, J., Porter, L. W., & Steers, R. M. Supervisory behavior and employee turnover: A field experiment. *Academy of Management Journal*, 1981, *24*, 249–259.

Latham, G. P., & Pursell, E. D. Measuring absenteeism from the opposite side of the coin. *Journal of Applied Psychology*, 1975, *60*, 369–371.

Latham, G. P., & Pursell, E. D. Measuring attendance: a reply to Ilgen. *Journal of Applied Psychology*, 1977, *62*, 234–236.

Lawler, E. E., III. *Pay and organizational effectiveness*. New York: McGraw-Hill, 1971.

Lawler, E. E. III, & Hackman, J. R. The impact of employee participation in the development of pay incentive plans: A field experiment. *Journal of Applied Psychology*, 1969, *53*, 467–471.

Lawler, E. E., III, Hackman, J. R., & Kaufman, S. Effects of job redesign on attendance. *Journal of Applied Social Psychology*, 1973, *3*, 39–48.

Lawler, E. E., Kuleck, W., Rhode, J., & Sorensen, J. Job choice and post decision dissonance. *Organizational Behavior and Human Performance*, 1975, *13*, 133–145.

Lee, S. M. An empirical analysis of organizational identification. *Academy of Management Journal*, 1971, *14*, 213–226.

Lefkowitz, J. Personnel turnover. *Progress in Clinical Psychology*, 1971, 69–90.

Levinson, H. Reciprocation: The relationship between man and organization. *Administrative Science Quarterly*, 1965, *9*, 370–390.

Levinson, H., Price, C. R., Munden, K. J., Mandl, H. J. & Solley, C. M. *Men, management and mental health*. Cambridge: Harvard University Press, 1962.

Locke, E. A. The nature and causes of job satisfaction. In M. D. Dunnette (Ed.), *Handbook of industrial and organizational psychology*. Chicago: Rand McNally, 1976.

Locke, E. A. The myths of behavior mod in organizations. *Academy of Mangement Review*, 1977, *2*, 543–553.

Locke, E. A., Sirota, D., & Wolfson, A. D. An experimental case study of the success and failures of job enrichment in a government agency. *Journal of Applied Psychology*, 1976, *61*, 701–711.

Lodahl, T., & Kejner, M. The definition and measurement of job involvement. *Journal of Applied Psychology*, 1965, *49*, 24–33.

Lundquist, A. Absenteeism and job turnover as a consequence of unfavorable job adjustment. *Acta Sociologica*, 1958, *3*, 119–131.

Malone, E. L. The non-linear systems experiment in participative management. *Journal of Business*, 1975, *48*, 52–64.

Mangione, T. W. Turnover: Some psychological and demographic correlates. In R. P. Quinn and T. W. Mangione (Eds.), *The 1969–1970 survey of working conditions*, Ann Arbor: University of Michigan, Survey Research Center, 1973.

March, J. G., & Simon, H. A. *Organizations*. New York: Wiley, 1958.

Marsh, R. M., & Mannari, H. Organizational commitment and turnover: A prediction study. *Administrative Science Quarterly*, 1977, *22*, 57–75.

Martin, J. Some aspects of absence in a light engineering factory. *Occupational Psychology*, 1971, *45*, 77–91.

Martin, T., Price, J., & Mueller, C. Job performance and turnover. *Journal of Applied Psychology*, 1981, *66*, 116–119.

McArthur, L. A. The how and what of why: Some determinants and consequences of causal attributions. *Journal of Personality and Social Psychology*, 1972, *22*, 171–193.

McDade, T. *Managerial perceptions of the cause of employee turnover: An attribution theory perspective*. Unpublished doctoral dissertation, University of Oregon, 1980.

Meister, D. *Behavioral foundations of systems development*. New York: Wiley, 1976.

Melbin, M. Organizational practice and individual behavior: Absenteeism among psychiatric aides. *American Sociological Review*, 1961, *26*, 14–23.

Metzner, H., & Mann, F. Employee attitudes and absences. *Personnel Psychology*, 1953, *6*, 467–485.

Miles, R. H., & Perreault, W. D. Organizational role conflict: Its antecedents and consequences. *Organizational Behavior and Human Performance*, 1976, *17*, 19–44.

Miller, D., & Porter, C. Effects of temporal perspectives on the attribution process. *Journal of Personality and Social Psychology*, 1980, *39*, 532–541.

Miller, D. T., & Ross, M. Self-serving biases in the attribution of causality: Fact or fiction? *Psychological Bulletin*, 1975, *82*, 213–225.

Miller, H. E., Katerberg, R., & Hulin, C. L. Evaluation of the Mobley, Horner, and Hollingsworth model of employee turnover. *Journal of Applied Psychology*, 1979, *64*, 509–517.

Mirvis, P. H., & Lawler, E. E., III. Measuring the financial impact of employee attitudes. *Journal of Applied Psychology*, 1977, *62*, 1–8.

Mobley, W. H. Intermediate linkages in the relationship between job satisfaction and employee turnover. *Journal of Applied Psychology*, 1977, *62*, 237–240.

Mobley, W. H. *Some unanswered questions in turnover and withdrawal research*. Paper presented at the 40th annual meeting of the Academy of Management, Detroit, August 1980.

Mobley, W. H., Griffeth, R. W., Hand, H. H., & Meglino, B. M. Review and conceptual analysis of the employee turnover process. *Psychological Bulletin*, 1979, *86*, 493–522.

Mobley, W. H., Horner, S. O., & Hollingsworth, A. T. An evaluation of precursors of hospital employee turnover. *Journal of Applied Psychology*, 1978, *63*, 408–414.

Moch, M., & Fitzgibbons, D. *Absenteeism and production efficiency: An empirical assessment*. Unpublished mimeo, University of Illinois at Urbana-Champaign, 1979.

Morgan, L. G., & Herman, J. B. Perceived consequences of absenteeism. *Journal of Applied Psychology*, 1976, *61*, 738–742.

Morris, J., & Koch, J. Impacts of role perceptions on organizational commitment, job involvement, and psychosomatic illnes among three vocational groupings. *Journal of Vocational Behavior*, 1979, *14*, 88–101.

Morris, J., & Sherman, J. D. Generalizability of an organizational commitment model. *Academy of Management Journal*, 1981, *24*, 512–526.

Morris, J., & Steers, R. M. Structural influences on organizational commitment. *Journal of Vocational Behavior*, 1980, *17*, 50–57.

Mowday, R. *Unmet expectations about unmet expectations: Employee reactions to disconfirmed expectations during the early employment period*. Paper presented at the 40th annual meeting of the Academy of Management, Detroit, August 1980.

Mowday, R. Viewing turnover from the perspective of those who remain: The influence of attitudes on attributions of the causes of turnover. *Journal of Applied Psychology*, 1981, *66*, 120–123.

Mowday, R., Koberg, C., & McArthur, A. *The psychology of the withdrawal process: A cross-validation of Mobley's intermediate linkages model of turnover*. Paper presented at the 40th annual meeting of the Academy of Management, Detroit, August 1980.

Mowday, R., & McDade, T. Linking behavioral and attitudinal commitment: A longitudinal analysis of job choice and job attitudes. *Proceedings of the 39th Annual Meeting of the Academy of Management*, Atlanta, 1979.

Mowday, R., & McDade, T. *The development of job attitudes, job perceptions, and withdrawal propensities during the early employment period*. Paper presented at the 40th annual meeting of the Academy of Management, Detroit, August 1980.

Mowday, R. T., Porter, L. W., & Dubin, R. Unit performance, situational factors, and employee attitudes in spatially separated work units. *Organizational Behavior and Human Performance*, 1974, *12*, 231–248.

Mowday, R. T., Porter, L. W., & Stone, E. F. Employee characteristics as predictors of turnover among female clerical employees in two organizations. *Journal of Vocational Behavior*, 1978, *12*, 321–332.

Mowday, R. T., & Spencer, D. The influence of task and personality characteristics on employee turnover and absenteeism. *Academy of Management Journal*, 1981, *24*, 634–642.

Mowday, R. T., Steers, R. M., & Porter, L. W. The measurement of organizational commitment *Journal of Vocational Behavior*, 1979, *14*, 224–247.
Management, July 1978.

Muchinsky, P. M. Employee absenteeism. A review of the literature. *Journal of Vocational Behavior*, 1977, *10*, 316–340.

Muchinsky, P. M., & Tuttle, M. L. Employee turnover: An empirical and methodological assessment. *Journal of Vocational Behavior*, 1979, *14*, 43–77.

Naylor, J. E., & Vincent, N. L. Predicting female absenteeism. *Personnel Psychology*, 1959, *12*, 81–84.

Newman, J. E. Predicting absenteeism and turnover. *Journal of Applied Psychology*, 1974, *59*, 610 615.

Newtson, D. Dispositional influence from effects of actions: Effects chosen and effects foregone. *Journal of Experimental Social Psychology*, 1974, *10*, 489–496.

Nicholson, N. Management sanctions and absence control. *Human Relations*, 1976, *29*, 139–151.

Nicholson, N., Brown, C. A., & Chadwick-Jones, J. K. Absence form work and job satisfaction. *Journal of Applied Psychology*, 1976, *61*, 728–737.

Nicholson, N., Brown, C. A., & Chadwick-Jones, J. K. Absence from work and personal characteristics. *Journal of Applied Psychology*, 1977, *62*, 319–327.

Nicholson, N., & Goodge, P. M. The influence of social, organizational and biographical factors on female absence. *Journal of Management Studies*, 1976, *13*, 234–254.

Nicholson, N., Wall, T., & Lischeron, J. The predictability of absence and propensity to leave from employees' job satisfaction and attitudes toward influence in decision making. *Human Relations*, 1977, *30*, 499–514.

Nisbett, R., & Ross, L. *Human inference: Strategies and shortcomings of social judgement*. Englewood Cliffs, N.J.: Prentice-Hall, 1980.

Noland, E. W. Attitudes and industrial absenteeism: A statistical appraisal. *American Sociological Review*, 1945, *10*, 503–510.

Nord, W. Improving attendance through rewards. *Personnel Administration*, November 1970, 37–41.

Nord, W. R., & Costigan, R. Worker adjustment to the four-day week: a longitudinal study. *Journal of Applied Psychology*, 1973, *58*, 60–61.

Nunnally, J. C. *Psychometric theory*. New York: McGraw-Hill, 1967.

O'Reilly, C., & Caldwell, D. Job choice: The impact of intrinsic and extrinsic factors on subsequent satisfaction and commitment. *Journal of Applied Psychology*, 1980, *65*, 559–565.(a)

O'Reilly, C., & Caldwell, D. *The commitment and job tenure of new employees: A process of postdecisional justification*. Paper presented at the 40th annual meeting of the Academy of Management, Detroit, August 1980.(b)

Orvis, B. R., Cunningham, J. D., & Kelley, H. H. A closer examination of causal inference: The roles of consensus, distinctiveness, and consistency information. *Journal of Personality and Social Psychology*, 1975, *32*, 605–616.

Oster, A. *Attitudes as mediators of the effects of participation in an industrial setting*. Unpublished doctoral dissertation, Wayne State University, 1970.

Owens, A. C. Sick leave among railwaymen threatened by redundancy: A pilot study. *Occupational Psychology*, 1966, *40*, 43–52.

Patchen, M. Absence and employee feelings about fair treatment. *Personnel Psychology*, 1960, *13*, 349–360.

Patchen, M. *Participation, achievement, and involvement in the job*. Englewood Cliffs, N.J.: Prentice-Hall, 1970.

Pedalino, E., & Gamboa, V. V. Behavior modification and absenteeism: Intervention in one industrial setting. *Journal of Applied Psychology*, 1974, *59*, 694–698.

Pettman, B. O. Some factors influencing labour turnover: A review of the literature. *Industrial Relations Journal*, 1973, *4*, 43–61.

Pettman, B. O. *Labour turnover and retention*. London: Wiley, 1975.

Pfeffer, J., & Lawler, J. The effects of job alternatives, extrinsic rewards, and commitment on satisfaction with the organization: A field example of the insufficient justification paradigm. *Administrative Science Quarterly*, 1980, *25*, 38–56.

Pocock, S. J., Sergean, R., & Taylor, P. J. Absence of continuous three-shift workers. *Occupational Psychology*, 1972, *46*, 7–13.

Porter, L. W., & Angle, H. L. Manager–organization linkages: The impact of changing work environments. In K. D. Duncan, M. M. Gruneberg, & D. Wallis (Eds.), *Changes in working life*. Chichester, England: Wiley, 1980.

Porter, L. W., Crampon, W. J., & Smith, F. J. Organizational commitment and managerial turnover: A longitudinal study. *Organizational Behavior and Human Performance*, 1976, *15*, 87–98.

Porter, L. W., & Lawler, E. E., III. Properties of organization structure in relation to job attitudes and job behavior. *Psychological Bulletin*, 1965, *64*, 23–51.

Porter, L. W., & Lawler, E. E. *Managerial attitudes and performance*. Homewood, Ill.: Irwin, 1968.

Porter, L. W., Lawler, E. E., & Hackman, J. R. *Behavior in organizations*. New York: McGraw-Hill, 1975.

Porter, L. W., & Perry, J. L. Motivation and public management: Concepts, issues, and research needs. In *Proceedings of the Public Management Research Conference*. Washington, D.C.: Brooking Institution, November 1979.

Porter, L. W., & Smith, F. J. *The etiology of organizational commitment*. Unpublished paper, University of California, Irvine, 1970.

Porter, L. W., & Steers, R. M. Organizational, work, and personal factors in employee turnover and absenteeism. *Psychological Bulletin*, 1973, *80*, 151–176.

Porter, L. W., Steers, R. M., Mowday, R. T., & Boulian, P. V. Organizational commitment, job satisfaction, and turnover among psychiatric technicians. *Journal of Applied Psychology*, 1974, *59*, 603–609.

Price, J. L. *The study of turnover*. Ames: Iowa State University Press, 1977.

Rabinowitz, S., & Hall, D. Organizational research on job involvement. *Psychological Bulletin*, 1977, *84*, 265–288.

Revans, R. Human relations, management and size. In E. M. Hugh-Jones (Ed.), *Human relations and modern management*. Amsterdam: North-Holland, 1958.

Rhodes, S. R., & Steers, R. M. *Summary tables of studies of employee absenteeism*. Technical Report No. 13, Graduate School of Management, University of Oregon, 1978.

Rhodes, S. R., & Steers, R. M. Conventional vs. worker-owned organizations. *Human Relations*, in press.

Roberts, K., Hulin, C., & Rousseau, D. *Developing an interdisciplinary science of organizations*. San Francisco: Jossey-Bass, 1978.

Robertson, G., & Humphreys, J. *Labor turnover and absenteeism in selected industries: Northwestern Ontario and Ontario*. Manpower Adjustment Study, Component Study No. 10, Ministry of Labour, Canada, 1978.

Robinson, D. *Alternate work patterns: Changing approaches to work scheduling*. Report of a conference sponsored by National Center for Productivity and Quality of Working Life and the Work in America Institute, Inc., June 2, 1976.

Rokeach, M. *The nature of human values*. New York: Free Press, 1973.

Ronan, W. A factor analysis of eleven job performance measures. *Personnel Psychology*, 1963, *16*, 255–268.

Rosen, H., & Turner, J. Effectiveness of two orientation approaches in hardcore unemployed turnover and absenteeism. *Journal of Applied Psychology*, 1971, *55*, 296–301.

Ross, L. The intuitive psychologist and his shortcomings: Distortions in the attribution process. In L. Berkowitz (Ed.), *Advances in experimental psychology* (Vol. 10). New York: Academic Press, 1977.

Rotondi, T. Organizational identification and group involvement. *Academy of Management Journal*, 1975, *18*, 892–897.

Rotondi, T. Identification, personality needs, and managerial position. *Human Relations*, 1976, *29*, 507–515.

Ruch, L. O., & Holmes, T. H. Scaling life change: Comparison of direct and indirect methods. *Journal of Psychsomatic Research*, 1971, *15*.

Salancik, G. R. Commitment and the control of organizational behavior and belief. In B. M. Staw and G. R. Salancik (Eds.), *New directions in organizational behavior*. Chicago: St. Clair Press, 1977.

Salancik, G. R., & Pfeffer, J. A social informtion processing approach to job attitudes and task design. *Administrative Science Quarterly*, 1978, *23*, 224–253.

Scheflen, K. C., Lawler, E. E., III, & Hackman, J. R. Long-term impact of employee participation in the development of pay incentive plans: A field experiment revisited. *Journal of Applied*

Psychology, 1971, *55*, 182–186.
Schneider, J. The greener grass phenomenon: Differential effects of a work context alternative on organizational participation and withdrawal intentions. *Organizational Behavior and Human Performance*, 1976, *116*, 303–333.
Schneider, B., & Dachler, H. P. *Work, family and career considerations in understanding employee turnover intentions*. Technical Report No. 19, Department of Psychology, University of Maryland, 1978.
Schriesheim, C. A., & von Glinow, M. A. *Predictors of employee job withdrawal: A closer look at the role of job satisfaction*. Working paper, University of Southern California, 1980.
Schuh, A. J. The predictability of employee tenure: A review of the literature. *Personnel Psychology*, 1967, *20*, 133–152.
Schwab, D. P., & Dyer, L. D. *Turnover as a function of perceived ease and desirability: A largely unsuccessful test of the March and Simon participation model*. Paper presented at the 34th annual meeting of the Academy of Management, Seattle, 1974.
Searls, D. J., Braucht, G. N., & Miskimins, R. W. Work values and the chronically unemployed. *Journal of Applied Psychology*, 1974, *59*, 93–95.
Seatter, W. C. More effective control of absenteeism. *Personnel*, 1961, *38*, 16–29.
Shaw, M. *Group dynamics* (3rd ed.). New York: McGraw-Hill, 1981.
Sheldon, M. E. Investments and involvements as mechanisms producing commitment to the organization. *Administrative Science Quarterly*, 1971, *16*, 142–150.
Sinha, A. K. P. Manifest anxiety affecting industrial absenteeism. *Psychological Reports*, 1963, *13*, 258.
Smith, A. L. Oldsmobile absenteeism/turnover control program. *GM Personnel Development Bulletin*, February 1972.
Smith, C. G., & Jones, G. The role of the interaction–influence system in a planned organizational change. In A. S.Tannebaum (Ed.), *Control in organizations*. New York: McGraw-Hill, 1968.
Smith, F. J. Work attitudes as predictors of specific day attendance. *Journal of Applied Psychology*, 1977, *62*, 16–19.
Smith, P. C., Kendall, L. M., & Hulin, C. L. *The measurement of satisfaction in work and retirement*. Chicago: Rand McNally, 1969.
Smulders, P. Comments on employee absence/attendance as a dependent variable in organizational research. *Journal of Applied Psychology*, 1980, *65*, 368–371.
Spencer, D. G., & Steers, R. M. The influence of personal factors and perceived work experiences on employee turnover and absenteeism. *Academy of Management Journal*, 1980, *23*, 567–572.
Spencer, D. G., & Steers, R. M. Performance as a moderator of the job satisfaction–turnover relationship. *Journal of Applied Psychology*, 1981, *66*, 511–514.
Spencer, D. G., Steers, R., & Mowday, R. *A partial replication and extension of the Mobley, Horner, and Hollingsworth model of employee turnover*. Unpublished manuscript, School of Business, University of Kansas, 1980.
Spiegel, A. H. How outsiders overhauled a public agency. *Harvard Business Review*, 1975, *53*(1), 116–124.
The spirited turnaround at Eastern Airlines. *Business Week*, October 1, 1979, pp.112–118.
Staw, B. M. Attitudinal and behavioral consequences of changing a major organizational reward. *Journal of Personality and Social Psychology*, 1974, *29*, 742–751.
Staw, B. M. *Two sides of commitment*. Paper presented at the National Meeting of the Academy of Management, Orlando, Florida, 1977.
Staw, B. M. Rationality and justification in organizational life. In B. Staw & L. Cummings (Eds.), *Research in organizational behavior* (Vol. 2). Greenwich, CT.: Jai Press, 1980. (a)

Staw, B. M. The consequences of turnover. *Journal of Occupational Psychology*, 1980, 1, 253–273. (b)

Staw, B. M., & Oldham, G. R. Reconsidering our dependent variables: A critique and empirical study. *Academy of Management Journal*, 1978, *21*, 539–559.

Steers, R. M. Antecedents and outcomes of organizational commitment. *Administrative Science Quarterly*, 1977, *22*, 46–56. (a)

Steers, R. M. *Organizational effectiveness: A behavioral view*. Santa Monica: Goodyear, 1977. (b)

Steers, R. M., & Mowday, R. Employee turnover and postdecision accommodation processes. In L. Cummings and B. Staw (Eds.), *Research in organizational behavior* (Vol. 3). Greenwich, CT.: JAI Press, 1981.

Steers, R. M., & Rhodes, S. R. Major influences on employee attendance: A process model. *Journal of Applied Psychology*, 1978, *63*, 391–407.

Steers, R. M., & Spencer, D. G. The role of achievement motivation in job design. *Journal of Applied Psychology*, 1977, *62*, 472–479.

Steiner, I. Perceived freedom. In L. Berkowitz (ed.), *Advances in experimental social psychology* (Vol. 5). New York: Academic Press, 1970.

Steiner, I. *Group processes and productivity*. New York: Academic Press, 1972.

Stephens, T. A., & Burroughs, W. A. An application of operant conditioning to absenteeism in a hospital setting. *Journal of Applied Psychology*, 1978, *63*, 518–521.

Stevens, J. M., Beyer, J., & Trice, H. M. Assessing personal, role, and organizational predictors of managerial commitment. *Academy of Management Journal*, 1978, *21*, 380–396.

Stevens, L., & Jones, E. E. Defensive attribution and the Kelley Cube. *Journal of Personality and Social Psychology*, 1976, *34*, 809–820.

Stockford, L. O. Chronic absenteeism and good attendance. *Personnel Journal*, 1944, *23*, 202–207.

Stogdill, R. M. *Handbook of leadership*. New York: Free Press, 1974.

Stoikov, V., & Raimon, R. L. Determinants of differences in the quit rate among industries. *American Economic Review*, 1968, *58*, 1283–1298.

Sussman, M. B., & Cogswell, B. E. Family influences on job movement. *Human Relations*, 1971, *24*, 477–487.

Taylor, S. E., & Fiske, S. T. Salience, attention and attribution: Top of the head phenomena. In L. Berkowitz (Ed.), *Advances in experimental social psychology* (Vol. 11). New York: Academic Press, 1978.

Terborg, J. R., Davis, G. A., Smith, F. J., & Turbin, M. S. A multivariate investigation of employee absenteeism. Technical Report No. 80-85, University of Houston, 1980.

Thibaut, J., & Kelley, H. *The social psychology of groups*. New York: Wiley, 1959.

Tjersland, T. *Changing worker behavior*. New York: American Telephone and Telegraph Company, Manpower Laboratory, December 1972.

Trist, E. L., Higgins, G., Murry, H., & Pollack, A. G. *Organizational choice*. London: Tavistock, 1965.

Turner, W. W. Dimensions of foreman performance: A factor analysis of criterion measures. *Journal of Applied Psychology*, 1960, *44*, 216–223.

Turner, A., & Lawrence, P. R. *Industrial jobs and the worker*. Boston: Harvard University Press, 1965.

Van Maanen, J. Police socialization: A longitudinal examination of job attitudes in an urban police department. *Administrtive Science Quarterly*, 1975, *20*, 207–228.

Van Maanen, J., & Schein, E. Toward a theory of organizational socialization. In B. Staw (Ed.), *Research in organizational behavior* (Vol. 1). Greenwich, CT.: JAI Press, 1979.

Vroom, V. *Work and motivation*. New York: Wiley, 1964.

Vroom, V. H., & Deci, E. L. The stability of post-decisional dissonance: A follow-up study of the job attitudes of business school graduates. *Organizational Behavior and Human Performance*, 1971, *6*, 36–49.

Walster, E., Berscheid, E., & Barclay, A. M. A determinant of preference among modes of dissonance reduction. *Journal of Personality and Social Psychology*, 1967, *7*, 211–216.

Wanous, J. P. Organizational entry: Newcomers moving from outside to inside. *Psychological Bulletin*, 1977, *84*, 601–618.

Wanous, J. P. *Organizational entry: Recruitment, selection and socialization of newcomers*. Reading, Mass,: Addison-Wesley, 1980.

Wanous, J. P., Stumpf, S. A., & Bedrosian, H. *Job survival of new employees*. Unpublished paper, New York University, 1978.

Waters, L. K., & Roach, D. Relationship between job attitudes and two forms of withdrawal from the work situation. *Journal of Applied Psychology*, 1971, *55*, 92–94.

Waters, L. K., & Roach, D. Job attitudes as predictors of termination and absenteeism: Consistency over time and across organizations. *Journal of Applied Psychology*, 1973, *57*, 341–342.

Waters, L. K., Roach, D., & Waters, C. W. Estimate of future tenure, satisfaction, and biographical variables as predictors of termination. *Personnel Psychology*, 1976, *29*, 57–60.

Watson, C. An evaluation of some aspects of the Steers and Rhodes' model of employee attendance. *Journal of Applied Psychology*, 1981, *66*, 385–389.

Weaver, C. N., & Holmes, S. L. On the use of sick leave by female employees. *Personnel Administration and Public Personnel Review*, 1972, *1*(2), 46–50.

Weiner, Y., & Gechman, A. S. Commitment: A behavioral approach to job involvement. *Journal of Vocational Behavior*, 1977, *10*, 47–52.

Weiner, Y., & Vardi, Y. Relationships between job, organization, and career commitments and work outcomes: An integrative approach. *Organizational Behavior and Human Performance*, 1980, *26*, 81–96.

Whyte, W. F. *Organizational behavior*. Homewood, Ill.: Irwin, 1969.

Wicklund, R. A., & Brehm, J. W. *Perspectives on cognitive dissonance*. Hillsdale, N.J.: Lawrence Erlbaum, 1976.

Woodward, N. The economic causes of labour turnover: A case study. *Industrial Relations Journal*, 1975–1976, *6*, 19–32.

World of Work Report. *Rising absenteeism in Sweden attributed to generous sick pay*, 1977, *2*(1), 12.

Wortman, C. B., & Brehm, J. W. Responses to uncontrollable outcomes: An integration of reactance theory and the learned helplessness model. In L. Berkowitz (Ed.), *Advances in experimental social psychology* (Vol. 9). New York: Academic Press, 1976.

Wright, J. *On a clear day you can see General Motors*. New York: Avon books, 1980.

Yankelovich, D. We need new motivational tools. *Industry Week*, August 6, 1979. (a)

Yankelovich, D. Work, values, and the new breed. In C. Kerr & J. M. Rostow (Eds.), *Work in America: The decade ahead*. New York, Van Nostrand, 1979. (b)

Yolles, S. F., Carone, P. A., & Krinsky, L. W. *Absenteeism in industry*. Sringfild, Ill.: Charles C Thomas, 1975.

Zanna, M. P. & Cooper, J. Dissonance and the attribution process. In J. H. Harvey, N. J. Ickes, & R. F. Kidd (Eds.), *New directions in attribution research* (Vol. 1). Hillsdale, N.J.: Lawrence Erlbaum, 1976.

Ziller, R. Toward a theory of open and closed groups. *Psychological Bulletin*, 1965, *64*, 164–182.

Author Index

Numbers in italic indicate the pages on which complete references are listed.

Subject Index